Financing Higher Education and Economic Development in East Asia

Financing Higher Education and Economic Development in East Asia

Edited by Shiro Armstrong and Bruce Chapman

ANU
THE AUSTRALIAN NATIONAL UNIVERSITY

E PRESS

E PRESS

Published by ANU E Press
The Australian National University
Canberra ACT 0200, Australia
Email: anuepress@anu.edu.au
This title is also available online at http://epress.anu.edu.au

National Library of Australian Cataloguing-in-Publication entry

Title:	Financing higher education and economic development in East Asia / edited by Shiro Armstrong and Bruce Chapman.
ISBN:	9781921666629 (pbk.) 9781921666636 (eBook)
Notes:	Includes bibliographical references.
Subjects:	Education, Higher--Economic aspects--East Asia. Education, Higher--East Asia--Costs. Economic development--Effect of education on.

Other Authors/Contributors:

Armstrong, Shiro.

Chapman, Bruce J. (Bruce James)

Dewey Number: 379.1214

Cover design and layout by ANU E Press

Contents

Part 3. Experience in East Asia

Preface

This book is the product of research collaboration between The Australian National University and Dhurakij Pundit University. It brings together new work—from a conference held in 2008 in Bangkok—on higher education financing by international experts on the issue from around East Asia.

The research collaboration between the ANU and DPU was initiated in August 2007 and involves biannual conferences with broad international participation and research and training exchanges. It aims to build capacity in the region through collaborative research and training and to share experience in the important areas of higher education financing and loans systems. It will encompass other key economic policy issues over time.

This volume addresses important issues to do with access to higher education and different models of its financing, and the analysis spans the East Asian region. It is enriched by diverse perspectives from vastly different starting points and by the historical and institutional settings in the East Asian region. The issues are set out in the context of the value of higher education in economic development and how it contributes to the capacities to adopt and adapt to new technologies and undertake institutional innovation. The established and well-functioning higher education loan and financing systems, such as those in Australia, and the experience of different systems tried—both in East Asia and in the United States—are brought to bear in this volume.

The ongoing research collaboration is led by Bruce Chapman and Peter Drysdale at the Australian end and Boonserm Weesakul in Thailand. We are grateful to Boonserm and his colleagues at DPU in Bangkok who were responsible for hosting the conference that reviewed the original research and to Peter Drysdale at the ANU for coordinating the program of research and the conference organisation. Our gratitude is also extended to the DPU management team including Charles Newton and especially Somsri Lathapipat, without whom this collaboration would not be possible.

The conference drew on the network and administrative work of the East Asian Bureau of Economic Research (EABER) and we are grateful to the member institutes and their researchers who contributed to the conference. The conference was made possible with the professional administrative input and expertise of Marilyn Popp, Aaron Batten, Alisa Maksamphan and Paitoon Sinralat.

We, and the EABER team, are especially grateful to all the contributors—the paper writers, discussants and referees—who collaborated so enthusiastically to bring this research to publication. Our debt to the authors in the volume is obvious. Sippanondha, Norman LaRocque, Aniceto Orbeta and Rangsit Sarachiti made substantial contributions to the chapters in this volume with their clarification of issues and refinement of ideas at the conference and in the process of preparation of the papers for publication. In addition, the volume benefited greatly from the background work and training conducted in Thailand and Australia by Piruna Polsiri, Rangsit Sarachitti and Thitima Sitthipongpanich. Finally, our special thanks to Kiatanantha Lounkaew and Dr Dilaka Lathapipat, who provided extremely valuable input on the training and intellectual aspects critical to the conference.

We are grateful to the *Economics of Education Review* Journal published by Elsevier that gave us permission to produce earlier versions of the three papers on Thailand as Chapters in this volume. The three papers were published in Volume 29, Issue 5, pages 685-721 (October 2010) of the Journal as: Bruce Chapman, Kiatanantha Lounkaew, Piruna Polsiri, Rangsit Sarachitti, Thitima Sitthipongpanich, *Thailand's Student Loans Fund: Interest rate subsidies and repayment burdens*; Bruce Chapman, Kiatanantha Lounkaew, *Income contingent student loans for Thailand: Alternatives compared*; and Somkiat Tangkitvanich, Areeya Manasboonphempool, *Evaluating the Student Loan Fund of Thailand*.

We are indebted to Kay Dancey and Jennifer Sheehan at CAP Cartography–GIS Services for their professional work on the charts. Duncan Beard and Lorena Kanellopoulos at ANU E Press did a fantastic job and we are very grateful for their patience with us throughout the process.

We would also like to thank Denis Cairney for excellent editorial assistance.

Shiro Armstrong and Bruce Chapman

June 2010

Canberra

1. Issues and Overview

Shiro Armstrong and Aaron Batten
Crawford School of Economics and Government,
The Australian National University

Human capital plays a key role in the development of all economies. A decade ago, discussions of education and development tended to be categorised by focusing on the importance of primary and secondary services. For example, it was thought more important to teach large amounts of people to read than to teach a small cadre liberal arts and high-level sciences. In an egalitarian sense, support for universities was seen as biased against poorer elements of society. These arguments have a degree of merit and, certainly, primary and secondary education are both important elements of the sector—not least because they feed directly into the quality of higher levels of education. But the lessons of recent economic history also highlight both the importance of strong higher educational outcomes obtained through universities and the need for delivering substantial economic support. The growth of Europe and the United States in particular can be attributed largely to the success of their universities. These knowledge-based economies require high levels of human capital, which influences a large number of economic outcomes and boosts long-term productivity. The current world economy is going to be increasingly dominated by knowledge-based industries over the coming decades. Agricultural, industrial and technical revolutions will all give way to increases in knowledge. Manufactures will continue to be displaced by services, and salary differences between knowledge-based and non-knowledge-based industries will continue to rise. The widening of these economic differentials highlights the importance of investing in knowledge and getting the fundamentals of each country's higher education sector right.

These developments are also placing increasing pressure on governments across the globe as citizens increase their demand for higher levels of human capital so that they can benefit from the growing knowledge-based economy. In addition, the constraints on investment in higher education within the region are in nearly all cases large. As such, the benefits must be weighed carefully against the large costs associated with a quality higher education sector—particularly in developing countries with tight fiscal constraints.

At present, the United States clearly dominates the university sector, and Lawrence Summers in Chapter 2 offers some important insights into how the sector should be run. First, the US university sector is intensely competitive—

as universities compete for the best students, faculty and rankings. This can sometimes be destructive but the fact of brutal competition forces a discipline and excellence that are present in US universities and not present in many other countries. Too often countries try too carefully to plan and manage their university sector, which undermines the sector's ability to drive for excellence. The second element is a governance model that maintains 'diamonds'. Judgments about the quality of staff and students are best made by experts in the field, but this can often lead to the self-perpetuation of ideas. It is difficult, for example, for incumbents to shut down mediocre activities and support ideas that diverge from their own. The challenge therefore is to draw on experts for identifying resources but to also maintain diversity.

The third great strength of the US system is its reliance on the private sector. The greatest universities are not public institutions, as the lion's share of resources comes from successful alumni. This mixture between the public and the private sector is a great stimulus to innovation within the university sector. Asia has the potential to build on these US lessons. As its wealth grows, so too does it ability to build universities that challenge the dominance of US universities and enhance the long-term development prospects of the region.

Ultimately, financing higher education systems must be focused on providing wide-scale access to higher education that is based on merit rather than economic status. Substantial efforts are required to attract the best students regardless of their life circumstances. This can act to help transform a society. Higher education is, however, about much more than simply teaching students technical skills. A quality higher education system must also be able to train students to question traditional dogma and assess views based on the strength of the argument rather than the person who is delivering it or what their status is in society. Fostering this type of environment, which challenges the current status quo, is a key role for quality universities as it promotes long-term improvements in entrepreneurship and productivity.

Higher education financing systems should thus aim to improve all aspects of higher education delivery. In all countries, this should include increasing both the quality and the quantity of access, helping to smooth consumption over time for consumers of higher education, and perhaps, most importantly, to widen access to those who are disadvantaged.

The Economics of Higher Education and its Financing Arrangements

Economic theory offers a number of lessons for a system that seeks to strengthen the quality of higher education while simultaneously promoting access. At present, access to higher education within East Asia is growing swiftly. This is a positive development. The expansion of access to higher education is, however, occurring largely through the expansion of the private sector. This is creating a number of challenges to the future dynamism of the sector. For example, private financing might preclude the enrolment of deserving students who do not have the ability to pay, and often evokes resentment among students who do. In Chapter 3, Nicholas Barr sets out the principles—from theory and practice—by which policy makers can make decisions regarding access to higher education and the growth of private and public institutions and address challenges of equity.

The economic case for government subsidies in the higher education sector is based largely on the large positive externalities involved in higher education. Market failure occurs because private-sector lending to finance tuition and prospective students' smooth consumption are unreliable, as banks are unable to generate collateral on human capital. This leads to suboptimal rates of borrowing and lending and, in the absence of government intervention, suboptimal levels of investment in higher education.

There are, however, a number of principles that must be incorporated into the system if government intervention into the higher education sector is to be effective at meeting its objectives. Barr gives lessons for policy design from economic theory combined with operational experiences. The first of these is that competition within all areas of the sector is highly beneficial, as the US case highlights. As in any market, competition benefits consumers when consumers are well informed. Within the higher education sector, the assumption of a well-informed consumer generally holds such that student choices, though not necessarily perfect, are better than those of central planners. The competition this creates encourages flexible institutional structures within the higher education sector and promotes adaptability to the prevailing economic and institutional environment. It is therefore important to promote competition and to better inform consumers where necessary so that these two dynamics reinforce each other.

Second, graduates should contribute to the cost of their degree so as to offer an allocative mechanism within the sector. Whilst higher education has large social benefits—albeit hard to quantify—it also has significant private benefits. Thus, it is both efficient and equitable that the graduate shares in the cost of higher education.

But sharing costs should not be vested with spurious accuracy, as it is impossible to measure the positive externalities generated through education systems. Determining the optimal trade-off between public and private financing of an individual's higher education thus should be determined not by scientific quantification but rather in relation to a country's overall fiscal envelope and the incumbent political and social values. Third, as mentioned, conventional loans are the wrong model for investment in human capital. They lead to inefficiently low borrowing and lending. They are also inequitable, in that these efficiency problems impact most on people from poor backgrounds, and minorities, who might be less well informed and therefore less prepared to risk a loan, if able to obtain one.

These principles offer a number of lessons for the role of government in designing optimal financing strategies for higher education. The first is that there is sufficient cause for the provision of taxpayer support for higher education. The second is that the government must regulate the system, both through a maximum level of fees and by ensuring that there is effective quality assurance (the role of government is to make sure that quality assurance happens, not necessarily to provide the service itself). Third is that government can play a role in allocating incentives towards the needs of the economy—for example, providing larger subsidies for certain subjects. Last, the government should be focused on policies that at all times seek to widen participation and access to the higher education sector for all segments of society.

Governments are thus faced with a range of possibilities for how to finance higher education support schemes. The first is a mortage-type bank-loan system (as used in Canada, the United States and the Student Loans Fund in Thailand). This helps to solve the default problem for the lender as the government enters the market to guarantee the loan and it provides finance simply and easily. But there are costs. These include the large expenses for taxpayers when people default, and the credit of government often means that banks are less likely to make sure people pay their debt. Also, government is forced in to a strict rationing system to try to maintain costs. Because repayments are based on time, those who enter the workforce in a low-paying job or who have poor labour-market outcomes at some stage will face a large repayment hardship, which could force default. There is also a credit risk for default for the students as it can ruin their credit rating and ability to finance into the future.

An increasingly popular option is the adoption of income-contingent loan schemes. Under this system, repayment is calculated as a portion of the graduate's (not student's) income in the future if and only if that graduate is earning over a threshold. This helps to fix the student default problem and lowers repayment hardships if the student enters a period of poor labour-market outcomes. These systems also act to smooth consumption over a person's life, as people pay more as their income goes up and less at times when income is low.

In terms of collection methods, ideally, income-contingent repayments should be collected alongside income tax or social security contributions on the basis of a person's current earnings. Thus, repayments instantly and accurately reflect changes in a person's economic circumstances. This approach is, however, administratively demanding. A different approach—less optimal in policy terms, but less demanding administratively and hence perhaps more realistic in some countries—is to base a person's loan repayments on his or her last completed tax return. It is also important to recognise that the ideal recovery rate for loans need not necessarily be 100 per cent as these loans can also offer insurance against low lifetime earnings. In fact, there have been no cases where a country's income-contingent loan scheme collects 100 per cent repayments, and that is by design, as it is not optimal to have 100 per cent repayments.

Income-contingent loan schemes do, however, have a number of risks. For instance, students can avoid repayment by not earning enough income despite living in high-income households, or in some cases leaving the country. Also, in developing countries in particular, postgraduate incomes are often not high enough to have sufficient rates of repayment over the life of the scheme.

Of course, the overarching issue with income-contingent loan schemes relates to implementation. Regional and global experiences suggest that this issue has been the key cause of failure in many income-contingent loan schemes. These lessons must, for example, be carefully applied to the unique institutional and historical environment that categorises each East Asian economy. In particular, they must be designed in reference to the administrative capacity of the relevant country. For example, a country should not consider starting a loan scheme without a reliable method of identifying individuals and the capacity to maintain records of amounts borrowed, cumulative borrowing and interest charges, and the value of each person's repayments.

The strength of income-contingent loan schemes is that they provide support and allow for variation in outcomes of students and do not place an excessively high burden on their ability to repay in the event of a poor outcome at the end of their higher education. These schemes are, however, notoriously difficult to get right and the world and region are littered with examples of failed income-contingent loan schemes. This highlights the importance of carefully assessing the validity and details of implementing such schemes before they are carried out. Means-tested scholarships have, for example, proven very difficult to administer due to the difficulty of assessing the ability to pay sometimes exorbitant administrative costs, corruption and high rates of default. Indeed, the failure of systems in the Philippines and Thailand highlights these risks to the development of income-contingent loans that do not take into account the administrative limitations of their incumbent institutional environment.

Once this is possible, the economics clearly points to the optimality of income-contingent loan schemes. It is important to recognise, however, that a pure focus on higher education financing systems as a means of improving human-capital outcomes understates the importance of undertaking reforms that strengthen the fiscal arrangements for the bureaucracy as a whole. There is, for example, a strong interdependence between aggregate fiscal policy, expenditure processes and the ability of government to provide optimal support for higher education.

A further issue is that in some countries it will be optimal to have student grants from government operating in combination with income-contingent loans. A 100 per cent repayment rate for an income-contingent loan scheme as a whole is effectively a commercial loan with no subsidy from the government. The lower the repayment rate of an income-contingent loan scheme, the closer it becomes to a grant or direct wealth transfer. Therefore, countries with very low repayment rates have the option of simply giving grant transfers instead of running a poorly performing and costly income-contingent loan scheme. There is also scope for a combination of grants and income-contingent loans.

Before making a decision about which type of scheme is most suitable, it is necessary to take into account each country's institutional setting and the contexts of each market for implementation and ongoing success of any financing regime. Collection is an important aspect, with not all countries able to collect repayments effectively. Policy design that exceeds a country's implementation capacity is not appropriate policy.

It is also important to recognise that policy regimes of allowing foreign institutions into countries and the financing schemes of higher education institutions are intertwined. Questions of whether governments should subsidise foreign-owned institutions, extend financing schemes to students of these institutions, and how these should be treated relative to domestic private-sector institutions are all complex issues that have not been adequately addressed in countries in the region yet.

Regional Experiences

Countries across the East Asian region have adopted a wide variety of approaches to financing their higher education sectors. There has also been a wide variety in both the successes and the failures of these approaches, which can offer a number of important lessons for the design of future strategies in the region and more broadly. In Chapter 4, Anthony R. Welch examines the rise of private higher education institutions and the implications for affordability and access in South-East Asia.

The regional experiences are especially important in the context of education becoming a much more widely traded and internationally delivered service, with the movement across borders of students, academics and even institutions.

Australia

The introduction of the Australian Higher Education Contribution Scheme (HECS) in 1989 has been highly successful. HECS incorporates an income-contingent loan for the payment of tuition through the income tax system, and was the first time that such an approach to student financing had been used internationally. A major issue for the adoption of HECS was the potential for the scheme to improve the access of the disadvantaged to Australian higher education, as private-sector lenders provide inefficient levels of loans given the uncertainty surrounding investments in human capital.

The intellectual architect of HECS, Bruce Chapman, explains the genesis and draws out the particular features of the Australian system in Chapter 5. There is evidence, as Chapman shows, to suggest that HECS has been associated with significant increases in the size of the higher education system and has proved to be administratively inexpensive. A major benefit of income-contingent loans in Australia is with respect to consumption smoothing for borrowers. For example, compared with the repayment of a similar bank loan, the burden of an income-contingent loan for students, as measured by the proportion of a graduate's income that is required to service the debt, can be far less than is the case for a bank loan. In addition, even though HECS means that students pay for a portion of their higher education—which had previously been free—extensive research into the implications of the scheme for the access of the poor to universities reveals that there have been no discernible effects. The second major impact of the HECS system is that for graduates receiving low incomes for some part of their lives there is considerable potential for the system to provide consumption smoothing. For situations in which former students experience very low incomes, the repayment of normal loans results in very high proportions of incomes being obliged to pay debt, and thus being unavailable for consumption. HECS has no such implication, and this is a critical benefit of an income-contingent loan.

Japan

In Chapter 6, Motohisa Kaneko takes a detailed look at higher education funding in Japan. Japan has been less successful than some places in the design and implementation of its higher education financing schemes despite undergoing radical changes over the past decade. For example, the Law for Incorporation of National University was enacted in 2004, transforming the legal status of the national universities as a kind of governmental facility to an independent legal entity. Private institutions have experienced a radical change in governmental subsidies, with their weight shifted from the mandatory current-cost subsidy to discretionary subsidies. In 2007, the current-cost subsidy fell from the previous year for the first time in 30 years. The government also revised the Private School Law to enhance accountability in governance and financing of private institutions. Yet, reforms are incomplete and the future institutional arrangements of the sector are uncertain.

There have been persistent demands for greater government expenditure on higher education, and one of the grounds for the argument was the low standing of Japan in international comparisons. On the other hand, there have been strong criticisms of this argument from the Ministry of Finance and various economic advisory committees. It is claimed that the low level of government expenditure does not constitute the main issue; after all, the government expenditure is financed by tax revenues—one of the main sources of which is taxes on individuals. Japan's higher education tends to be financed through direct contribution from households, not through tax and government expenditure. Whether this is optimal in Japan's case is part of an ongoing debate, and the international and regional experiences have not been brought to bear.

Japanese higher education is also faced with the effects of demographic change, a shrinking population and declining absolute enrolments. The direct consequence of the shrinking market will be the prospect of institutional closure. Some institutions are already facing a decline in applicants, and in a number of cases the freshman class has failed to fill the legal sitting capacity. The situation will be further aggravated over the next decade. Despite the large number of institutions in the high and medium-risk groups, there have been very few cases of closure for directly fiscal reasons. Many institutions appear to have sizeable margins in their current revenue over costs. Some of them have succeeded in slashing costs by either decreasing the number of employees or reducing wage levels. Nonetheless, the prospect of closure is definitely looming.

Kaneko makes clear that after a half-century of robust expansion, higher education in Japan is clearly at a crossroad. In order to respond to the new challenges, it has to undergo a significant transformation in which changes in financing assume the critical role. The policy management of a transition to fewer students has important implications for the Japanese higher education sector. Opening up further to international trade in education services is another issue that will have to be debated in addition to the improvements in the financial accessibility for prospective students. All of these developments involve a number of issues over which there are significant differences of opinion. In this sense, Japanese society is struggling to find a definite direction for higher education finance towards the future.

China

The Chinese higher education sector has also been undergoing rapid transformation in recent years as the economy increasingly integrates itself into the global knowledge economy. The rapidly growing economy, increasing job opportunities and the demands of a modern society have resulted in large unmet student demand for financial assistance to attend higher education institutions in China—as measured by the gap between loan applications and approvals in the adoption of the country's student loan policy in 2004. In addition, the coverage of the financial assistance is very small across the sector and has declined in recent years. In total, the student loan coverage rate increased from 2.7 per cent of total students in 2004 to 6.6 per cent in 2005 but then dropped again, to 4.6 per cent, in 2006.

The scale and pace of growth of the Chinese higher education sector are unprecedented and present policy makers with some acute challenges. Wei Jianguo and Wang Rong outline the problems and challenges in Chapter 7. At present, there are two major challenges to improving the effectiveness and size of the Chinese education sector. The first step is in defining the financial responsibilities of government for its elite and non-elite institutions. The second regards efforts that need to be made in the future to strengthen and improve the existing public higher education system or enhance the role of the non-public sector. Central to both of these challenges is improving China's student financial-aid system so that it can both channel the best students into the sector in a non-discriminatory way and provide adequate resources for the sector to remain competitive and meet the labour-market demands of the economy.

The State Council implemented a new policy for student financial aid in 2007. This policy allocated $7.1 billion in earmarked funds annually to student financial aid (including aid for students in vocational middle schools). This has included a dramatic increase in the coverage of the National Scholarship Program to approximately 20 per cent of all students in the sector at approximately RMB2000 per recipient per annum.

In addition, in order to promote the development of the student loan program, the Ministry of Education, the Ministry of Finance, the People's Bank of China and the China Banking Regulatory Commission mandated a new policy for the student loan program in June 2004. This new policy both extended the repayment period of the loan, reducing repayment hardships, and allowed recipients to receive loan waivers if they voluntarily chose to work in less-developed regions or less-attractive professions for a set time after graduation. The new policy also reformed the way to identify banks that are eligible to provide student loans using bidding and implementing collaboration between the banks and higher education institutions to improve the competitiveness of the sector. Finally, it introduced a risk compensation fund, whereby the government and the higher education institution each pays 50 per cent of the fund to commercial banks.

The Chinese higher education sector still, however, faces a number of significant challenges in addressing the country's shortage of highly skilled labour, which can drive entrepreneurship and productivity into the future. As is the case in other countries, in China, the governance and accountability of the sector remain as the core determinants of whether the sector can adequately meet the needs of the country's rapidly growing economy. The government has made some significant moves towards decentralising the sector. For instance, since 1998, about 200 regular higher education institutions that used to belong to central ministries and agencies have been transferred to the jurisdiction of local governments. This has had a large impact, with the proportion of college enrolment in centrally controlled higher education institutions dropping from 20 per cent in 2000 to 10 per cent in 2006. There is, however, little evidence to suggest that locally run institutions perform any better or are more efficient than centrally controlled ones. Ultimately, setting up appropriate institutional structures that ensure that the sector remains accountable to the people it serves and adaptable to the changing demands of a rapidly growing economy will prove to be the biggest determinant of China's ability to meet its higher education needs.

Indonesia

Teguh Yudo Wicaksono and Deni Friawan outline in Chapter 8 the challenges the Indonesian higher education sector faces. Indonesian higher education institutions have expanded rapidly in the post-independence era (since 1945). In more recent decades, participation rates in higher education have, however, tended to stagnate. Access to tertiary education is also very unequal. In 2006, for example, the participation rate of students from the lowest 40 per cent income group was only 2.67 per cent, compared with about 33.9 per cent for the richest 20 per cent. In part, this is a result of a large share of the cost of higher education still being borne by parents and students as well as the flow-on effects from low participation rates in secondary education. Notably, the percentage of national education expenditure to gross domestic product (GDP) increased from 2.4 per cent in 2001 to 3.8 per cent in 2007, but this is still well below other countries in the region such as Malaysia (8.1 per cent) and Thailand (4.6 per cent). In addition, tertiary education received only less than 10 per cent of the total education budget—lower than primary education (75 per cent) and secondary education (15 per cent).

In large part, the stagnation of access to higher education access stems from a number of failed attempts at financing arrangements in the sector. In the 1980s, student loans were implemented under the so-called '*Kredit Mahasiswa Indonesia*' (KMI; Indonesian Student Loan) scheme, which provided government-backed loans to selected disadvantaged groups. After a few years, however, default rates reached up to 95 per cent and this scheme began to place an excessively high burden on government resources and was subsequently cancelled. This failure was caused largely by the moral hazard of the borrowers, a poor administration system and a lack of strong political support to impose more effective collection standards on students.

More recently, the government has sought to improve the funding of the sector by increasing resources for direct means-assessed scholarship payments—particularly to private higher education institutions, although public institutions are still the major beneficiaries. Even after being augmented with substantial private contributions, these scholarship programs were having an insufficient impact on the overall access of students to the higher education sector. In 2006, the Sampoerna Foundation in conjunction with the International Finance Corporation (IFC) and Bank International Indonesia (BII) also began to try to reinvent and rejuvenate the student loan program by offering advances of up to Rp200 million (approximately US$20 000).

Perhaps the biggest constraint on the quality and access of Indonesia's higher education institutions, however, which cannot be corrected by student loan systems, has been the lack of proper long-term planning and vision for the sector. The universities suffer from internal inefficiency and poor initiatives, particularly in research, and lack clear lines of public accountability. Undoubtedly, these problems have brought negative impacts on quality, efficiency and the relevance of higher education in the country. The goals of widening access and improving the quality and quantity of higher education institutions are thus far from being achieved.

Facing these issues, the government, through the Directorate General for Higher Education (DGHE), has taken some major reform efforts. These have included moves to increase the autonomy of public university governance structures, clarifying funding mechanisms, particularly between private and public higher education institutions, as well as reforming the curriculum content so that it is more in line with the national development context. Ultimately, it will be the ability of these reforms to create an environment in Indonesia that allows the sector to make effective policy decisions that will determine whether the renewed financial loan scheme will prove a success or lead to another failure.

The Thai Case

The last three chapters of the volume are concerned with the Thai case. The rapid expansion of the higher education sector in Thailand and the policy failures and successes make for valuable case studies. In Chapter 9, Somkiat Tangkitvanich and Areeya Manasboonphempool give an overview and outline the problems faced, the policy measures undertaken to date, and also assess the success and failure of each. Piruna Polsiri, Rangsit Sarachitti and Thitima Sitthipongpanich conduct analysis in Chapter 10 that shows repayment burdens for the Thai Student Loans Fund (SLF) under different scenarios of interest rate subsidies. Their chapter is a contribution to the understanding of the Thai case but also to the analysis of interest rate subsidies and repayment hardship in the higher education literature. Bruce Chapman and Kiatanantha Lounkaew in Chapter 11 compare alternatives in Thai income-contingent student loans.

Since the early 1900s, the number of higher educational institutions in Thailand has increased to nearly 800 institutions with the total number of students enrolled reaching 2.5 million. With a 41 per cent gross enrolment ratio, the country ranks second only to Japan and is ranked higher than much wealthier countries such as Malaysia and Hong Kong. The public sector plays a very dominant role in this education provision, enrolling more than four-fifths of total students.

To cope with this rapid enrolment expansion, the Thai education financing system has needed a number of reforms. During the past three decades, continued efforts have been made to transform major limited-admission public universities into autonomous universities. The purpose of this was to provide administrative flexibility to these universities, aiming to enhance their quality to an international level. So far, however, only seven public universities have been successfully transformed, with only a few more in the pipeline.

In addition to the direct provision of higher education by public institutions, the Thai government has also provided loans to students since 1996 under the SLF scheme. The main objective of the SLF is to increase the opportunities for students from low-income families to continue their study. Other objectives are to promote more equal income distribution in the long run and to develop a demand-side financing system by increasing the capacity of households to contribute more resources to education. The SLF loans cover tuition fees, educational-related expenses and other living expenses. Only high-school or tertiary-level students whose family's income is less than B150 000 per annum are eligible to apply for the loan. During the first 10 years of its operation, the SLF has lent to more than 2.6 million students, with the loan value totalling nearly B200 billion.

In practice, however, despite its high cost, the SLF seems to have increased the educational opportunities of the borrowers only from families with income below the poverty line. Since this group constitutes only 13 per cent of the total borrowers, the income threshold set by the SLF appears to be far too high. The current SLF scheme also contains many flaws. For example, its loan-screening system is far from perfect, it fails to disburse loans on time, it has a very poor collection mechanism and it is still based on the supply-side financing paradigm. Analysis shows also that it has not significantly influenced the decisions of high-school students to continue their studies to a higher level, except for the poorest group, who were a minority among the recipients. In addition, the SLF is suffering from a serious financial sustainability problem due to its very low recovery rate.

The SLF was temporarily abolished and replaced with the Thai Income Contingent Allowance and Loan (TICAL) scheme under the Thaksin government in 2006— with the SLF reintroduced following the 2007 election. The TICAL, which was modelled after the income-contingent loan scheme in Australia, is different from the SLF in many important ways. First, it allows only undergraduates but not high-school students to borrow. In addition, it sets no conditions on the household income of the borrowers. This means that all undergraduate students in any field may apply for a loan. Second, it covers only tuition fees, not other education-related and living expenses. Third, it does not require the borrowers to start repaying until their incomes reach B16 000 a month (the minimum income threshold for the payment of income tax). The repayment rate is contingent upon the borrowers' incomes, and is progressively increased with higher income. Fourth, there is no interest charged under the TICAL scheme, but the outstanding debt will be adjusted by inflation from the first year of borrowing. Finally, the revenue department is responsible for collecting the repayment.

The shift to the TICAL brought about many important improvements, especially a potentially more effective repayment collection system. Moreover, it was based on a demand-side financing paradigm that promoted more choices for students. The TICAL was not, however, without its problems; it still unnecessarily subsidised the borrowers by charging a zero real interest rate. In addition, the TICAL by itself could not bring about the overall changes to the educational financing system unless other complementary reforms were also undertaken.

Hidden costs in the SLF make up a large portion of the total implicit subsidy received by students. The Thai SLF is relatively soft in terms of payment hardships under poor post-education outcomes. It is also very generous in terms of the implicit subsidy. This means that a large amount of public money is required to maintain the system. If you remove a lot of the hidden benefits of the scheme, such as grace periods and income thresholds, the system becomes a lot more inexpensive but dramatically increases the burden on students. Having said this, the current scheme is prohibitively expensive for the Thai government and reform needs to be implemented whilst still maintaining widespread access to quality higher education for all economic groups.

Perhaps most importantly, policy certainty is a prerequisite for the long-term development of the system. Frequent policy reversals will not only bring about confusions to all stakeholders, they will also raise questions about the government's commitment to any loan programs, thus undermining the credibility and integrity of the scheme. Another important lesson is the importance of strengthening public financial management, which not only allows the government to implement a more effective higher education financing system, but also has a number of other equally important positive effects on the economy. Within this process, to avoid haphazard policy changes, policy makers should seek consensus from broad-based stakeholders before making any more major policy changes in the future.

Conclusion

Higher education and an appropriate financing system that helps to overcome market failures are essential components of a country's ability to integrate into the increasingly knowledge-based global economy.

The question is how to arrange the resources to make sufficient investment in education that is accessible to everyone while also improving the quality of the education that is delivered. This is not an easy problem particularly in the early stages of economic success when resources are stretched towards achieving many objectives. The focus of research is on the various strategies that have been used to promote the expansion of accessibility to higher education for the populations around the region. There is much policy experience in addressing these questions from other countries in the region and, taken together, these experiences can illuminate the challenges and options in different countries. The first of these is the ultimate role of government within the sector to correct a market failure that occurs from the existence of the large positive externalities derived from a highly educated, capable workforce. Large positive externalities lead to sub-optimal levels of investment in education under free-market conditions. This is also amplified by the inability of individuals to use human capital as collateral to make investments in their own education.

Such a situation creates a clear role for government to intervene in the higher education sector, but, as with all interventions, these must be carefully planned. One key element of this planning must be a clear recognition of what the government wishes to achieve from its intervention as this will play a large role in the optimal type of intervention. Ultimately, there are three main objectives of government intervention into the higher education sector. These include increasing the quantity and quality of and access to higher education. Consumption smoothing is an important aspect that helps facilitate this.

Economic theory also offers a number of lessons for the design of higher education schemes that can achieve the objectives of government. These include elements such as the importance of competition—both amongst universities and amongst those wishing to attend. This raises the importance of promoting access to the sector for people from all segments of society regardless of economic background.

It is also important for government to recognise the strengths and weaknesses of different types of support systems. Loan schemes are not well designed to directly benefit the poor. They are best designed to increase resources to the higher education sector and to provide an element of consumption smoothing, which will benefit mainly middle-income students. Grant-based or interest rate subsidy schemes, on the other hand, are better suited to improving access to higher education—particularly for poorer segments of society.

The big question is whether a country is capable of implementing and administering a student loan or higher education support scheme. Countries need a number of characteristics, such as strong political support, which is long term, enough bureaucratic capacity to ensure an effective administration as well as widespread public acknowledgment of the need for a higher education system.

It is also important to highlight the importance of country specificity in the design, implementation and, ultimately, the effect of higher education financing schemes. Israel attempted to import a scheme directly from another country without adjusting it to Israel's institutional settings with predictable adverse consequences. If Thailand were to implement a scheme similar to Australia's or New Zealand's it would be unlikely to generate either the same outcomes or the same level of debt repayment. One reason for this might be, for example, that local incomes are not high enough in Thailand to allow for sufficient rates of repayment. As noted in the previous section, the main policy conclusions of successes in the implementation of income-contingent loans across the region need to be handled with care. In some countries, the institutional framework might be currently inappropriate to allow efficient, even workable, collection of income-contingent loans. If this is the case, fruitful policy reform would seem to involve improvements in public-sector management. The Australian case, for example, offers some useful insights into the application of higher education financing in Thailand but should not be taken to suggest that income-contingent loans are a panacea to international higher education funding challenges. In many countries, there are important institutional difficulties to be overcome in the successful adoption of such approaches.

Part 1. Education and Development: The role of higher education

2. Education and Development: The role of higher education

Lawrence Summers

Harvard University

This chapter provides an American perspective on issues affecting higher education in China. It discusses how the work of universities is so important to the development of nations, and reflects on the success of the US system and what lessons can be taken from this system for higher education in other parts of the world.

Discussions of higher education and development took an odd turn about a generation ago from which we are only now recovering. It came to be a fashionable idea that emphasis should be placed on primary and secondary services, rather than on tertiary services. The argument was made that from an equity point of view, it was more important to teach more people to read than to teach a small cadre the liberal arts. The argument was made from the point of view of mass economic development. Strengthening primary and secondary schools for the many was more important than strengthening universities for the few. The argument was made that in a fundamental sense, there was something unegalitarian about support for universities, especially since the majority of students entering the system were the children of what quite likely had been privileged families. None of the arguments is entirely without merit, and to suggest that higher education should be emphasised at the expense of primary and secondary education is not the point. It does seem that the lessons of recent economic history point in a very compelling way towards the importance of strong universities—and universities that receive substantial public support.

This is not a new idea. Economic historians who have studied the growth of Europe assign a very significant role to what took place in universities. In the United States, the land-grant colleges established during the Lincoln administration—with the objective of spreading education and in particular promoting research into more productive agriculture and the dissemination of agricultural technologies—are generally regarded as having made an important contribution to US economic success.

Most evidence would suggest that the current world economy is going to be a knowledge economy to a much greater extent than any we have seen to date. As the agricultural revolution gave way to the Industrial Revolution, increasingly the Industrial Revolution is giving way to a kind of information

19

revolution. Alan Greenspan made that point in a very powerful way by noting that even as the value of the US gross product had increased, its total mass had quite substantially decreased. We are replacing semi-conductive steel with semiconductors; we are replacing manufactured products with services. All you have to do is look at the results of the market to see the impact of knowledge. Salary differentials between those with high-school degrees and no high-school degree, those with college degrees and no college degree, graduate degrees and college degrees, those with training at first-rate institutions versus those with training at second-rate institutions—all of these economic differentials have widened very substantially, and that suggests the high importance of the increase in the supply of highly skilled workers.

Bill Clinton was fond of remarking that you could not have employees without having employers. Or, as he sometimes put it, he hoped that there would be many more millionaires in the United States at the end of his term than there were at the beginning. He expressed that hope because he recognised that people who started successful businesses, who built successful institutions, generated enormous externalities by employing large numbers of people. If there is going to be that leading edge in any country, it is going to depend critically on that country's system of higher education, because in today's economy, the majority of such people are going to be those who have received sophisticated education at the undergraduate level and perhaps even the graduate level.

The case in countries such as the United States or those in Europe is that a large fraction of the benefits of higher education derive from enabling entrepreneurs to push the frontier of science with commercial application. In emerging markets, the largest fraction of the benefit will probably derive from facilitating the adoption and dissemination of new technologies. In either event, successful practically oriented institutions of education are crucial to the success of any country competing in today's global economy.

There are other reasons why strong institutions of higher education are important to the work of nations. Strong institutions of higher education that promote access, that enable access without regard to financial circumstances or the ability to pay, that provide large numbers of spaces for those who are most able, regardless of their connections or their family's wealth, are also important guarantors of the kind of social mobility that promotes a healthy society.

These are only some of the reasons why the work of universities is very important in any society. One of the major differences between the economy of today and the industrial economy of a generation ago is that a contemporary economy has to be based much more on the authority of ideas and much less on the idea of authority. The most successful organisations today are not those based on strong hierarchical commanding control; they are based on organisations and companies that reorganise themselves every six months or every two years. They are based on organisations whose strategy can be altered, whose traditional dogma can be questioned by any part of the organisation, by anyone who has something to contribute. It is this kind of culture that universities, at their best, are very good at fostering.

As President of Harvard University, I taught a freshman seminar and one of the topics we covered was capital flows and capital flows to emerging markets—an issue I would be very much engaged in at the US Treasury. And it was with great pleasure that I remember the meaning of the seminar, at which a freshman who had been at Harvard for six weeks and who was asked to summarise that week's readings said very calmly that he had read Professor Summer's lecture and he had found it very interesting, although the data, in his view, did not come close to proving the conclusions. And I thought, what a remarkable and positive thing that a seventeen-year-old who had been at Harvard for all of six weeks felt entirely free saying that the President did not really know what he was talking about on an issue for which he had led policy for his country. To be sure, I did not agree with the student and I made clear why I did not agree, but I thought that kind of open dialogue, which is encouraged in universities, is something that does not get fostered in many institutions and it is something that universities are very, very good at doing. New knowledge pushing back the frontiers of science with commercial application, providing equal opportunity, modelling the kinds of open organisations and the kinds of open structures that promote creativity and entrepreneurship—these are the great contributions that universities make to societies.

Universities make another contribution. To be sure it is not a contribution they have always made. They prompt reflection by society on what their deepest values are, what their true nature is, ways in which they can be better. The United States and Europe are very different places because of the events of the 1960s. In the United States there would be a very different attitude towards women and race if the changes in university policy that were very much at the vanguard of questions of inclusion had not taken place. It might be an exaggeration to say that what is good for a country is good for its universities and what is good for its universities is good for the country, but when one looks at different emerging markets, one has the sense that looking back one or two generations at which countries have succeeded and which have not, the ones that have been most successful will tend to be the countries that were most successful in fostering terrific educational experiences for the people in their late teens and early twenties who in 25 or 30 years are going to be their nation's leaders in every sphere. That is why the development of educational institutions is so important.

When looking at the data of the top-ranking universities in the world, it is clear that US universities are a very substantial fraction of the top group—whether that is the top five, the top 10, the top 25, the top 50 or the top 100. There are few other sectors where that would be the case. It certainly would not be the case in almost any area of manufacturing activity today. It would be the case in very few service-sector activities. It is worth considering what it is about the US system that contributes to that great strength. This can be summarised in three primary factors.

First, the US university system is intensely competitive. Universities compete for the best students; they compete for the best faculty; they compete to have the highest rankings whenever anyone constructs a system of rankings. That competition can sometimes be destructive but in the fullness of it, the fact of brutal competition for the best students and the best faculty forces a discipline and excellence that are present in US universities and are sometimes less present in others. As such, the capacity to maintain a competitive environment and what the competitive environment depends on is the availability of choice—the fact that professors are free to move from one university to another without regard to any kind of national plan, the fact that students have multiple options and that the best students are able to choose the universities that they wish to go to. This competition among universities, as among businesses, is a very powerful spur to quality. Too often countries beyond the United States have a carefully planned and managed system that does not provide those kinds of incentives for competition and therefore miss a drive for excellence of the kind that has proven so powerful in the United States.

A second strength of the US university system—though it is one on which improvements are certainly possible—is a governance model that maintains dynamism. A university is a very difficult kind of institution to govern, because many of the most important judgments—judgments about what is going to be taught in a physics class or a history class or a literature class, judgments about who is the best scholar to hire—are judgments that really are best made by experts in those fields and not by general leaders. Yet, at the same time, when judgments are made by the incumbents in a field, you tend, as in any area of human activity, to get self-perpetuation. So the challenge is to find a governance model that draws on local expertise, draws on experts, but at the same time ensures accountability for excellence. University governance models go wrong in two ways. In some cases in the United States, and certainly in many cases abroad, universities are governed too much like any other part of the public sector. There are elaborate bureaucratic rules governing promotion, compensation and decision making that preclude the kind of dynamism, flexibility and rapid movement to opportunity that success and knowledge-based activities require. If universities cannot be run like departments of motor vehicles, it is also true that it is very dangerous when universities are run by their staff. In too many places, university presidents are chosen or renewed on the basis of votes of faculty, students and staff. In such a context—which would be unthinkable in a modern corporation—it is very difficult for a leader to make difficult choices, to shut down mediocre activities or to reallocate resources from lower-productivity activities to higher-productivity activities. The challenge is to find leadership that is empowered vis-a-vis those who work in the institution but at the same time understand that empowerment is a very different thing to the ability to dictate precisely what is going to happen. Private universities in the United States with trustees—often trustees who are involved in providing substantial resources to the university—strike this compromise as well as it has been struck. It is a constant battle, however, and one that requires constant vigilance, but it is a critical issue that must be monitored.

A third strength of the US system is its substantial reliance on the private sector. Great institutions such as Harvard, the University of Chicago and Stanford University are not public institutions. They certainly do receive support for research and for financial aid for students from the government. But the lion's share of their resources comes from loyal alumni—from people who have been highly successful and have chosen to allocate resources to support their activities. That mixture of the public and the private sector is often a source of tension in the United States, but it is also a great spur to innovation. It is hoped that around the world over the next generation we will see the John Harvards, the Lyman Stanfords, the Andrew Carnegies and the John. D. Rockefellers who will step forward and provide the leadership for creating academic institutions that will be a source of national strength for many years into the future.

3. Financing Higher Education: Lessons from economic theory and operational experience[1]

Nicholas Barr[2]

London School of Economics

This chapter talks about how to pay for teaching at universities. It does not talk about financing research or about any particular country. Instead, its purpose is to offer a tool kit for policy makers thinking about reform.

The chapter sets out lessons for policy design from economic theory and the experience of developed countries. Economic theory, however, is not enough. Policy design that outstrips a country's capacity to implement it effectively is bad policy design. This chapter therefore deliberately goes beyond theory to include lessons about implementation. The chapter concludes with discussion of the resulting system.

The Backdrop

Higher education matters—and always will—because knowledge for its own sake is important. But, in sharp contrast with 50 years ago, now higher education matters also for national economic performance and for individual life chances. Technological advance has driven up the demand for skills. To compete internationally, countries need mass high-quality higher education.

That immediately raises the question of how to pay for it. Countries typically pursue three goals in higher education: larger quantity with good access, higher quality, and constant or falling public spending. It is possible to achieve two but only at the expense of the third. Systems can be

- large and tax financed, but with worries about quality (France, Germany, Italy)
- high quality and tax financed, but small (the United Kingdom until 1989)
- large and good quality, but fiscally expensive (Scandinavia).

---

1   This chapter is a shortened version of Barr (2008), which draws on earlier writing—notably Barr (2004a)—much of it growing out of work over many years with Iain Crawford (see Barr and Crawford 2005).

2   Professor of Public Economics, London School of Economics and Political Science, Houghton Street, London WC2A 2AE, UK. Tel: +44 20 7955 7482; fax: +44 20 7955 7546. Email: <N.Barr@lse.ac.uk>; <http://econ.lse.ac.uk/staff/nb>

There is nothing illogical about the last option, but it is unsustainable in most countries, not least because of competing fiscal pressures connected with population ageing (see Barr and Diamond 2008), advances in medical care, and increased international competitive pressures ('globalisation'). Thus, the only realistic way of achieving all three objectives is to supplement public finance with private finance. The scale of the task should not be underestimated. In South Korea, the participation rate in tertiary education is 82 per cent; total spending on tertiary education is 2.6 per cent of gross domestic product (GDP)— double the average for the EU19 of 1.3 per cent; and *private* spending on tertiary education is significantly higher than *total* (public plus private) spending in any Organisation for Economic Cooperation and Development (OECD) country except the United States and Canada (OECD 2006:Table B2.1b; all figures for 2003).

A related issue is how to promote quality. Part of the story is adequate finance, but there is also the issue of how to ensure that resources for higher education are used efficiently. As discussed later, competitive systems of higher education tend to produce higher quality, at least as measured by world rankings.

Lessons from Economic Theory

This section sets out three central lessons from economic theory for a system that seeks to strengthen the quality of higher education while simultaneously promoting access: competition is beneficial; graduates should contribute to the cost of their degree; and well-designed loans have core characteristics.

Competition is Beneficial

The case for competition in higher education is not ideological, but rooted in the economics of information.

Fifty years ago, richer countries generally had small university systems offering degrees in a limited range of subjects. In that world it was possible, as a polite myth, to assume that all universities were equally good and hence to fund them broadly equally. Today there are more universities, more students and much greater diversity of subjects. As a result, the characteristics and the costs of different degrees at different institutions vary widely, so that institutions need to be funded differentially—a problem too complex for any central planner. A mass system in an increasingly complex world needs a funding mechanism that allows institutions to charge differential fees to reflect different costs and objectives. Central planning is no longer feasible.

Central planning is also no longer desirable. It is a standard proposition in welfare economics that competition benefits consumers when consumers are well informed (Barr 2004b:Ch. 4). Students (in sharp contrast with schoolchildren or people with complex medical problems) are potentially well-informed consumers, and thus able to make choices that conform with their interests and those of the economy. Though that proposition is robust, there is an important exception: people from disadvantaged backgrounds might not be fully informed, emphasising the need for action to promote access. It should be noted that the same analytical approach can lead to very different conclusions for school education (Barr 2004b:Chs 13, 14).

Graduates Should Contribute to the Cost of their Degree

Higher education creates benefits beyond those to the individual—benefits in terms of growth, the transmission of values, and the development of knowledge for its own sake—justifying continuing taxpayer subsidies. But there are also significant private benefits—in terms of higher earnings, more satisfying jobs and/or greater enjoyment of leisure time—making it efficient and equitable for graduates to bear some of the costs.

Though the previous paragraph is uncontentious as far as it goes, policy makers—especially in ministries of finance—are keen to know the answers to two questions

- what is the efficient level of spending on education
- what is the efficient level of taxpayer subsidy?

These questions are important but unfortunately can be answered only indicatively. The conclusion of a very different literature (Barr 1999; Sen 1999) is that it is not possible to quantify a value-free definition of poverty. Instead, the decision about where to pitch the poverty line depends on social choice constrained by fiscal realities. Analogously, problems—of concept and of measurement—mean that the benefits to education cannot be quantified in any definitive way.

Quantitative Arguments

In principle, it is efficient to devote resources to tertiary education to the point where their marginal social value equals their marginal social costs. Though it is possible to measure the costs of education, there are several reasons why there is no definitive way of quantifying social benefits: measuring outputs and inputs faces major problems; and, even were these to be resolved, causality is problematic. The arguments summarised briefly below are set out more fully in Barr (2000).

First, output cannot be measured, because there is no single definition of a 'good' education. Test scores are imperfect measures even where output is defined narrowly as technical achievement; they fail to capture the broader benefits of education to the individual; and they take no account of a range of external benefits, including shared values. That the broader benefits are largely unmeasurable does not make them unreal.

Second, there are problems connecting output to educational inputs. Measuring inputs is not easy. It is possible to measure the quantity of teachers' and pupils' time, buildings, and so on, but much harder to measure the quality of teachers, natural ability and the quality of parenting. A second problem is establishing the production function that connects inputs and outputs. Studies tend to assume (since no other assumption is available) that schools have a single, simple objective: maximising pupils' test scores. Though analytically tractable, this approach is flawed; it implies, for example, that a school should stop teaching children who are not capable of passing tests.

A third set of problems relates to establishing causality. The discussion above implicitly assumes that education increases individual productivity. What is known as the screening hypothesis questions the causal link—at least for post-primary education—arguing that education is associated with increased productivity but does not cause it.[3] The argument has two elements.

- Individual productivity could be the result of natural ability rather than post-primary education (analogously, good health could be due more to a naturally strong constitution than to medical intervention).
- Firms seek high-ability workers but, prior to employing them, cannot distinguish high-ability from low-ability workers.

The two elements together suggest that there is no social benefit from post-primary education, but a private benefit for individuals, who face incentives to make themselves stand out. The screening hypothesis argues that post-primary education does exactly that: it gives a signal to prospective employers that it is in the individual's interest to acquire.

It is clear that the hypothesis does not hold fully. It fails where education includes professional training such as medicine. It also fails where there is more than one type of job; if skills and job characteristics are heterogeneous, education has a social benefit as a device for matching workers and jobs. The extent to which the hypothesis has some validity is an empirical matter, but is clouded by the measurement problems already discussed—notably of such factors as natural ability and family background.

---

3 The large literature on this and other aspects of the economics of education is surveyed by Blaug (1976, 1985) and Glennerster (1993).

Qualitative Arguments

Thus, it is not possible to quantify external benefits; hence there is no definitive answer to questions about the optimal size of the sector or the efficient level of taxpayer subsidy.

There are, however, powerful qualitative arguments for increasing investment in human capital. Technological advance is a key driver. Though technological change reduces the need for some skills (user-friendly computers), it mostly increases the demand for skilled workers. In addition, skills date quickly. The 'information age' can be taken to mean a need for education and training that is larger than previously, more diverse and repeated, given the need for periodic retraining.

Demographic change offers a second reason for increased investment in education. The rising proportion of older people foreshadows increased spending on pensions, medical care and long-term care. Part of the solution is to increase output sufficiently to meet the combined expectations of workers and pensioners.[4] If workers are becoming relatively more scarce, the efficient response is to increase labour productivity. Demographic change is thus an argument for additional spending on investment both in physical and in human capital.

For these reasons, the qualitative case for expanding higher education and continued taxpayer support is strong.

Alongside the case for expansion is a strong case for cost sharing, given the evidence on the private benefits of higher education. It is a standard proposition in economic theory that it is efficient (and usually also equitable) if a person pays for the private benefits he/she receives. Beneficiaries, however, should bear those costs when they can afford them—when they are graduates—and not as students, leading directly to the third set of lessons from economic theory.

Well-Designed Loans Have Core Characteristics

Two lines of argument support widespread student loans. As noted, it is not feasible to rely on taxation to finance high-quality mass higher education. As well as being infeasible, tax finance is also undesirable, for at least three reasons. First, in most countries it has not significantly widened access. The record in the United Kingdom in this regard is shameful: in 2002, 81 per cent of children with parents from professional backgrounds went to university; the comparable figure for children from poorer backgrounds was 15 per cent (UK Education and Skills Select Committee 2002:19). Second, tax finance has not generally been able to protect quality; the days are gone when the higher education sector was

---

4   On the analytics, see Barr and Diamond (2008).

small and competing claims on public funds less powerful. Finally, tax finance is generally regressive; participating in higher education is a matter of choice, and that choice is highly skewed to the better off.

Thus, the case for loans is twofold: well-designed loans bring in private-sector sources (graduates' repayments) to supplement tax revenues; and they address the regressivity of tax finance.

Characteristic 1: Income-contingent repayments

How should loans be designed? A central element is that they should have income-contingent repayments—that is, repayments calculated as x per cent of the borrower's subsequent earnings until the loan has been repaid, rather than $X a month.[5]

There are both efficiency and equity gains from this approach. The equity argument is that loans with income-contingent repayments protect low earners because insurance against inability to repay is an integral part of their design. In efficiency terms, such loans address important imperfections in capital markets whose implications were first explored by Milton Friedman (1955).

To illustrate, when someone buys a house, she normally borrows from a private lender. Similar loans exist for cars. Why has the private market not provided analogous loans for borrowing to finance investment in human capital?

Home loans are relatively low risk for both borrower and lender.

1. The person who buys a house generally knows what he is buying.

2. The house is unlikely to fall down and is, in any case, insurable.

3. The real value of the house will generally (though not always) increase.

4. The existence of a physical asset reduces risk for the borrower; if his income falls, making repayments impossible, he can sell the house and repay the loan.

5. The house acts as physical collateral, reducing risk for the lender, who can if necessary repossess the asset—thus, loans are available with only a small risk premium.

Thus, it is not surprising that a market solution exists. The contrast with human capital is clear. Though many applicants to university are well informed, this is not the case in families where no-one has been to university, violating (1). A qualification can 'fall down', violating (2), since students might fail exams.

---

5   For fuller discussion, see Barr (2001:Chs 11, 12), and for an early proposal with loan repayments based on social security contributions, see Barnes and Barr (1988).

Though the real rate of return to a degree continues to be high, there is a variance around the average so that the same is not necessarily true for all students, violating (3). In addition, there is no collateral. Thus, someone who has borrowed to finance a degree but then experiences low earnings does not have the option to sell the qualification, violating (4), and can therefore borrow, if at all, only at a substantial risk premium, violating (5). One solution is to introduce collateral in the form of a guarantee—say, from a parent—but this runs counter to the drive to widen access.

Friedman (1955) recognised these capital-market imperfections explicitly:

> [I]n a non-slave state, the individual embodying the investment cannot be bought and sold. But even if he could, the security would not be comparable. The productivity of...physical capital does not...depend on the co-operativeness of the original borrower. The productivity of the human capital quite obviously does...A loan to finance the training of an individual who has no security to offer other than his future earnings is therefore a much less attractive proposition than a loan to finance, say, the erection of a building...
>
> A further complication is...the inappropriateness of fixed money loans to finance investment in training. Such an investment necessarily involves much risk. The average expected return may be high, but there is wide variation about the average. (Friedman 1955:137)

The solution proposed by Friedman is that the government would provide the investment capital, in return for which

> [t]he individual would agree in return to pay to the government in each future year x per cent of his earnings in excess of y dollars for each $1,000 that he gets in this way. This payment could easily be combined with payment of income tax and so involve a minimum of additional administrative expense. (Friedman 1955:140)

Thus, the efficiency case for income-contingent repayments is that they address important capital-market imperfections: borrowers from disadvantaged backgrounds might be badly informed about the value of a degree; and all borrowers face substantial uncertainty. Thus, there are technical problems on the demand side of the market for loans and, as a result, borrowing to finance investment in human capital will be inefficiently low.

On the supply side, lenders are uncertain about the riskiness of an applicant for a loan and will therefore charge a risk premium. A risk premium assessed by a well-informed lender is efficient (analogous to higher automobile insurance premiums for bad drivers). But lenders are not well informed about the riskiness of an applicant. The problem is compounded by the potential for adverse selection, since the borrower is better informed than the lender about his or her degree of riskiness. For example, the lender cannot be certain that the borrower will become an accountant rather than an actor, or that the borrower will work hard. Adverse selection leads to two sets of ill effects. Private lenders will charge a risk premium that is inefficiently high. In addition, they face incentives to lend only to the best risks (analogous to incentives to cream-skimming facing private medical insurers). An obvious way to do so is to lend only to students who can provide security—for example, from a home-owning parent.

In sum, borrowing to finance a degree has technical characteristics that differ substantially from borrowing to buy a house. Conventional loans are the wrong model for investment in human capital. They lead to inefficiently low borrowing and lending. They are also inequitable, in that these efficiency problems impact most on people from poor backgrounds, women and ethnic minorities, who might be less well informed and therefore less prepared to risk a loan. In addition, these groups are likely to be on the wrong end of cherry-picking by lenders. The interest of lenders is in secure loans; the national interest is in the optimal quantity and mix of investment in human capital. In a world of perfect information, the two interests coincide; with imperfect information, they do not.

Characteristic 2: Large enough

A second feature of well-designed loans is that the loan should be large enough to cover fees and, in developed countries, living costs, thus providing efficient consumption smoothing, resolving student poverty and promoting access by making higher education free at the point of use.

Characteristic 3: A rational interest rate

Finally, loans should attract an interest rate broadly equal to the government's cost of borrowing. The question of interest rates bears examination. A number of countries, including the United Kingdom, offer loans at a zero real interest rate—a rate lower than the government has to pay to borrow the money.[6] Thus, there is a blanket interest subsidy. In a system with income-contingent repayments, this policy achieves not a single desirable objective. The subsidy is

---

6 Australia has a system in which students may pay a tuition charge (say, A$6000) either through a loan with a zero real interest rate or by paying tuition charges up-front at a 25 per cent discount (that is, A$4500). Thus, students pay a zero real interest rate at the margin but also a fixed element (in that they are liable to repay A$6000—A$1500 more than those who pay up-front). The effect of the discount is to introduce a positive real interest rate on average. The balance between the marginal element (the zero real interest rate) and the fixed element (the discount) determines the size of the resulting real interest rate. Irrespective of the balance, a marginal subsidy is likely to be distorting even if offset by an average charge.

enormously expensive in fiscal terms. Because of the resulting fiscal pressures, loans are too small, harming access. The subsidies also crowd out university income, harming quality. Finally, the subsidies are deeply regressive.

The regressivity point merits attention.

- The subsidies do not help students (graduates, not students, make repayments).
- In a well-designed system, they give relatively little help to low-earning graduates, since unpaid debt is eventually forgiven.[7]
- They do not help high-earning graduates early in their careers; with income-contingent loans, monthly repayments depend only on earnings, thus the interest rate *has no effect on monthly repayments*, but only on the duration of the loan.
- Thus, the major beneficiaries are successful professionals in mid career, whose loan repayments are switched off earlier than would otherwise be the case because of the subsidy. This is not the target group that policy makers had in mind.

In contrast, *targeted* interest subsidies have much to commend them.

In sum, income-contingent repayments improve efficiency by protecting borrowers and lenders from the uncertainty of a loan that is not secured by physical collateral; borrowers are protected because monthly repayments are calibrated to the borrower's subsequent earnings, and lenders are protected from the risk of an unsecured loan, not least because repayments are collected alongside income tax. Income-contingent repayments also protect access because the loan has built-in insurance against inability to repay. Note that what is being discussed is not a tax, which goes on forever, but a genuine loan, for which repayments cease once the principal plus interest have been repaid. Income-contingent repayments have a profound effect that is insufficiently understood.

The Resulting Policy Strategy

These theoretical considerations suggest a general strategy for efficiency and equity with three elements: variable fees, well-designed loans, and active measures to promote access. The strategy is potentially applicable to all countries that have the capacity to implement it—a centrally important topic discussed later.

---

7   In the United Kingdom, any loan that has not been repaid after 25 years is forgiven. Income-contingent repayments protect against low current income; the 25-year rule protects against low lifetime income.

Element 1: Variable fees

There are three arguments for variable fees (OECD 2004:Ch. 4, 2005:Ch. 3, 2008)

- they promote quality by making funding open ended,[8] thus increasing the volume of resources going to higher education
- they promote quality by strengthening competition, thus improving the efficiency with which the extra resources are used
- counter-intuitively, they are also fairer: why should a student at a small local university be required to pay the same fee as one at a world-class institution?

The argument for competition is rooted in the idea that students in higher education are broadly well informed and that their information can be further improved. The argument is not for law-of-the-jungle competition but for regulated markets.

The obvious argument against fees is that they deter students from poor backgrounds. That is true of up-front fees, but not where students go to university free and make a contribution only after they have graduated. This brings us to the second part of the strategy.

Element 2: A well-designed loan scheme

Student support is through loans with income-contingent repayments. The loan entitlement should be large enough to cover fees and, if possible, also living costs, and should carry a rational interest rate. If, however, someone has extended spells out of the labour force, his or her loan can spiral upwards. Thus, though there is a strong case against blanket interest subsidies, there are good arguments for targeted interest subsidies for people with low earnings or out of the labour force.

If loans are large enough to cover fees, the package resembles 'free' higher education financed through taxation. Students pay nothing at the time they go to university. Part of the cost is paid through taxation and part through their subsequent income-contingent repayments. The viewpoint of the ministry of finance is somewhat different. Though loans bring in private resources in the longer term, a loan system, by definition, has up-front costs because it lends the money first and receives repayments later. Thus, depending on a country's fiscal situation, there can be advantages if students can borrow from private sources, but—particularly in a developing country—private lenders will charge

---

8 If there are no fees, the ministry of finance controls the total volume of resources going to higher education. With fees set centrally by central government the same is true; if rising fee income is offset by declining taxpayer funding, the total volume of resources going to higher education does not change (this is what happened in Australia over the 1990s). With variable fees, in contrast, universities have an instrument with which they can respond to any decline in public funding, hence funding becomes open ended.

a substantial risk premium unless there is a government guarantee; and if there is a government guarantee, the loans will be classified as public spending. As discussed later in this chapter, potential solutions exist in this highly technical area, but require considerable care in design.

Element 3: Action to promote access

Assume that all students are well informed and have a good school education. In that case, a good income-contingent loan is all that is needed. In most countries, however, not all students are well informed. In particular, the group for whom we want to promote access is not well informed. More is needed. Most people argue that what is needed is 'free' higher education. The evidence, however, points in a different direction. The primary driver of participation in higher education is attainment in school. The sharp socioeconomic gradient in participation in the United Kingdom has already been noted. Yet controlling for the quality of high-school grades, the gradient disappears; of those with good high-school graduation grades, 90 per cent progressed to higher education, irrespective of socioeconomic background (UK Office for National Statistics 2004:Fig. 2.15).

What does this imply for policy to improve participation? Exclusion, it can be argued, has four roots: lack of education, lack of information about university, lack of aspirations, and lack of money. A well-designed strategy should address all four.

Raising attainment: access fails when someone drops out of school early, usually for reasons that started much earlier. More resources are needed earlier in the system, not least because of the growing evidence (Feinstein 2003) that the roots of exclusion lie in early childhood. A central element in widening participation is to strengthen pre-university education, from nursery school onwards.

Increasing information and raising aspirations: a series of policies addresses both. Action to inform schoolchildren and raise their aspirations is critical. Relevant activities include mentoring by university students, visit days, Saturday schools, summer schools, and the like.

More money: policies include financial support to encourage teenagers to complete high school, and grants and scholarships to cover some or all costs at university. Both policies could be supported by financial incentives to universities to widen participation.

Policy Design: Lessons from international experience

There are important lessons about tuition fess and about student loans. It is also useful to inquire about other sources of private finance.

Lessons about Fees

As noted earlier, competition benefits consumers when they are well informed. This line of argument suggests that each university should be able to set the level of its tuition fees and other charges. That, however, does not mean that the optimal solution is complete deregulation. Liberalising fees in a 'big-bang' way can be politically destabilising. In 1992, New Zealand introduced fees set by universities, but made mistakes. First, reform was to some extent big bang. Student loans were new, and fees, though not new, were fully liberalised. Second, though the system included targeted interest subsidies, more could have been done to assist low earners. Third, the government failed to explain—and to continue to explain—the reforms and, in particular, the considerable advantages of income-contingent repayments. As a result, as nominal student debt increased over time, so did political pressures. The scheme was diluted in 2000.

A second lesson is that the opposite policy direction—no liberalisation—is also a mistake. Higher education with no or low fixed fees creates two problems. Quality suffers because the education budget has to compete with other budgetary imperatives; and within the education budget, universities compete with nursery education, school education and vocational training. As a result, real funding per student tends to decline. Access also suffers. If places are scarce, middle-class students tend to get them; and if places are not scarce, the need to finance a mass system typically creates concerns about quality and means that resources to promote access are limited.

Lessons about Loans

Discussion focuses on four lessons: income-contingent loans do not harm access; interest subsidies are expensive; positive real interest rates are politically feasible; and the design of the student loan contract matters.

Income-contingent loans do not harm access. Australia introduced a system of income-contingent loans in 1989 to cover a newly introduced tuition charge. Chapman and Ryan (2003) point to increased participation overall since 1989 and, superimposed on that trend, that women's participation grew more strongly than men's, and that the system did not discourage participation by people in the lowest socioeconomic groups. This result is what theory would predict: income-contingent repayments are designed explicitly to reduce the risks borrowers face, and fees supported by loans free resources to promote access.

A second lesson is that interest subsidies are expensive. The UK system charges an interest rate equal to the inflation rate—that is, a zero real rate, which is less than the government has to pay to borrow the money. The interest subsidy is expensive: for every £100 the government lends, between £30 and £35 is never repaid simply because of the interest subsidy (Barr 2002:paras 33–7). In other words, the interest subsidy converts nearly one-third of the loan into a grant. New Zealand offers parallel evidence (see Barr 2004a).

Positive real interest rates, however, are politically feasible—examples include Hungary, the Netherlands, Norway and Sweden. It is interesting that in those countries, in contrast with the United Kingdom, the interest rate has not been the subject of much political discussion.

Finally, contract design is important. International labour mobility is high and likely to increase, creating problems of default when a person emigrates. In Australia, loan repayments are part of a person's tax liability, so that someone outside Australia is not liable to make repayments. With interest subsidies, this is a particularly costly mistake. In the United Kingdom, the individual loan contract includes the collection of repayments through the tax system, but does not exempt a person outside the country. Though default and administrative costs for people working abroad are somewhat higher, the effect is not large. There is no question of emigration causing a repayment black hole.

Why Not Other Sources of Private Finance?

Why the emphasis on private finance through student loans? There are, of course, other potential sources of private finance.

- Family resources: parents might wish to help their children and the children might wish to accept that help. But not all parents are willing or able to help, and those least likely to do so are those with little or no experience of university. Major reliance on family resources thus runs counter to widening participation.
- A student's earnings while a student: time spent earning money is at the expense of studying and other aspects of student life. There is nothing wrong with this approach, but taken too far it conflicts with the quality of study.
- Employers: it is often argued that employers should contribute. But with today's fluid labour markets, the incentive facing each employer is to let others pay for training and then try to poach the resulting trained workers.

As a standard proposition in economic theory, given the presence of an externality, employer contributions will be sub-optimal.

- Entrepreneurial activity by universities: this approach is often advocated; however, few universities make much money this way, and many waste resources trying. Again, there is nothing wrong with this approach, but its usefulness is overestimated.

- Philanthropic donations: often advocated, the benefits from this approach, again, are overestimated. The approach works well for some US universities, but produces major resources for very few institutions even in the United States, and, outside the United States, as with entrepreneurial activities, it would usually run at a loss if the relevant resources were accounted for properly.[9]

In sum, the potential for other sources of private finance should not be overestimated. Loans—that is, the student's future earnings—are the only large-scale and socially equitable source of private finance, provided they can be implemented effectively.

Lessons about Implementation[10]

Implementation: The policy maker's blind spot

As mentioned at the start of this chapter, strategic policy design is important but, on its own, is not enough. Implementation is of equal importance. Loans are not easy to implement, so the international landscape is littered with failed schemes. Many countries have a woeful record of collecting repayments. It is one thing to design a good loan system, quite another to make sure that the money is paid promptly and accurately to the right people and that repayments are collected effectively. After introductory discussion, we consider the prerequisites for an effective loan system, before outlining the tasks that are necessary to create and run a scheme, illustrating some of the problems that can arise where implementation fails; we then discuss an implementation myth.

---

9   There is an incentive to overstate the resources brought in by fundraisers. The relevant amount is not total donations, but only donations that would not have happened without the effort of the fundraisers. There is also often double counting—for example, where the research arm of a university and the fundraising arm both claim an incoming amount in full.

10   I am grateful to Hugh Macadie for the material on which the sections 'Prerequisites for a Loan System' and 'The Necessary Tasks' draw.

Effective reform rests on a tripod of skills: strategic policy design, political implementation, and administrative/technical implementation.[11] In many ways, policy design is the easy task. The more difficult part is to make a scheme work in practice—in both political and administrative terms.

Most people are not aware of implementation, or, when they are, they underestimate what is involved. The idea that if one understands a policy one can establish a program for implementing it—a view to which academics are perhaps particularly prone—is generally false. A person with one of the skills frequently fails to grasp the importance of the other two. Academics frequently ignore politics and administration. Politicians might give too little weight to the coherence of a policy strategy or to meeting its administrative requirements— for example, by allowing enough time and including an adequate administrative budget. Technical experts might take a narrow approach or oppose reforms for other reasons.

Prerequisites for a Loan System

Political Prerequisites

Implementing student loans has obvious political dimensions. Though largely taken for granted once they have become established, their initial introduction was turbulent in many countries. In the United Kingdom, the introduction of student loans in 1990 provoked enormous demonstrations, though today, loan design is part of my undergraduate teaching. In 2004, in the crucial parliamentary vote on a bill to introduce variable tuition fees, a government with a parliamentary majority of 160 won by five votes. In Australia, similarly, the proposal to introduce an income-contingent charge in 1989 to pay for part of tuition costs provoked considerable commotion, but the system is now regarded as part of the landscape.

The experience of the United Kingdom and Australia illustrates the need for robust political capacity. That capacity is necessary not only at the time the scheme is introduced, but on a continuing basis. As the New Zealand case shows, initial momentum for reform can falter for lack of continuing action by government to sustain support. Political pressures and populist politics can combine to introduce expensive and regressive blanket interest subsidies.

Technical Prerequisites

A country should not embark on a loan scheme unless and until it has

---

11   For fuller discussion, see Barr and Crawford (2005:Ch. 16).

- a reliable method of identifying individuals—a responsibility of national government
- the capacity to maintain records of amounts borrowed, cumulative borrowing and interest charges, and the value of each person's repayments; this task is the responsibility of the loans administration
- the capacity to collect repayments; income-contingent repayments are best collected by the tax or social security authorities; relying on educational institutions to collect loan repayments does not work well; in addition to collecting repayments within the country, it is necessary also to have the capacity to collect repayments from graduates working in other countries
- the capacity to track the income of each borrower; ideally this is the task of national government through personal income tax or social security contributions.

The first three elements apply to any loan scheme. As discussed in more detail in the section 'Banks are Good at Collecting Repayments', a country that cannot implement income-contingent repayments will generally also have difficulties collecting conventional loan repayments.

The Necessary Tasks

If a country has the technical capacities outlined above, a further series of requirements has to be in place to: a) establish a loan scheme; and b) run it.

Establishing an Effective Scheme

In order to establish a new scheme

- enough time must be allowed from the passage of legislation to the delivery of loans to the first cohort of borrowers; a large number of schemes fail at this first hurdle
- strong political sponsorship is essential—someone must have the vision and power to ensure that the policy happens as proposed
- clear ownership is also essential—for example, by the ministry of education
- the introduction of a loan system is not an event, but a process. Thus, political support has to be strong when the system is being established and continuing when it is in operation.

A further series of requirements is more narrowly technical, including ensuring that there are enough people with the necessary skills, legislative preparation, information technology (IT) development, and effective project management.

A number of problems are common.

- The political timetable for the introduction of a scheme is often incompatible with the timetable necessary for administrative purposes. A problem besetting UK governments is that they consistently underestimate the time, skills and energy necessary to make policy work. The United Kingdom is far from alone in making this error.

- Policy makers might introduce changes to the scheme once work is under way. Such changes are often incompatible with the planned administrative structure.

- Ownership of the scheme might be unclear or diffuse.

Running a Scheme

As already noted, running a scheme once it has been established involves identification of the student, record keeping (amounts borrowed, repayments, accumulation of interest), and collection of repayments within the country and from graduates working abroad.

More specifically, at the time a student first takes out a loan it is necessary to establish her identity reliably; to provide her with information about her entitlement and about the operation of the loan; to establish the size of the loan to which she is entitled, which will require information about the degree she is taking (fees might be higher for some subjects than others), the university at which she is studying (some universities might be more expensive than others, either in terms of fees or living costs), and perhaps also her own income and that of her parents (if the size of the loan to which a student is entitled is income tested); and to establish that she actually turns up at the relevant university.

During the time a student is at university, it is necessary to establish that she continues her studies (and perhaps to keep track of her grades), and to keep track of the dates and amounts of further borrowing.

After the student has left university, it is necessary to

- keep track of him or her through changes of name, address, job, family circumstance (for example, if this is relevant to qualifying for a targeted interest subsidy), and country

- collect repayments, liaising as necessary with the tax authorities if that is the main route by which repayments are collected

- collect repayments in other ways for people who are outside the country

- ensure that any concessions on repayment are granted

- pursue delinquent repayments

- answer queries

- record repayments and calculate the outstanding balance

- keep borrowers notified of the balance of their loans
- arrange for collection of repayments to cease once the loan has been repaid.

Depending on how the loan scheme is financed, the loans administration might also need the skills to operate in financial markets.

A Different Way of Implementing Income-Contingent Repayments

Ideally, income-contingent repayments should be collected alongside income tax or social security contributions on the basis of a person's current earnings. Thus, repayment instantly and accurately reflects changes in a person's economic circumstances.

This approach—as in Australia, New Zealand and the United Kingdom—is, however, administratively demanding. A different approach—less good in policy terms, but less demanding administratively and hence perhaps more realistic— is to base a person's loan repayments on his or her last completed tax return. Since tax returns are filed only at the end of the tax year, and then require time for the authorities to process them, repayments reflect a person's earnings only with a lag. This is not a major problem where earnings do not change much, but fails to give automatic protection where a person's income falls—for example, when someone loses their job or leaves paid work to have a child. For such cases, it is necessary to have an additional procedure whereby the person can apply for a reduction of his or her loan repayment. This is the arrangement in Sweden (which certainly has the capacity to collect repayments on a current basis) and Hungary (where policy makers intend to move to collection on the basis of current income once they have sufficient confidence in the robustness of the—still new—system of personal income tax).

The least demanding way to approximate income contingency is the system in the Netherlands. The default arrangement is that the borrower repays in equal annual instalments for a fixed period after graduation (that is, mortgage-type repayments). But the system includes provision for someone with low earnings to be allowed a lower repayment. Note, however, that this approach does not avoid the need to measure a person's income—a task that many countries are not able to do well.

Illustrations

Merely to list these requirements indicates the size of the task. The following tales illustrate the importance of implementation and the predictable problems that arise when policy makers ignore practicalities or accept excessively optimistic predictions about the ease of solving implementation problems.

- Some institutions have a large peak in communications—for example, tax returns around the filing deadline, or student loan applications at the start of the academic year. How does a paper-based system deal with tasks such as opening large numbers of envelopes?

- In an electronic system, the analogous question is whether the system can cope with a huge peak without crashing.

- If a loan scheme processes loan applications by optically scanning handwritten paper applications, can the system cope with an application that has spent two weeks folded in a student's pocket or has a large coffee stain on it?

- Does the system have a way of coping where an applicant for a loan misspells (paper-based) or mistypes (electronic) his or her own name (this is not fanciful)?

- Can the system cope with a massive peak of phone inquiries—for example, by automatically moving staff at the student loans administration from other tasks to the phones at such times. Again, this is not fanciful. If any element in the system breaks down (for example, a delay in disbursing loans), there will be a surge of telephone inquiries; if nothing is done, a breakdown in disbursement is rapidly followed by a breakdown in the system of telephone inquiries.

Given the wide array of institutional requirements both to establish and to run a scheme,

> it is not surprising that successful income-contingent loans in advanced economies—including Australia, New Zealand, the Netherlands, Sweden, and the United Kingdom—are not echoed in poorer countries. Chile and South Africa have such schemes on a small scale, with repayments collected by universities, a method that has proved unsatisfactory. Both schemes have met with some success, but would be fiscally costly on a larger scale. Thailand is planning to introduce an income-contingent loan scheme in 2006, the success of which will depend greatly on the effectiveness of income tax collection. Designing a cost-effective repayment mechanism in poorer countries should be at the top of the policy-maker agenda. (World Bank 2006:Box 3.7)

'Banks are Good at Collecting Repayments': An implementation myth

It is often argued that one way to sidestep these problems is to ask banks to organise the scheme as a conventional loan, with fixed monthly repayments and short repayment duration. This approach, it is argued, does not depend on tax collection, and can therefore be effective in a country without an effective income tax system. That argument is profoundly mistaken.

Mortgage Repayments Require a Fairly Sophisticated Collection Mechanism

Commercial banks have expertise in collecting repayments for loans that are: a) short term; and/or b) secured on a physical asset. This is the point Friedman made 50 years ago. Neither applies to student loans. There are good reasons for wanting student loans to have a fairly long duration: it is efficient if the lifetime of a loan bears a rational relationship to the lifetime of the asset being financed by the loan—thus, there are 25-year home loans but three-year car loans; and a longer repayment period makes possible smaller monthly repayments and/ or larger loans. In addition, as noted, there is no security for borrowing to finance human capital. For both reasons, collection by banks is likely to be administratively demanding and requires some sort of government guarantee.

Government Guarantees to Private Lenders Create Problems

If, however, the guarantee is not generous, banks will decline to get involved. But if the guarantee is sufficiently generous, it creates problems of moral hazard, since banks have no incentive to pursue repayments vigorously, not least because they have no desire to alienate people who will become their best customers. Thus, the incentive structure is inimical to effective collection, leading to high default rates.

A second problem arising from government guarantees is what is known as the classification problem. There are international guidelines for national accounting that determine whether spending is public or private (IMF 2001; for non-technical discussion, see Barr 2001:Ch. 14). If students borrow money from banks, but the government guarantee is generous, the government, in effect, takes the risk of default. Thus, there is no risk transfer and, under international guidelines, lending by banks to students counts as *public* borrowing. The US system—with a government guarantee for loans that are classified as private— ignores the rules. Ignoring the rules is not an option for developing countries.

The classification problem is central to discussion of ways of bringing private finance into post-compulsory education as, for example, in Hungary. This topic is rarely discussed and little known, but a developing country ignores it at its peril.

A Public Collection Agency?

On the face of it, public collection of conventional repayments might work better. This approach, however, requires considerable administrative capacity. Even where that administrative capacity exists, the public sector ends up running a student loan collection agency *and* a tax collection system, raising the question of whether resources devoted to collecting mortgage-type student loan repayments might not be used better to bolster the effectiveness of the tax system. In the United Kingdom, the need for the Student Loans Company to conduct an annual reconciliation of individual accounts with the tax authorities helped to strengthen the effectiveness of both institutions.

Mortgage Repayments Require a Capacity to Implement an Income Test

Whether collected by a public or private agency, mortgage repayments require an income test. If repayments (say, $100 a month) are unrelated to a person's income, a mechanism is needed to protect people with low or no earnings, for equity reasons, to ensure that the scheme remains politically viable, and to protect the credibility of the collection mechanism. But the corollary is that the agency organising repayments has to be able to establish a person's income. This is a difficult task of measurement and enforcement even in an advanced country, let alone in a poorer country that does not have an effective tax system (which was the argument for having mortgage-type loans in the first place). An income test, in short, will be administratively demanding and costly. With a mortgage scheme, these costs will be *in addition* to those of the tax system.

In sum, mortgage-type loans, for the well-established reasons discussed earlier, work well for physical assets such as housing. With lending for human capital, in contrast, the theoretical arguments suggest that they expose both borrower and lender to excessive risk and uncertainty. The outcome is inefficient because it wastes talent and inequitable because capital-market imperfections bear most heavily on the least well off. Separately, mortgage loans are considerably more demanding administratively than is generally realised.

The Resulting System

It is important to be clear that the resulting system is not—and should not be—a free market. It is a regulated market. Universities set fees, but with a maximum fee level established by government. There is continued taxpayer support for teaching. Students apply to the institutions and courses of their choice.

Lessons About the Role of Government

Economic theory and international experience both suggest that a well-designed system has a continuing, important role for government

- to provide taxpayer support for higher education
- to regulate the system, both through a maximum level of fees and by ensuring that there is effective quality assurance (the role of government is to make sure that quality assurance happens, not necessarily to provide the service itself)

- to set incentives—for example, larger subsidies for certain subjects
- to ensure that there is a good loan scheme
- to adopt policies to widen participation.

Lessons About the Design of Student Loans

Economic theory offers a series of conclusions.

- Loans should have income-contingent repayments.
- Untargeted interest subsidies prevent the achievement of any desirable policy objective. The default interest rate should be the government's cost of borrowing, in combination with targeted interest subsidies.
- If untargeted interest subsidies are avoided, there should ideally be no income test for loan entitlement.
- There needs to be a thoughtful choice of the level of income at which loan repayments start and the repayment rate as a fraction of a person's income.
- The design of the loan contract should ensure that emigrants and others outside the tax net are required to make repayments.

International experience offers complementary lessons.

- Income-contingent loans do not harm access (Australia, New Zealand, the United Kingdom, Hungary).
- Interest subsidies are expensive (New Zealand, the United Kingdom).
- Positive real interest rates are politically feasible (the Netherlands, Sweden, Norway, Hungary).
- The design of the loan contract matters.
- The design of the loan matters; it is possible, with care, to design a system with income-contingent repayments but mainly private finance, as in Hungary.

References

Barnes, J. and Barr, N. 1988, *Strategies for Higher Education: The alternative white paper*, Aberdeen University Press for the David Hume Institute and the Suntory-Toyota International Centre for Economics and Related Disciplines, London School of Economics and Political Science, London.

Barr, N. 1999, 'Comments on "Economic Policy and Equity: An Overview" by Amartya Sen', in V. Tanzi, K.-Y. Chu and S. Gupta (eds), *Economic Policy and Equity*, International Monetary Fund, Washington, DC, pp. 44–8.

Barr, N. 2000, 'The benefits of education: what we know and what we don't', in *Economic Growth and Government Policy*, Papers presented at a HM Treasury seminar, 11 Downing Street, HM Treasury, London, 12 October 2000, pp. 33–40, <http://www.hm-treasury.gov.uk/media/132BF/252.pdf>

Barr, N. 2001, *The Welfare State as Piggy Bank: Information, risk, uncertainty and the role of the State*, Oxford University Press, Oxford and New York, <http://www.oxfordscholarship.com/oso/public/content/economicsfinance/0199246599/toc.html>

Barr, N. 2002, *Funding higher education: policies for access and quality*, Post-16 Student Support, Sixth Report of Session 2001–2002, HC445 (TSO, 2002), House of Commons, Education and Skills Committee, UK, pp. Ev 19–35.

Barr, N. 2004a, 'Higher education funding', *Oxford Review of Economic Policy*, vol. 20, no. 2 (Summer), pp. 264–83.

Barr, N. 2004b, *The Economics of the Welfare State*, (Fourth edition), Oxford University Press, UK, and Stanford University Press, Calif. [also in Korean].

Barr, N. 2008, 'Financing higher education: lessons from developed economies, options for developing economies', in J. Linn and B. Pleskovic (eds), *Annual World Bank Conference on Development Economics 2008, Regional: Higher education and development*, The World Bank, Washington, DC.

Barr, N. and Crawford, I. 2005, *Financing Higher Education: Answers from the UK*, Routledge, London and New York.

Barr, N. and Diamond, P. 2008, *Reforming Pensions: Principles and policy choices*, Oxford University Press, New York and Oxford.

Blaug, M. 1976, 'The empirical status of human capital theory: a slightly jaundiced survey', *Journal of Economic Literature*, September, pp. 827–56, reprinted in Blaug, M. 1987, *The Economics of Education and the Education of an Economist*, Edward Elgar, Aldershot, UK, pp. 100–28.

Blaug, M. 1985, 'Where are we now in the economics of education?', *Economics of Education Review*, vol. 4, no. 1, pp. 17–28, reprinted in Blaug, M. 1987, *The Economics of Education and the Education of an Economist*, Edward Elgar, Aldershot, UK, pp. 129–40.

Chapman, B. and Ryan, C. 2003, *The access implications of income contingent charges for higher education: lessons from Australia*, Discussion Paper No. 463, April, Centre for Economic Policy Research, The Australian National University, Canberra.

Feinstein, L. 2003, 'Inequality in the early cognitive development of British children in the 1970 cohort', *Economica*, vol. 70, no. 277, pp. 73–98.

Friedman, M. 1955, 'The role of government in education', in R. A. Solo (ed.), *Economics and the Public Interest*, Rutgers University Press, New Brunswick, NJ, pp. 123–44.

Glennerster, H. 1993, 'The economics of education: changing fortunes', in N. Barr and D. Whynes, *Issues in the Economics of the Welfare State*, Macmillan, London, pp. 176–99.

International Monetary Fund (IMF) 2001, *Government Finance Statistics Manual 2001*, International Monetary Fund, Washington, DC, <http://www.imf.org/external/pubs/ft/gfs/manual/index.htm>

Organisation for Economic Cooperation and Development (OECD) 2004, *OECD Economic Survey of the UK 2004*, Organisation for Economic Cooperation and Development, Paris.

Organisation for Economic Cooperation and Development (OECD) 2005, *OECD Economic Survey of the UK 2005*, Organisation for Economic Cooperation and Development, Paris.

Organisation for Economic Cooperation and Development (OECD) 2006, *Education at a Glance: OECD indicators 2006*, Organisation for Economic Cooperation and Development, Paris.

Organisation for Economic Cooperation and Development (OECD) 2008, *Thematic Review of Tertiary Education: Synthesis report*, Organisation for Economic Cooperation and Development, Paris.

Sen, A. K. 1999, 'Economic policy and equity: an overview', in V. Tanzi, K.-Y. Chu and S. Gupta (eds), *Economic Policy and Equity*, International Monetary Fund, Washington, DC, pp. 28–43.

UK Education and Skills Select Committee 2002, *Post-16 Student Support*, Sixth Report of Session 2001–2002, HC445, TSO, London.

UK Office for National Statistics 2004, *Focus on Social Inequalities, 2004 Edition*, TSO, London.

World Bank 2006, *World Development Report 2007: Development and the next generation*, The World Bank, Washington, DC.

4. Finance, State Capacity, Privatisation and Transparency in South-East Asian Higher Education

Anthony R. Welch
University of Sydney

Key dilemmas underpin the development and expansion of higher education in South-East Asia. On the one hand are the tensions between the desire to expand the quantity of higher education while at the same time improving quality. On the other is the issue of enhancing access while improving equity. While all of the five states treated in this chapter (Indonesia, Malaysia, the Philippines, Thailand and Vietnam) share the goal of extending access to higher education as part of their wider social and economic development goals, none is in a position to provide public higher education to all who aspire to it, especially at a price they can afford. (The last is particularly significant: as is seen below, it is already the case, for example, that fees for high-demand courses in some public higher education institutions in Indonesia outstrip those in the private sector; Welch 2007a:680.)

Hence, across the region, private higher education is growing swiftly. This expansion is clearly widening access, although often at fee levels that, being much higher than those that commonly apply at public higher education institutions (HEIs), further exclude the poor. At the same time, the growth of private higher education is also sharpening quality issues, as well as problems in governance systems within the sector that are, in cases such as the Philippines, Indonesia and Vietnam, already stretched to capacity.

This chapter examines the rise of private-sector HEIs in South-East Asia, and some of the issues associated with the changing balance and blurring borders of public and private higher education: finance, state capacity, governance, and transparency. The context for South-East Asian society and higher education is also rehearsed, including the relatively peripheral place occupied by the five South-East Asian higher education systems, within the global knowledge system. What is argued is that, while the spread of private higher education is undoubtedly opening up access, the high fee levels demanded effectively preclude enrolment by the poor, who are now also being squeezed by rising fee levels at public HEIs. Selected examples are given of differential funding and fee regimes, from the public and private sectors.

The Functions of Higher Education

According to Manuel Castells (1993), all societies throughout history designate specific roles and functions for universities. Not only do these roles and functions change over time, depending on a given society's prevailing history, culture, ideology or politics, they are also not always congruent, hence Castells refers to universities as 'dynamic systems of contradictory functions'. He identifies four principal functions, each of which has implications for access and equity.

1. Universities might be assigned the responsibility for training bureaucracies and the provision of a highly skilled labour force. Most clearly evident in classical China, this was also their primary goal in Vietnam's early Confucian period—for example, when institutions of higher learning were devoted to preparing students for the imperial system of examinations, which, for the successful, led to the state bureaucracy (Welch 2008a). While this strategy was in principle open to all, in practice, males drawn from noble families were the most common source of scholars.

2. A somewhat different function of universities can be to act as social sorting mechanisms to select and train scientific, economic, political and educational elites. In such cases, the selection, socialisation and development of networks among other cadres all help to distinguish these elites from the rest of the society. Historically speaking, the French example is pertinent here, as also is its paler colonial imitation in Vietnam. Santo Tomas University—the Philippines institution founded in 1611—also served this function, albeit for the colonial elite. This function stands in contradiction to most principles of access and equity.

3. Universities are often assigned the duty of acting as ideological apparatuses, responsible (among other institutions) for the formation and dissemination of the societal or state ideology. Here again, the role of Ho Chi Minh thought and Marxist–Leninist thought in contemporary Vietnam and the national ideology of *Pancasila* in Indonesia since independence are arguably illustrative. In principle, this function can open access to new aspirants, based on their ideological purity (but could well close that same door to well-qualified aspirants whose ideological orthodoxy is suspect).

4. Universities also function to generate new knowledge. This is a more modern trend attributable to the successful incorporation by German universities of the research seminar and modernist subjects such as maths, science and technology into their curriculum in the nineteenth century (Welch 1980), and, somewhat later, US science-oriented universities' close involvement in scientific and technological (including military) development and economic growth. Once again, this function does not exclude the poor or dispossessed,

but an examination of the social class characteristics of elite German and US institutions over time, for example, reveals a strong class bias. Much the same can be said of the characteristics of leading universities in South-East Asia, which are in general more concerned with teaching than knowledge creation.

In summary, Castells' taxonomy of roles and functions yields a broad outline of goals that are set for universities to perform

- train skilled labour as demanded by the society
- cultivate elites
- generate and transmit ideology
- create and apply new knowledge.

Here, however, while ambitions and aspirations among developing countries are usually great, they often suffer from something of a disadvantage, relative to their counterparts in the developed world, where, as indicated below, the concentration of various kinds of resources, and a longer history of research and development, give the latter important competitive advantages.

The ongoing ability to successfully manage the sometimes contradictory functions of Castells' typology is one crucial index of success for developing countries in achieving growth, reform, equity and social integration. Castells does not distinguish here between public and private institutions, but the addition of private universities into this sometimes volatile mix, including the regulation of this developing sector, further complicates an already difficult task, as is seen below. While it is acknowledged that, in a context that includes significant privatisation of public-sector HEIs (Welch 2007a, 2007b), and widespread globalisation of higher education, the former sharp divisions between public and private are no longer tenable, and, moreover, that different dimensions of private higher education also exist (Kim et al. 2007; Marginson 2007; Thaver 2003), the specification of these different dimensions is beyond the scope of this chapter. Official government definitions of private higher education are referred to throughout.

All of the states embraced by the following analysis can be considered part of the global South. Yet despite the fact that four of the South-East Asian Five countries in this analysis can be seen to fall within the low-income category (Malaysia's GDP per capita level now places it into a middle-income category), all five have ambitious plans to extend higher education to larger proportions of their populace, who are in turn pressing their governments for more and more places for their children, and more institutions of higher education. This is for at least two reasons, each of which relates to Castells' taxonomy above.

The first is that higher education is seen by all five governments, as well as international organisations such as the Organisation for Economic Cooperation and Development (OECD), the World Bank and the Asian Development Bank (ADB), as critical to the supply of the highly skilled personnel who, in a more post-Fordist world, are said to be the foundation of the new knowledge economies that supposedly characterise the twenty-first century (World Bank 2002a). Governments of all five nations would subscribe to the following statement that summarises the role of higher education in forging the twenty-first century knowledge economy: 'The quality of knowledge generated within higher education institutions, and its availability to the wider economy, is becoming increasingly critical to national [and one could add international ARW] competitiveness' (World Bank 2000b:9).

Governments of developing nations, especially in South-East Asia, tend to see universities not merely as institutions of great national and international prestige (and also as important repositories of national culture), but, crucially, as springboards to the future, perhaps in concert with key industries such as information technology (IT), engineering and science, with which many of its better established universities are now engaged in cooperative or contract research. Just as information and communication technology (ICT) is seen as critical to development priorities, so too higher education is increasingly seen (especially in a more neo-liberal, economically rational world; Pusey 1991) as a driver of economic growth, putatively even enabling developing nations to leap ahead in their ongoing quest for development (World Bank 2002b). (As seen below, however, the parallel with higher education goes further, since this fervent aspiration is not so easily achieved, at least in the short term.)

As indicated, however, this rationale for higher education is not limited to states (termed by economists the 'social rate of return'), but also obtains at the level of the individual (the 'individual rate of return'). Many individuals in the developing world see university education as a chance to secure a good white-collar job, and perhaps to provide a passport to a postgraduate opportunity at an overseas university and/or the chance to work and live abroad. While this does not hold true for all who wish to pursue higher education (after all, significant numbers of students still pursue degrees that are almost bound to keep them poor—such as in the performing or fine arts, or in the less remunerative areas of the humanities, including history, languages or philosophy), it is more likely to hold true for those who enrol in the key areas such as engineering, the sciences, IT and business.

But there are important differences in poorer, developing countries where, as in Vietnam, for example, public universities can provide places for at most about 10 per cent of qualified applicants, fuelling a demand for private universities that is likely only to increase and perhaps lead to some distortions in fields of study. Thus, for example, the intense pressure to gain entry leads to access becoming an end in itself: numbers of students end up studying subjects in which they have little interest, thus adding to the concerns about the efficiency and quality of the higher education system. Or, private institutions offer only a restricted range of popular subjects, particularly languages, IT and business studies, which are cheaper to provide (Levy 2007).

Compared with lower levels of education, tertiary education is particularly expensive to provide, and even more so in the mission-critical departments and faculties of IT, engineering and science:

> By their very nature, science and technology have always demanded significant and ongoing investment to establish, maintain and expand the 'engine' of physical infrastructure—including laboratories, libraries and classrooms. They also need a rich [and expensive] fuel of textbooks, computers, equipment, and other supplies. (World Bank 2000b:71)

This is less the case in the area of business, although even here, to establish an internationally reputable, well-staffed business school takes both time and considerable investment. To develop Stanford Business School or INSEAD in France to their current level took time, planning and a considerable, ongoing injection of resources—something often unavailable in developing countries.

The South-East Asian Context

In order to appreciate the context for South-East Asian higher education, it is important to remind ourselves here of several key elements of the socioeconomic context that are relevant to considerations of financing access and equity. South-East Asia embraces about 540 million people, with a combined GDP of US$610 billion (or US$1.9 billion in purchasing power parity dollars/PPP$), and with very wide disparities—both across the region and within countries. Per capita GDP ranged from US$9120 (Malaysia) to US$2300 (Vietnam) in 2005 (UNDP 2005:20). Females make up 49 per cent of the total population, while more than 56 per cent of the population still inhabits rural areas. Almost half the substantial numbers employed in agriculture are women; Human Development Index (HDI) rankings ranged from 59 (Malaysia) to 112 (Vietnam) in 2002 (UNDP 2005).

Of the five nations considered in this analysis, all are developing countries, while only Malaysia can be considered middle income. As well, while all five have recovered significantly from the calamitous effects of the regional financial crisis of the late 1990s, the gap between rich and poor continues to increase. Overall, this does not mean that the poor are becoming poorer, but rather that the rich are making greater gains: 'By and large...increases in inequality are not..."the rich getting rich and the poor getting poorer." Rather, it is the rich getting rich faster than the poor' (ADB 2007:6).

Table 4.1 summarises key human development indicators for the South-East Asia Five, over the period 1990–2002, including expenditures on education.

What can be seen from the table is that none of the five countries figures all that highly within overall HDI rankings, although there are significant differences among the five, with Indonesia and Vietnam—the two poorest—placed significantly below the other three. Indonesia and Thailand showed the greatest fall in HDI rankings over the period, but Malaysia also fell. Much of this decline can be attributed to the severe effects of the regional financial crisis of the late 1990s, from which affected economies have only recently emerged. Only Vietnam emerged from this financial crisis with its HDI ranking unchanged (UNDP 2005:20). Darkening this picture of limited resources are the debt levels carried by the majority of the five. While Vietnam's debt, expressed as a percentage of GDP, is relatively low, at 3.4 per cent, the ratios for all the other countries are much higher: Indonesia, 9.8 per cent; Malaysia, 8.5 per cent; Philippines, 10.9 per cent; and Thailand, 15.6 per cent (UNDP 2005:27). Additionally, in the case of Indonesia, expenditure on the military, expressed as a percentage of GDP, is as high as that for education (UNDP 2005:27). Such factors form an important part of the context and impose clear limits upon public-sector efforts in higher education: 'Expenditures on debt servicing and military spending tend to crowd out social expenditures' (UNDP 2005:26).

While all countries (including Vietnam, whose data are absent in Table 4.1) show a rise in public expenditure on education over the period 1990–2002, this needs to be put into perspective. First, compared with public expenditure on education by the European Union, for example (5.41 per cent for the EU15, and 5.14 per cent for the Accession 12), investment levels are modest for four of the five (UNDP 2007). Moreover, the apparently high proportion of the national budget expended on public education in Malaysia revealed in Table 4.1 is misleading, since in effect Chinese and Indian Malaysians (who together make up one-third of its population) are effectively excluded from the public sector in higher education (Tierney 2008; Welch 2008b), thereby heavily reducing access and equity. The same is true when proportions of public expenditure on tertiary education are examined, as seen in Table 4.2.

Table 4.1 Human development indicators, South-East Asia Five, 1990–2002

Country	HDI 1990	HDI 2002	HDI rank 2002	Life expectancy at birth 2002	Education index 2002	GDP per capita (PPP$) 2002	Public expenditure on education (% of GDP) 1990	Public expenditure on education (% of GDP) 2002
Indonesia	0.623	0.692	111	78.0	0.80	3230	1.0	1.3
Malaysia	0.720	0.793	59	73.0	0.83	9120	5.2	7.9
Philippines	0.719	0.753	83	69.8	0.89	4170	2.9	3.2
Thailand	0.707	0.768	76	69.1	0.86	7010	3.5	5.0
Vietnam	0.610	0.691	112	69.0	0.82	2300	...	...

Source: UNDP (2005:20).

Table 4.2 Current public expenditure on tertiary education as proportion of total public expenditure on education

Country	Percentage of public education budget expended on tertiary sector
Indonesia	19
Malaysia	35
Philippines	14
Thailand	20
Vietnam	...

Source: UNDP (2007:266–7).

While significant variation is evident in the above data, the percentages are generally low compared with high human development countries (UNDP 2007). Once again, the exception is Malaysia, which spends 35 per cent of its public education budget on the tertiary sector; but, as seen above, funds are effectively cordoned off for ethnic Malays (*Bumiputras*).

In general, while rates of primary completion have shown significant growth, net secondary enrolment rates among the South-East Asia Five range from 58 per cent in Indonesia to 76 per cent in Malaysia (UNDP 2007). Many of those who do not complete secondary schooling, thereby rendering themselves ineligible for higher education, are from the poor.

Poverty is also a significant issue that constrains the development of the public higher education sector in South-East Asia; actual poverty rates vary from 9 per cent in Vietnam to more than 14.1 per cent in the Philippines, and 16.6 per cent for Indonesia (ADB 2005; World Bank 2007a:8). As measured by the GINI Index, inequality, particularly between rural and urban groups, is high relative to other world regions. Compared with the EU15, for example, which embraces a significant range of different contexts, all of the South-East Asia Five reveal relatively high indices, as evident in Table 4.3.

Table 4.3 GINI coefficient for the South-East Asia Five, compared with the EU15

Country/region	GINI index	Most recent data
Indonesia	34.3	2002
Malaysia	49.2	1997
Philippines	46.1	2000
Thailand	43.2	2000
Vietnam	36.1	1998
EU15	24.7–38.5	...*

* EU data cannot be given for a specific year since the category includes a number of countries for which data stem from different years.

Source: UNDP (2005:26).

In effect, what this means is that access by marginalised groups such as the urban and rural poor lags behind that of the overall population, in a context in which regional governments spend too little on the delivery of services to the poor.

In addition, spiralling costs of basic commodities such as food and fuel in 2007 and 2008 have meant that larger amounts are being taken from national budgets to support significant sections of the population hardest hit by swiftly rising prices. In an effort to offset rising unrest among the poor, for example, Indonesia increased the price of subsidised rice by 60 per cent in April 2008, but also expanded eligibility—beyond the 19 million individuals who already qualify for 5 kg of subsidised rice monthly (SMH 2008). Millions of the poorest Filipinos—currently allocating almost all their income to buy rice—are barely being kept afloat by government food subsidies. Following similar action by Indonesia, Vietnam—traditionally a major exporter of rice—has imposed export restrictions (SMH 2008). The above measures do not merely reduce the discretionary income of poor families available for education, including higher education, they also significantly constrain state budgets for social and educational programs.

Last, it is important to note that, in addition to the factors indicated above, pressure upon tertiary education provision in the South-East Asian context also stems from the demographic profile of all five countries, in terms of both the relative youth of their populations and the high fertility rates (relative to developed nations). The implications of each can be seen in Table 4.4.

Table 4.4 Demographic pressures on higher education, by country

Country	Total population (millions) 1975	Total population (millions) 2000	Antnual population growth rate (%) 1975–2000	Population under 15 (% of total) 2000
Malaysia	12.3	22.2	2.4	34.1
Thailand	41.1	62.8	1.7	26.7
Philippines	42.0	75.7	2.4	37.5
Indonesia	134.6	212.1	1.8	30.8
Vietnam	48.0	78.1	2.0	33.4

Source: Compiled from UNDP (2002).

Simply responding to this demographic pressure—and rising aspiration levels for higher education—is a difficult task for each of the South-East Asia Five, even apart from questions of institutional quality.

A final index of development consists of foreign direct investment (FDI) inflows, which, while revealing remarkable changes over recent decades (including the substantial impact of the regional financial crisis of the late 1990s), remain modest (compared with China's current FDI inflow for 2006, for example, of some US$72 billion). Some of this investment capital flows into South-East Asian higher education, as do some of the remittances—which, in the case of the Philippines, are extraordinarily high—but evidence is not systematic (Welch 2008b).

Table 4.5 FDI inflows, South-East Asia Five, 1970–2003

Country	1970	1980	1990	2000	2003
Indonesia	83	180	1092	–4550	–597
Malaysia	94	933.9	2611	3787.6	2474
Philippines	–1.04	–106	550	1345	319
Thailand	42.8	293.9	2575	3350.3	1802
Vietnam	0.07	17.9	180	1289.0	1450

Source: UNCTAD (2004).

All of the dimensions treated above significantly constrain growth in state capacity and substantial expansion of public higher education.

North–South Differences in Higher Education and Research

Thus, while the ambition and commitment of the South-East Asia Five, and more generally among countries of the global South, to expand access to higher education in these key areas—and at the same time to build world-class departments and institutions—are undoubted and ubiquitous, the question of how far and fast they can move on this front is a genuine one. This is all the more the case when one considers that many developing countries, including the majority of the countries in this survey (except the Philippines, whose impressive tertiary enrolment ratio of 30 per cent in 1995—albeit including many low-quality HEIs—bears comparison with many OECD countries) had a tertiary enrolment ratio in the second-lowest category of all internationally (between 5 and 15 per cent) in 1995 (World Bank 2000b:12–13), while quality among many HEIs is still problematic in all five.

What the above context adds up to is that the existing scientific gap between South and North is huge, and growing—exacerbated by trends that are examined below. This is not surprising, in light of some basic statistics. The North, for example, has something like 10 times the proportion of research and development (R&D) personnel (scientists and technicians) per capita of the South (3.8 per cent, compared with 0.4 per cent), and spends about four times the proportion of GDP on R&D—2 per cent compared with 0.5 per cent (World Bank 2000b). Most recent data further underline major disparities on a variety of knowledge indices, as seen in Table 4.6.

Table 4.6 National innovation indices, by country, region and level of development

Country	Average years of schooling	Researchers per million	Quality of scientific research institutions	University–industry research collaboration
South-East Asia	6.6	210	4.1	3.6
Indonesia	4.7	207	3.9	3.4
Malaysia	7.9	299	5.0	4.7
Philippines	7.6	48	3.3	2.7
Thailand	6.1	287	4.0	3.6
Developed-country average	9.5	3616	5.1	4.4

Source: World Bank (2006:134).

Particularly with respect to researchers per million of population, the average difference is more than seventeen-fold, while in no South-East Asian country is the difference from the developed-country average less than twelve-fold.

Table 4.7 reveals significant ongoing disparities in R&D, in terms of both spending and proportion of GDP.

Table 4.7 R&D expenditure levels and as a percentage of GDP, 2002 (R&D spending 2002; R&D as a percentage of GDP)*

Country	US$ billion (PPP)	Percentage of world	1992	2002
South-East Asia	3.3	0.4	0.1	0.2
Indonesia	0.3	0.0	0.1	0.1
Malaysia	1.5	0.2	0.4	0.7
Philippines	0.4	0.0	0.2	0.1
Thailand	1.1	0.1	0.2	0.2
Developed-world average	645.8	77.8	2.3	2.3

* Regional data are the sum of R&D divided by the sum of PPP GDP

Source: World Bank (2006:116).

In addition, the North registers some 97 per cent of all patents registered in the United States and Europe, and, together with the newly industrialising countries of East Asia, accounts for 84 per cent of all scientific articles published (World Bank 2000b:69). Further data from the US Patent Office reveal a continuing wide gap in terms of performance with respect to patents.

Table 4.8 US patents granted, by region, country and level of development (number of patents; patents per 100 000 people)

	1990–94	2000–04	1990–94	2000–04	% change
South-East Asia	31	140	0.01	0.04	15.3
Indonesia	6	15	0.00	0.01	8.8
Malaysia	13	64	0.07	0.28	15.3
Philippines	6	18	0.01	0.02	10.4
Thailand	6	43	0.01	0.07	20.9
Developed world (average)	104 170	168 017	12.88	19.58	4.3

Source: World Bank (2006:123).

It is of course important to acknowledge that such indices as the Science Citation Index (SCI), Social Science Citation Index (SSCI), Engineering Index (EI) and the like are skewed in favour of English-language journals (thereby adding linguistic disadvantage to the existing disparities of wealth). Notwithstanding this additional burden for the South-East Asia Five, it is illustrative to note the following publication differentials (Table 4.9).

Table 4.9 Papers and citations, by country, 1980s and 1990s

Country	No. of papers 1981	No. of papers 1995	No. of citations 1981–85	No. of citations 1993–97
Indonesia	89	310	694	3364
Malaysia	229	587	1332	3450
Philippines	243	294	1379	2893
Thailand	373	648	2419	8398
Vietnam	49	192	203	1657

Source: World Bank (2000b:125–7).

Comparative figures help put this into perspective: Australian publications for 1995 totalled 18 088, and for Japan 58 910. Citation counts for each country in 1993–97 were 301 320 and 930 981, respectively. More recent data show that higher education across South-East Asia contributes much less to total R&D performance than among developed nations, as indicated in Table 4.10.

Table 4.10 R&D performance by sector

Country	Business	Government	Higher education
South-East Asia	51.3	22.1	15.7
Indonesia	14.3	81.1	4.6
Malaysia	65.3	20.3	14.4
Philippines	58.6	21.7	17.0
Thailand	43.9	22.5	31.0
Developed world (average)	62.9	13.3	27.0

Source: World Bank (2006:120).

Table 4.10 shows that, with the exception of Thailand, the higher education sector contributes little more than half of total R&D performance, relative to the average of developed nations, while in the case of Indonesia, it is about one-sixth, at 4.6 per cent.

These stark disparities exist, notwithstanding the existence of traditions of great respect for education and the role of the teacher in society that obtain in much of Asia, and East and South-East Asia particularly, and despite the venerable forms of learning that long obtained in countries such as Vietnam (where Ha Noi's *Van Mieu* [Temple of Literature]—founded in 1070, and more recently refurbished by American Express—contains the stelae of scholar-priests of many centuries ago) and Thailand (which exhibits a longstanding Buddhist tradition of commitment to learning) (Bovornsiri et al. 1996:55–7).

What the above data reveal is that, notwithstanding the highest annual GDP per capita growth rate of any world region in recent decades (World Bank 2006:38–9), very high aspirations for higher education at both individual and social levels, and a high commitment to learning, among South-East Asian nations, existing levels of infrastructure in higher education limit the capacity for knowledge creation— indicated by Castells as the fourth key function of the modern university.

The Rise of Private Higher Education

It is important to consider the implications of the above here. Given a young population (as seen above, only one of the South-East Asia Five has less than 30 per cent of its population under the age of fifteen, and in the case of the Philippines it is closer to 40 per cent), rising levels of aspiration for higher education, and a tight budgetary context, the state is less and less likely to be able to satisfy demand for tertiary entry. How far is this likely to fuel demand for private higher education? And, if so, what does this mean for equity in countries where, under the influence of globalisation and structural adjustment, the gap between the rich and poor— already large—is only widening (Mok and Welch 2003)?

Baseline data, against which to measure change, consist of the differing proportion of public and private higher education enrolments in the South-East Asia Five countries about a decade ago, as indicated in Table 4.11.

Table 4.11 Distribution of students in public and private institutions of higher education, South-East Asia Five countries, 1997–98

Country	Public	Private
Indonesia	44	59
Malaysia	100	0
Philippines	25	75
Thailand	60	40
Vietnam	100	0

Source: Gonzales (1999:116).

A striking index of change in South-East Asian higher education is the extent to which this picture has altered over the past decade. Notwithstanding the substantial diversity of political systems within the South-East Asia Five (ranging from a socialist polity adapting to the demands of a market economy and recent entry to the World Trade Organisation in Vietnam, to long-term crony-capitalist regimes such as the Philippines), private higher education in the region has grown apace.

Both the dynamism of the region and the incompleteness of the data preclude the development of a current table comparable with the above. Nonetheless, indices of change are telling. While private higher education in the Philippines was already dominant, it has continued to grow, so that the proportion of private HEIs has remained more than 75 per cent (Welch 2008b). Vietnam has announced strikingly ambitious targets to expand higher education, which entail vigorous growth of the private ('people's') higher educational institutions. (Following China, the term 'socialisation' is preferred to 'privatisation'.) Effectively, private-sector HEIs doubled their share of enrolments in Vietnam over the three years from 1996–97 to 1998–99 (Welch 2007b), while Le and Ashwill (2004) report that, by 2002–03, there were 23 private HEIs, enrolling 24 500 students (about 12 per cent of the total of 200 000 new enrolments). By 2020, government plans are for 40 per cent of all enrolments to be private ('non-public') (Hayden and Thiep 2004). In Malaysia, there are now 11 private universities registered, with a similar number of colleges, while private enrolments in higher education now significantly outnumber those in the public sector, if diploma and certificate levels are taken into account (MOHE 2006). In Indonesia, too, private higher education has grown, although with total private enrolments now estimated to be 1.9 million, of a total of 3.4 million (Buchori and Malik 2004; Welch 2007a), the proportion might not have increased.

Table 4.12 reveals the extent of change over the past decade or more.

4. Finance, State Capacity, Privatisation and Transparency in South-East Asian Higher Education

Table 4.12 Numbers and types of HEIs, South-East Asia, 2007

Country	Public			Private			Total
	Degree	Non-degree	Subtotal	Degree	Non-degree	Subtotal	
Indonesia	-	-	81	-	-	2431	2516
Malaysia	18	40	58	22	519	541	599
Philippines	424	1352	1776	1363	2045	3408	5184
Thailand	66	-	66	54	401	455	521
Vietnam	201	-	201	29	-	29	230

Source: ADB (2008:45, citing SEAMEO 2007).

Fees and Funding

Funding and fees are each an important factor in the expansion of private higher education. Given that although specific policies differ across the region, state funding for private higher education remains minimal (some countries choose to make land or other facilities available, and in some instances allow private HEIs to compete for discretionary funds), and that perhaps 90 per cent of the income of private HEIs comes from fees, issues of quality—already problematic—remain a concern. Compared with this is the situation of public HEIs in Indonesia, for example, which still gain about two-thirds of their budget from the state (Purwadi 2001; Welch 2007a).

There are also direct implications for access and equity, since fee levels for private HEIs are at least 50 per cent higher, and are often at least three times higher, than those at public HEIs (Welch 2007a, 2007b), which are usually still of higher quality. For example, when per capita income level in Indonesia was at US$880 in the mid 1990s, fees (which account for only an estimated 15–20 per cent of total costs) ranged from about US$100–400 at public HEIs, and from US$100–1000 in private institutions. (While fee levels have changed, the patterns of difference between public and private have not.) Making matters worse was the differential impact on the poor. World Bank data for 1995 showed that higher education was already well beyond the reach of many: average household expenditure on higher education per student in West Java, for example, was 84.6 per cent of total per capita expenditure levels. The average, however, conceals the differential impact on social strata, which ranged from 79.1 per cent for the highest quartile to 151.5 per cent for the lowest quartile (Welch 2007a).

Two factors increase the squeeze on the poor. The first is the effect of very different schooling retentivity rates. In Indonesia, for example, many 'students from poorer families fail to complete secondary school, and efforts to target the few poor students who do, for scholarships, have largely proved unsuccessful' (Welch 2007a). Second is the trend by many public HEIs—themselves squeezed in an era of rising enrolments but declining per-student funding from the state—to raise their fees, particularly for high-demand courses. In Indonesia, for example, it is now possible to pay more for specific high-demand courses—for example, in engineering—at a major public university than would be paid at a quality private HEI (Welch 2007a). The phenomenon known in Indonesia as '*Jalur Khusus*' (special path, or special passage) gives entry to perhaps 10 per cent of enrollees, upon payment of a fee that might be double that paid at a decent private HEI (Welch 2007a). The effects on the poor—for whom entry to a good public HEI was, however difficult, their only hope of an affordable place at a quality institution—are obvious.

In Vietnam, the relatively recent category of HEI known as 'people's universities' (a term that disguises the fact that they are, for all intents and purposes, private institutions) attracts no funds from the state, and they are entirely dependent upon fees and donations (although they might be given land by the government, or permission to purchase land at a discount).

Distinct political ideologies make a difference to higher education policies in each of the five cases, although at least three factors moderate these differences. The first are the powerful homogenising effects of economic globalisation and structural adjustment, which, as has been argued elsewhere, are moving many systems in a similar direction, albeit at different paces and to differing degrees (Welch and Mok 2003). The second is the gap between official rhetoric and actual practice in each case. Although following the example of its powerful and sometimes troublesome northern neighbour, Vietnam chooses to call its private universities 'people's universities', they are in many ways little different in form and function to private institutions in other countries. The third homogenising effect is the rise of global English (Crystal 1997; Wilson et al. 1998), which is exerting pressure on teaching and research regimes—and not merely regionally.

State Capacity and Governance in Higher Education

What implications do the data and trends indicated above yield for the governance of regional higher education? Clearly, the fact that, with the exception of Malaysia, the South-East nations included here are each among the low-income category, and that additionally each of them suffered substantially in the fallout from the regional economic crisis of the late 1990s, imposes limits on both the quality of teaching and learning and the capacity of the public sector to respond to demand. Table 4.13 shows shifting levels of GDP growth among the South-East Asia Five before, during and after the regional economic crisis.

Table 4.13 GDP growth rates, South-East Asia Five countries, 1996–99 and 2005 (per cent)

Country	Growth rate 1996	Growth rate 1997	Growth rate 1998	Growth rate 1999	Growth rate 2005
Indonesia	8.0	4.5	−13.7	0.2	5.5
Malaysia	8.6	7.5	−7.5	5.4	5.3
Philippines	5.8	5.2	−0.5	3.2	5.0
Thailand	5.5	8.4	−10.0	4.2	5.2
Vietnam	9.3	8.2	3.5	4.2	7.5

Sources: World Bank (2000a, 2005); IMF (2001:Table 3, p. 35).

While Table 4.13 reveals significant economic regrowth among all of the South-East Asia Five, especially compared with the depths of the late 1990s, recent analyses predict that the 'global fallout from the US financial crisis' will reduce growth rates for 2008 in all of the South-East Asia Five, with the exception of Thailand (The Australian 2008).

What this means for universities throughout South-East Asia is that there is still much ground to be made up. None of the universities in the South-East Asia Five, for example, was among the top-500 universities listed in the Shanghai Jiaotong index of leading research universities (MOHE 2006:263–73). That said, of course, each country has cherished icons of higher education among its ranks: Vietnam National University, the University of the Philippines, the University of Indonesia, Chulalongkorn University and the University of Malaysia.

More than knowledge creation is, however, limited by relative lack of resources, infrastructure and training. The lack of income and infrastructure in education also affects regulatory capacity in higher education (notably, the various national agencies or departments charged with regulation and quality assurance) (Welch 2007a, 2007b). While regional higher education systems grow apace, particularly in the private sector, as was seen above, it is not clear that regulatory capacity, and in some cases transparency, has always grown in parallel, in either size or strength.

Internationally, a significant element of higher education reforms in recent years has been changes to governance. As the goals of higher education have been revised, against the background of a complex and shifting environment, so too has the governance of higher education (Amaral et al. 2002, 2003; OECD 2003). A key element common to many systems of higher education, including in the Asia-Pacific, is the move towards devolution, from a pattern of strong centralisation. While governments retain a strong interest in higher education, and in particular its capacity to contribute to national economic development, devolution to institutional level is seen as a means to ensure flexibility and diversity. In Indonesia, for example, educational decentralisation in higher education was trialled via a pilot scheme in five public HEIs, which were accorded the new status of 'Badan Hukum Milik Negera' (BHMN; 'State-Owned Legal Institution') (Welch 2007a). By virtue of this new status, the selected HEIs were authorised to create new patterns of student recruitment, which would, inter alia, have the effect of garnering greater financial support from students and their families.

At the same time, however, HEIs are caught in something of a dilemma. On the one hand, the increasing mismatch between ever increasing enrolment demand and limited state capacity means that public HEIs are being pressured to diversify their income sources, while the private sector expands to respond to unmet demand. Both trends are evident in the South-East Asian systems treated here. This might, however, add little if anything to teaching quality or research output; indeed, there is evidence in several South-East Asian systems that it could weaken each, with academics from the public sector either being poached to work in the private sector or increasingly moonlighting there (Welch 2007a).

On the other hand, while governments tout the virtues of devolution, institutions find themselves pressured by more intricate regulatory architecture, which sets real limits on their capacity to implement devolution effectively. While state funding per student plateaus, or even declines, governments demand more and more accountability—a process that has been characterised as like accountancy, as 'rule by performance indicator' increasingly burdens academic work and life (Welch 1998). In the process, devolution has been characterised as a form of 'centralised decentralisation' (Lee and Gopinathan 2004; Mok 2004). Many critics seriously question the extent to which the much-touted institutional freedom to run their own affairs is genuine, or illusory, against such a backdrop. Certainly, regional evidence shows that decentralisation of governance (Aspinall 2004) and education at other levels has not been without its problems (Amirrachman et al. 2008; Surakhmad 2002), while in higher education, too, problems persist, as is seen below.

The Impact of Limited Infrastructure

In a curious irony, it can be argued that the increasing demands of governance impose real limits on governability in South-East Asian universities. While regionally devolution has been accompanied by increased demands for performance data, and a move to discretionary funding for which HEIs must compete, little or no additional personnel or other resources have been made available to respond to such trends. At the same time, governments, too, are under pressure, often with very limited resources available within agencies and ministries charged with the regulation of quality and propriety in higher education. Given the less-developed status of all but one of the South-East Asia Five, personnel with which to perform such regulatory tasks are limited, and high-level training of such staff cannot always be assumed.

This has long been problematic, but has become more so in light of several factors. The rise of mass higher education systems, and larger numbers of institutions, makes the mechanics of ensuring quality control difficult, even in the public system. The rise and complexity of the private sector, sketched above, have made the job even more complex, with in some cases the total number of HEIs nationally rising to more than 1000. Most recent figures for Malaysia show 533 private HEIs of non-university status (MOHE 2006:257), while in Indonesia, for example, there are two categories of private HEIs: *'terakreditasi'* (accredited) and *'tidak terakreditasi'* (non-accredited). The latter are quite widespread. Geographic dispersal adds to these difficulties—although in the early 1990s, some 25 per cent of all private HEIs were still located either in Jakarta (16.4 per cent) or East Java (9.6 per cent) (Pardoen 1998:28). The proliferation in recent years of private HEIs (PHEIs) well outside the major cities itself yields its own difficulties:

> [S]uch a big number of PHEIs presents problems, especially when dealing with the quality control of the education they offer…the controls sound weak due to the fact that monitoring activities are not easy, and necessitate a high cost because some of the PHEIs are in scattered areas. Generally, the problems of monitoring PHEIs lead to several particulars concerning government policies, quality control and financial matters. (Hardihardaja 1996:42)

Last, the rise of transnational higher education and cross-border programs and institutions makes the regulatory challenge even tougher (Knight 2007) for already hard-pressed national regulatory agencies. While many transnational institutions and programs act ethically, and are of high quality, there are numerous regional examples of bogus 'cyber universities' and virtual-diploma mills.

Transparency: The impact of corruption

It must also be acknowledged that South-East Asia is not free of corruption, and that this also at times permeates higher education. While most university staff— both academic and administrative (sometimes they are the same individuals)— throughout the region work hard under challenging conditions, including the aforementioned poor remuneration rates and very limited resources, there are some who perform less honourably.

Transparency International's 2006 Corruption Perceptions Index points to a strong correlation between corruption and poverty, with a concentration of impoverished states at the bottom of the ranking. 'Corruption traps millions in poverty', according to the chair of Transparency International, Huguette Labelle. 'Despite a decade of progress in establishing anti-corruption laws and regulations, today's results indicate that much remains to be done before we see meaningful improvements in the lives of the world's poorest citizens' (Transparency International 2006).

The 2006 Corruption Perceptions Index (Transparency International 2006) is a composite index that draws on multiple expert opinion surveys that poll perceptions of public-sector corruption in 163 countries around the world—the greatest scope of any Corruption Perceptions Index to date. Countries are scored on a scale from zero to 10: zero indicates high levels of perceived corruption, while 10 indicates low levels of perceived corruption.

A strong correlation between corruption and poverty—evident in the results of the 2006 Corruption Perceptions Index—affects the South-East Asia Five significantly. Public-sector wages in all but Malaysia are poor, and moonlighting is common. Indeed, the correlation between poverty and corruption is underscored by the fact that only Malaysia scored 5.0, while others ranged from 3.6 (Thailand) and 2.6 (Vietnam) to 2.4 (Indonesia) and 2.5 (Philippines). Moreover, there is evidence that, while some among the South-East Asia Five have made progress in controlling corruption in recent years (notably, Malaysia and Thailand), the situation has worsened in Indonesia, Vietnam and the Philippines (UNDP 2005:41). As seen below, higher education is not immune to such effects.

Westcott's (2001) analysis of corruption in South-East Asia provides some examples of the general effects of pervasive corruption (International Herald Tribune 2001). He cites, for example, the estimate of Thailand's National Counter-Corruption Commission (NCCC) that up to 30 per cent of government procurement budgets could be lost due to corrupt practices. At the lower end, this would almost equal the entire budget of the Ministry of Agriculture. At the upper end, it would exceed the combined budgets of Agriculture and Public Health (Westcott 2001:252). Data from Vietnam cite reports showing that nearly one-third of Vietnam's public investment expenditure in 1998—equivalent to 5 per cent of GDP—was lost to fraud and corruption, and the situation has not improved since then (Westcott 2001:258). As elsewhere in South-East Asia, in Vietnam, the situation is not helped by poor public-sector pay and widespread moonlighting (Welch 2007a, 2007b).

Education effects at all levels, especially for the poor, are clearly evident, as illustrated in the following example taken from the Philippines:

> Corruption…has an impact on the health and education of the poor…it reduces test scores, lowers national ranking of schools, raises variation of test scores within schools, and reduces satisfaction ratings…corruption affects public services in different ways than urban areas, and…harms the poor more than the wealthy. (UNDP 2005:44)

Specific effects on higher education are revealed in the two following examples. The first occurred within Indonesia, where a private HEI's Faculty of Engineering, facing an upcoming evaluation of its facilities by the national regulatory authority (BAN), and well aware that its level of engineering infrastructure was inadequate, adopted a strategy designed to circumvent the problem. Unwilling to accept the consequences of a poor rating, the Faculty of Engineering approached local engineering firms to borrow numerous items of major equipment. The day after the successful inspection, which ultimately yielded a satisfactory B rating, all items of equipment were returned, leaving students just as bereft of much necessary equipment as before. Such stories are not uncommon: 'Many private schools provide engineering education without sufficient equipment to support the curriculum and end up compromising the quality of their graduates' (Buchori and Malik 2004:262). The need for a more effective regulatory regime is now widely acknowledged against a background of a widespread culture of corruption (known in Indonesia as KKN: 'Korrupsi, Kollusi and Nepotism') that has the capacity to undermine the effectiveness of quality-assurance procedures (Kompas 2002; Transparency International: <http://www.transparency.org>). Indeed, one of the impacts of devolution in Indonesia in recent years is sometimes said to be the export of corruption to the local level (Amirrachman et al. 2008).

The second set of examples comes from Vietnam, where, in 2001, serious problems surfaced at certain private HEIs. At least two difficulties became apparent in the course of the official police investigation. Each also arguably related to their status as non-state institutions, ineligible for public funds. The first issue was that of over-enrolment, in a situation in which the Ministry of Education and Training (MOET) sets legally defined enrolment limits for such institutions. Dong Do University was found by MOET to have over-enrolled to the tune of 2.8 times its MOET quota. Thus, for the academic year 2001–02 alone, Dong Do had enrolled 4205 students, rather than its allotted 1500. Interestingly, however, the problems had been known for some years: 'The Dong Do University scandal first surfaced in October 1998 when officials of the Ministry of Education and Training found that the number of students admitted to the university far surpassed the permitted figure' (Viet Nam News 2002a).

The second issue was one of entry standards. While this could be seen as simply an issue of quality, it was alleged in 2001 that the leaders of Dong Do had been routinely accepting bribes from students or their families in order to secure entry to the institution. This, too, is strictly illegal, but allegedly occurred in an effort to boost the numbers of enrolments and income levels.

Once again, the official MOET investigation did indeed uncover substantial breaches: papers were given marks of eight or nine out of 10, at times by unqualified markers, when their real grade was assessed as being as low as 0.5. Several dozen students were accepted for enrolment without even being on the list of students for selection. Another 380 had no upper secondary graduation certificates at all. All in all, some 80 per cent of students accepted for enrolment at Dong Do were found to have scores lower than those reported by the

University Council, while some had had their marks increased by re-scoring. The investigating team also found, beyond these serious breaches of procedure, that the university had failed to build any facilities, offices or classrooms in seven years of operation or to invest in enhancing the quality of academic staff. Facilities were assessed as not meeting the standards of a university (*Lao Dong*: <http://www.laodong.com.vn>).

As a result of this investigation, Dong Do's 2002 enrolments were deemed cancelled, and the university was given strict instructions to end such illegal practices. The Ha Noi police were called in to conduct an investigation and, if necessary, proceed to prosecutions against the rector and other senior staff responsible. The deputy chair of its board of management was subpoenaed 'for his involvement in [one] of the biggest scandals to date in the education sector' (Viet Nam News 2002a, 2002b). The former director of its training department was also charged.

At times, too, gamekeeper has turned poacher. In a separate case in 2002, two senior MOET officials—both at deputy minister level—were either reprimanded or sacked after their involvement in the 'Asian International University' (AIU) scam was revealed. Both officials were linked with the 'bogus university, which set up shop in Vict Nam, and enrolled thousands, awarding worthless paper degrees' (Viet Nam News 2002c). After being in operation for five years, AIU, which was established in 1995 in cooperation with Hanoi University of Foreign Languages, ceased pretending to be a university, leaving more than 2000 students stranded, having lost hundreds of thousand of dollars (Le and Ashwill 2004). In another incident, the so-called American Capital University (ACU) offered an MBA program, together with a partner: the variously titled Singapore (later Senior) Management Training Centre. Both institutions are now defunct—again, leaving numbers of students thousands of dollars out of pocket (Ashwill 2006).

What are the implications of the above examples for access and equity? The Indonesian example clearly raises issues of access, since if the process of accreditation had proceeded in a transparent manner, the ability of the institution to recruit would have been crippled. Equity is also implied, since under the current regime, students are being denied access to good-quality engineering education, notably through lack of relevant facilities and equipment. Of the Vietnamese cases, Dong Do could be said to represent widening of access—albeit illegally—but at the cost of quality, since students were able to enter at scores well below those normally deemed acceptable. The cases of the bogus AIU and ACU represented a loss of both access and equity, leaving many families out of pocket, having paid fees in good faith to institutions that proved in the end to be little more than shopfronts.

Conclusion: Blurring borders, changing balance

If, as is evident above, expanding access to higher education is occurring largely through expansion of the private sector—as is currently the case in many parts of the world (Altbach 1999)—the question of the impact of such a new balance on equality must be addressed:

> [T]here is another important downside to private financing—it may preclude the enrolment of deserving students who do not have the ability to pay, and often evokes resentment among students who do. Means-tested scholarship and loan programs are one possible approach to addressing this problem, but they have proven very difficult to administer due to the difficulty of assessing ability to pay, sometimes exorbitant administrative costs, corruption and high rates of default. (World Bank 2000b:57)

The ongoing failure of student loans in the Philippines and Thailand illustrates such difficulties (Welch 2008b). At the very least, there is a heightened need for regulation and quality assurance (QA) in such a new context, in which there are likely to be a growing number of domestic and international private providers, some of whom are worthy and others of whom are little more than shopfronts or (cyber) diploma mills. As indicated above, already the rector of one of the larger and more longstanding 'people's universities' in Vietnam has been placed under police investigation, allegedly both for exceeding his enrolment quota by a huge margin and for taking bribes to allow students with poor marks to enrol. In Indonesia, and in others of the South-East Asia Five countries, further examples of corrupt practices and cheating exist. Such stratagems were driven, at least in part, by the need—or greed—for funding, as well as poor public-sector pay and a culture in which lack of transparency is widely accepted.

Despite the undoubted need for careful regulation of the higher education sector, and the importance of promoting quality, it will not be easily or simply accomplished:

> [I]n most developing countries, no clearly identified set of individuals or institutions is working to ensure that all the goals of the country's higher education sector will be fulfilled. A coherent and rational approach toward management of the entire higher education sector is therefore needed...Policymakers must decide on the extent to which they will guide the development of their country's higher education sector, and the extent to which they think that market forces will lead to the establishment of and operation of a viable system. Overall, the Task Force believes that government guidance is an essential part of any solution. (World Bank 2000b:58)

The case of the Philippines, where, as was seen above, until recently more than 80 per cent of all HEIs were private, illustrates the difficulty clearly. In a political system in which every legislator sees it as part of their legacy to create an HEI that will be named after them, the proliferation of small, poor-quality institutions is a longstanding problem. Faced with this difficulty, efforts were made during the 1980s to introduce a national system that regulated the establishment and operations of private HEIs. The ensuing stout opposition by the private sector, many sections of which argued that the regulations threatened the financial viability of their institutions, forced the abandonment of the scheme, and a reversion to a laissez-faire pattern occurred. It is for such reasons, for example, that all but a few HEIs in the Philippines—public and private—are regarded by both domestic experts and external accreditation agencies as falling well short of international degree-level standards.

Finally, given the swiftness and the extent of the transformation, which are seeing public HEIs introducing fees, at times quite high, and employing all available strategies—and stratagems—to diversify their funding base, are the boundaries between public and private likely to be as clear in the future as in the past? Just as transnational HEIs and programs are breaching national borders on an unprecedented scale, are we likely to see a further blurring of borders between public and private in higher education?

Private higher education is one of the most dynamic and fastest-growing segments of post-secondary education at the start of the twenty-first century. A combination of unprecedented demand for access to higher education and the inability or unwillingness of governments to provide the necessary support has brought private higher education to the forefront. Private institutions—with a long history in many countries—are expanding in scope and number and are increasingly important in parts of the world that have relied on the public sector. A related phenomenon is the 'privatisation' of public institutions in some countries. With tuition and other charges rising, public and private institutions look more and more similar (World Bank 2000b:58).

In such circumstances, the challenge to access and equity in higher education in South-East Asia remains substantial. The second function of universities listed above by Castells—the selection and training of elites—is being distorted by increases in fees, which are excluding the poor both from both private and, increasingly, from public HEIs. Adding to the problem is corruption—an ongoing problem, with clear implications for access and equity. Hence, while the rise of private higher education ensures that access to higher education will continue to expand (albeit less so in the Philippines where access is already substantial), equity, particularly in terms of access to good-quality higher education for the poor, will likely continue to be quite limited.

References

Altbach, A. 1999, 'Private higher education: themes and variations in comparative perspective', in *Private Prometheus: Private higher education and development in the twenty-first century*, Greenwood Publishing, Santa Barbara, Calif.

Amaral, A., Jones, G. and Karseth, B. (eds) 2002, *Governing Higher Education: National perspectives and institutional governance*, Kluwer Academic Publishers, Dordrecht.

Amaral, A., Meek, L. and Larsen, I. (eds) 2003, *The Higher Education Managerial Revolution?*, Kluwer Academic Publishers, Dordrecht.

Amirrachman, A., Syafi'i, S. and Welch, A. 2008, 'Decentralising Indonesian education. The promise and the price', in J. Zajda (ed.), *Centralisation and Decentralisation in Education*, Springer, Amsterdam.

Ashwill, M. 2006, 'US institutions find fertile ground in Vietnam's expanding higher education market', *International Higher Education*, vol. 44, no. 6 (Summer), pp. 13–14.

Asian Development Bank (ADB) 2001, *Education sector policy paper*, (Draft), Asian Development Bank, Manila.

Asian Development Bank (ADB) 2005, *South East Asia Annual Report2005*, Asian Development Bank, Manila, <www.adb.org/Documents/ReportsAnnual_Report/2005/part010900.asp>

Asian Development Bank (ADB) 2007, *Key Indicators. Inequality in Asia*, vol. 38, Asian Development Bank, Manila.

Asian Development Bank (ADB) 2008, *Education and Skills: Strategies for accelerated development in Asia and the Pacific*, Asian Development Bank, Manila.

Aspinall, E. 2004, 'Indonesia: transformation of civil society and democratic breakthrough', in M. Alagappa (ed.), *Civil Society and Political Change in Asia*, Stanford University Press, Calif., pp. 61–96.

Bovonsiri, V., Uampuang, P. and Fry, G. 1996, 'Cultural influences on higher education in Thailand', in K. Kempner and W. Tierney (eds), *The Social Role of Higher Education*, Garland, New York, pp. 55–77.

Buchori, M. and Malik, A. 2004, 'Higher education in Indonesia', in P. Altbach and T. Umakoshi (eds), *Asian Universities. Historical perspectives and contemporary challenges*, The Johns Hopkins Press, Baltimore, pp. 249–78.

Castells, M. 1993, 'The university system: engine of development in the new world economy', in *Improving Higher Education in Developing Countries*, Economic Development Institute of the World Bank EDI Seminar Series, The World Bank, Washington, DC.

Crystal, D. 1997, *English as a Global Language*, Cambridge University Press, UK.

Gonzales, A. 1999, 'Private higher education in the Philippines', in P. Altbach (ed.), *Private Prometheus: Private higher education and development in the twenty-first century*, Greenwood Press, Santa Barbara, Calif., pp. 103–25.

Guardian Weekly 2002, 'English in schools divides Malaysia', 26 September – 2 October, TEFL Supplement, *Guardian Weekly*.

Hardihardaja, J. 1996, 'Private higher education in Indonesia: current developments and existing problems', in W. Tong-In and Y. Wang (eds), *Private Higher Education in Asia and the Pacific. Final report*, UNESCO PROAP and SEAMEO RIHED, Bangkok.

Hayden, M. and Thiep, L.-Q. 2004, 'A 2020 vision for higher education in Vietnam', *International Higher Education*, vol. 44, no. 6 (Summer).

International Herald Tribune 2001, 'In many Asian countries, public anger at corruption is on the rise', 22 January, *International Herald Tribune*.

International Monetary Fund (IMF) 2001, *Vietnam selected economic indicators*, IMF Country Report No. 01/59, International Monetary Fund, Washington, DC.

Kim, S., Gilani, Z., Musisi, N., Texeira, P. and Landoni, P. 2007, 'Rethinking the public–private mix in higher education: global trends and national policy challenges', in P. Altbach and P. McGill Peterson (eds), *Higher Education in the New Century*, Sense, Rotterdam, pp. 79–108.

Knight, J. 2007, 'Internationalisation. A decade of challenges and changes', *International Higher Education*, vol. 50 (Winter), pp. 6–7.

Kompas 2002, '*Tampa Kontrol, Peningkatan Anggaran Pendidikan Bisa Berbahaya* [Without controls, increasing the education budget could be dangerous]', 15 August, *Kompas*.

Le, N.-M. and Ashwill, M. 2004, 'A look at nonpublic higher education in Vietnam', *International Higher Education*, vol. 36, no. 6 (Summer), pp. 16–17.

Lee, M. and Gopinathan, S. 2004, 'Centralized decentralization of higher education in Singapore', in K.-H. Mok (ed.), *Centralization and Decentralization: Educational reforms and changing governance in Chinese societies*, Kluwer Academic Publishers, Dordrecht, pp. 117–36.

Levy, D. 2007, 'Private higher education: patterns and trends', *International Higher Education*, vol. 50 (Winter), pp. 7–9.

Marginson, S. 2007, 'The public private divide in higher education: a global revision', *Higher Education*, vol. 53, pp. 307–33.

Ministry of Higher Education (MOHE) 2006, *Report by the Committee to Study, Review and Make Recommendations Concerning the Development and Direction of Higher Education in Malaysia*, Ministry of Higher Education, Kuala Lumpur.

Mok, K.-H. (ed.) 2004, *Centralization and Decentralization: Educational reforms and changing governance in Chinese societies*, Kluwer Academic Publishers, Dordrecht.

Mok, K.-H. and Welch, A. 2003, 'Globalization, structural adjustment and educational reform', in K.-H. Mok and A. Welch (eds), *Globalisation and Educational Re-Structuring in Asia and the Pacific*, Palgrave Macmillan, London, pp. 1–31.

Organisation for Economic Cooperation and Development (OECD) 2003, *Education Policy Analysis 2003*, Organisation for Economic Cooperation and Development, Paris.

Pardoen, S. 1998, *Assessment of Private Investment in Private Higher Education in Indonesia. The case of four private universities*, Centre for Societal Development Studies, Atma Jaya Catholic University, Jakarta.

Purwadi, A. 2001, 'Impact of the economic crisis on higher education in Indonesia', in *Impact of the Economic Crisis on Higher Education in East Asia*, IIEP/UNESCO, Paris.

Pusey, M. 1991, *Economic Rationalism in Canberra. A Nation-building state changes its mind*, Cambridge University Press, UK.

South East Asian Ministers of Education Organisation (SEAMEO) 2002, *Private Higher Education: Its role in human resource development in a globalised knowledge society*, South East Asian Ministers of Education Organisation, Bangkok.

Surakhmad, W. 2002, Decentralising education: a strategy for building sustainable development, Presented to Conference on Autonomy in Education in the Indonesian Context, The Australian National University, Canberra, 29 September.

Sydney Morning Herald (SMH) 2008, 'We fill our tanks, while they can't fill their stomachs', 19 April, *Sydney Morning Herald*.

Thaver, B. 2003, 'Private higher education in Africa. Six country case studies', in D. Teferra and P. Altbach (eds), *African Higher Education. An international reference book*, The Johns Hopkins Press, Baltimore, pp. 53–60.

The Australian 2008, 'East Asia faces testing times', 2 April, *The Australian*.

Tierney, W. 2008, Forms of privatization: globalization and the changing nature of tertiary education, Unpublished ms.

Transparency International 2006, *Corruption Perceptions Index 2006*, Transparency International, Berlin.

United Nations Committee on Trade and Development (UNCTAD) 2004, *World Investment Report 2004. The shift towards services*, United Nations, New York and Geneva.

United Nations Development Programme (UNDP) 2001, *Human Development Report 2001. Making new technologies work for human development*, United Nations Development Programme/Oxford University Press, New York.

United Nations Development Programme (UNDP) 2002, *Human Development Report 2002. Deepening democracy in a fragmented world*, United Nations Development Programme, New York.

United Nations Development Programme (UNDP) 2005, *Southeast Asia Human Development Report. Regional economic integration and regional cooperation in Southeast Asia: deepening and broadening the benefits for human development*, United Nations Development Programme, New York.

United Nations Development Programme (UNDP) 2007, *Human Development Indicators 2007/2008*, United Nations Development Programme, New York.

Viet Nam News 2002a, 'Enrolment irregularities bring on suspensions at Dong Do University', 14 January, *Viet Nam News*.

Viet Nam News 2002b, 'Police grill professor over Dong Do University scandal', 19 June, *Viet Nam News*.

Viet Nam News 2002c, 'Officials fall in school scandal', 7 October, *Viet Nam News*.

Welch, A. R. 1980, 'Ideology, sociology and education. Some developments and relationships', *Australian and New Zealand Journal of Sociology*, vol. 16, no. 2, pp. 71–81.

Welch, A. 1998, 'Education and the cult of efficiency: comparative reflections on the reality and the rhetoric', *Comparative Education*, (Special Issue on International Policy), pp. 157–75.

Welch, A. 2005, 'South Korean higher education: internationalised or globalised?', in K.-H. Mok and R. James (eds), *Globalisation and East Asian Higher Education*, Eastern Universities Press, Singapore, pp. 34–67.

Welch, A. 2006, Ho Chi Minh meets the market. Public and private higher education in Viet Nam, Presented to Australian and New Zealand Comparative and International Education Society Annual Conference, Canberra, December.

Welch, A. 2007a, 'Blurred vision. Public and private higher education in Indonesia', *Higher Education*, vol. 54, pp. 665–87.

Welch, A. 2007b, 'Ho Chi Minh meets the market. Public and private higher education in Viet Nam', *International Education Journal. Comparative Perspectives*, vol. 8, no. 3, pp. 35–56.

Welch, A. 2008a, 'Internationalising Vietnamese universities: retrospect and prospect', in G. Harman, M. Hayden and T. Pham (eds), *Modernising Vietnamese Higher Education*, Springer, Amsterdam.

Welch, A. 2008b, *Higher Education in SE Asia. Changing balance, blurring borders*, Routledge, London.

Welch, A. and Mok, K.-H. 2003, 'Conclusion: deep development or deep division?', in K.-H. Mok and A. Welch (eds), *Globalisation, Educational Re-Structuring and Educational Reforms in Asia and the Pacific*, Palgrave Macmillan, London, pp. 333–56.

Westcott, C. 2001, *Combatting Corruption in Southeast Asia*, Asian Development Bank, Manila.

Wilson, M., Qayyam, A. and Boshier, R. 1998, 'World wide America: manufacturing web information', *Distance Education*, vol. 19, no. 1, pp. 109–41.

World Bank 2000a, *East Asia: Recovery and beyond*, The World Bank, Washington, DC.

World Bank 2000b, *Higher Education in Developing Countries. Peril and promise*, Task Force on Higher Education and Society, The World Bank, Washington, DC.

World Bank 2002a, *Constructing Knowledge Societies. New challenges for tertiary education*, The World Bank, Washington, DC.

World Bank 2002b, *Vietnam—Selected economic indicators, 1995–2001*, The World Bank, Ha Noi.

World Bank 2005, *East Asia Update*, The World Bank, Washington, DC.

World Bank 2006, *An East Asian Renaissance. Ideas for economic growth*, The World Bank, Washington, DC.

World Bank 2007a, *Inequality in Asia. Key indicators 2007 special chapter. Highlights*, The World Bank, Washington, DC.

World Bank 2007b, *Key Indicators 2007. Volume 38: Inequality in Asia*, The World Bank, Washington, DC.

Part 2. Experience in Developed Economies

5. The Australian University Student Financing System: The rationale for, and experience with, income-contingent loans

Bruce Chapman
Crawford School of Economics and Government,
The Australian National University

Introduction and Background

In 1989 the Australian government introduced an income-contingent loan for the payment of public-sector higher education[1] tuition charges, known as the Higher Education Contribution Scheme (HECS). The debt is repaid through the income tax system and, at the time, it was the first scheme of its kind. Since then similar arrangements have been adopted in, among other countries, New Zealand (1991), South Africa (1991), the United Kingdom (2006), Thailand (2006) and Israel (planned for 2008). As well, there is currently active consideration of potential higher education financing reforms towards income-contingent loans in Germany, Canada and a host of other countries. It is not an exaggeration to suggest that there is an ongoing quiet revolution internationally in higher education financing towards the adoption of income-contingent loans.

This chapter examines the basis of income-contingent loans for higher education financing, focusing on the Australian experience with HECS.[2] A key aspect of the discussion is an analysis of the benefits in concept, and a difficulty in practice, of income-contingent loans. A major issue for the adoption of HECS was the potential for the scheme to reduce the access of the disadvantaged to Australian higher education; an extensive review of the literature illustrates that this has not eventuated. As well, there is evidence to suggest that HECS has been associated with significant increases in the size of the higher education system and has proved to be administratively inexpensive.

---

1 Practically all Australian universities are in the public sector.
2 For simplicity, the discussion does not include consideration of the period since 2005, when the scheme was made much more complex. The essential aspect of HECS—income-contingent repayment of the debt— remains. For analysis of the likely effects of the changes introduced in 2005, see Beer and Chapman (2004).

An important issue explored in this chapter concerns the benefits of income-contingent loans with respect to consumption smoothing for borrowers. A hypothetical empirical exercise illustrates that, compared with the repayment of a similar bank loan, the burden of an income-contingent loan for students—as measured by the proportion of a graduate's income that is required to service the debt—can be far less than is the case for the bank loan.

The analysis should not be taken to suggest that income-contingent loans are a panacea for international higher education funding challenges. This is because in many countries there are important institutional difficulties to be overcome in the successful adoption of such approaches.

A Brief History of the Introduction of HECS[3]

1973 to 1986

Australian universities required students to pay fees until 1973, when they were abolished. But before then the majority of students had fee obligations exempt through the receipt of scholarships awarded on the basis of academic merit. Fee abolition meant that from the early 1970s to the late 1980s Australian universities were financed without any direct contribution from students.

This policy stance changed significantly in 1987 with the institution of the Higher Education Administration Charge (HEAC), a small up-front fee on all university students of A$250 in 1987 terms—a charge that did not vary with respect to either discipline or course load. In symbolic terms, the institution of HEAC was significant in that it represented government endorsement of the charging of fees, and thus set the scene for more radical reforms involving user pays.

The revenue raised from HEAC was trivial in comparison with the total costs of higher education—amounting to about only 3 per cent of teaching costs. In 1987, it remained the case that taxpayers provided practically all of the finances for higher education. At this time, a conjunction of forces made it inevitable that the government would move financing arrangements towards increased contributions from students. These forces were as follows.

---

3   The discussion of this section is based on description from Chapman and Ryan (2002).

First, over the 1980s there was a significant increase in year 12 (the final year of high school) completion rates, but there was not a commensurate expansion in higher education places. This resulted in the political problem of large and growing queues of qualified prospective students.

Second, while this problem could have been solved with increased Commonwealth budget outlays, the Labor government was intent on fiscal parsimony and not prepared to spend the additional taxpayer resources necessary to finance additional university places (see Edwards et al. 2001).

Finally, and perhaps most importantly with respect to the political process, at least two cabinet ministers—John Dawkins and Peter Walsh—were strongly in favour of student fees on grounds of redistribution. Their view was that a system that did not charge higher education students was regressive; after all, universities were paid for by all taxpayers, yet students both came from relatively privileged backgrounds and, as graduates, received relatively high personal economic benefits. It is important to record that Walsh and Dawkins were then, respectively, in charge of the critical ministries of finance and higher education.

The Introduction of HECS

In 1987, John Dawkins invited the author of this chapter to prepare a report outlining the costs and benefits of different approaches to the introduction of a user-pays higher education system for Australia. The report presented analyses of several financing mechanisms, including up-front fees with scholarships, up-front fees with government-subsidised bank loans, and an income-contingent charge system. The paper recommended the last of these, with repayments to be made via the direct tax system. Details were provided of how such a system might work, including possible fee levels and repayment parameters.

The minister believed that this report would have a difficult reception—for three reasons. First, the Australian Labor Party (ALP) in government had abolished university fees in 1973, and this had happened under the larger-than-life Labor icon former Prime Minister Gough Whitlam. Second, at that time, the Labor Party platform included a statement to the effect that 'all education should be free of charge'. Third, the income-contingent payment system recommended was both radical and untested: there was no similar scheme internationally, and thus no empirical or political basis to assess its likely economic, social and administrative implications.

Minister Dawkins' response was to set up a committee chaired by a popular former state Labor Premier, Neville Wran, to examine the relative merits of potential options. It was clear from the terms of reference that the government's intent was to set the scene for the introduction of charges.

In May 1988, the Wran committee recommended that all Australian undergraduates should be required to pay a uniform charge, with the timing and level of payment dependent on income. This became policy in 1989, with the income-contingent feature of HECS being unique internationally. At that time, the first repayment threshold was about A$50 000 per annum in 2007 terms.

Labor lost power in 1996, but the new conservative government maintained the essence of HECS. In 1997, however, charge levels were increased by about 40 per cent on average, differential charges by course were introduced and the first income threshold at which graduates began to repay their loans was decreased to just less than $30 000 per annum in 2007 terms. The last decision was reversed in 2005, at which time the government also allowed some price discretion and extended HECS to cover full-fee-paying domestic students.

The Advantages of, and a Difficulty with, Income-Contingent Loans[4]

The Failure of Capital Markets for the Financing of Higher Education

Some might be tempted to ask why government intervention is required with respect to higher education financing. Why not impose charges at the point of entry and allow prospective students without access to the financial resources needed to pay the tuition to borrow the finances from banks?

The problem is that commercial banks will not in general be interested in providing loans to finance human-capital investments. The concern of a bank lending in these circumstances is that, unlike many other purchases from a prospective debtor, there is no saleable collateral in the event of default—such as would be the case for the housing-capital market—and there is no slavery market in which to sell the human capital being developed. As well, and as recognised in Barr (2001) and Chapman (2006), investment returns from higher education are highly variable and uncertain. This implies a real risk to a bank with respect to default in the situation of former students receiving low incomes.

---

4   Much of the discussion in this section follows that of Chapman et al. (2007).

The governments of many countries (for example, the United States, Canada and the Netherlands) address these problems by acting as a guarantor for student loans, and by paying the interest on the debt for the period before the borrower's graduation. A problem inherent in this approach is that because the loans are government guaranteed, defaults imply additional government subsidies, which can be very high.[5] What now follows examines other issues pertinent to a comparison between income-contingent and bank loans.

Income-Contingent Repayment and Default Protection

Instead of allowing some prospective students access to a bank loan with a government guarantee, other countries (including Australia, New Zealand and the United Kingdom) have adopted income-contingent loan systems, in which the former student repays the debt through the tax system, with repayments being dependent on income. Making repayments conditional on future income has a special advantage over other typical debt-repayment schemes—a point now explored.

One advantage of an income-contingent repayment approach is that it avoids the basic problem of the usual type of loan offered by banks. Unlike income-contingent loans, normal bank loans require repayments to be made over a specified period—for example, the term of the loan. Usually no weight is given to the consequences of a borrower's low income; the contract specifies that principal debt and interest payments have to be repaid within a given time.

The essential difference between income-contingent and bank-style loans is that the income-contingent variety serves to protect prospective students from the costs of the exigencies associated with the financial returns to educational investments. So income-contingent loans offer a form of 'default insurance', such that former students do not have to bear the costs of reneging on their debt as a result of periods of low future incomes. This is quite different to a bank-style loan, in which the costs of defaulting exist and could be very high, particularly if the borrower is locked out of other borrowing markets (most notably for housing) through damage to credit reputations.

Default protection with income-contingent repayment overcomes a fundamental problem for prospective borrowers inherent in other loan schemes. With income-contingent approaches, there is unlikely to be any concern about prospective students being unable to repay a loan or making repayment under financial duress.

---

5   See Harrison (1995) for data on US student loan defaults.

Income-Contingent Repayment and Consumption Smoothing

A related problem for students with bank loans concerns possible consumption difficulties associated with fixed repayments. If the expected path of future incomes has a high variance, a fixed level of a debt payment will be associated with a high variance of disposable (after debt repayment) incomes. The point can be illustrated with the following simple example, with much more detail being presented in section five below.

Imagine that a student incurs a debt with fixed monthly repayments of $500 after graduation, say, for five years. If her monthly income is expected to be a constant amount of $5000 after tax then the debt is also a constant proportion of income—in this case, 10 per cent. It is more likely to be the case that she expects her income to increase over time, as a result of promotions, for example, implying that the bank repayment would be expected to fall as a proportion of disposable income. For this example, the bank loan should not be expected to significantly affect her welfare.

But in the event of misfortune, such as job loss or sickness, the former student's income stream might be far less stable than for the above circumstances. For example, imagine that the student experiences a monthly after-tax income stream of $5000 for the first year, but only $1500 for the second year. In this case, her *ex post* loan obligations turn out to be 10 per cent of income initially, but then reach 33.3 per cent of income. The fixed loan-repayment obligation is then associated with the likelihood of significant consumption hardships. Moreover, the uncertainty of future earnings has a greater potential to discourage loan take-up from those expecting to not have access to alternative finances in the event of low future incomes, and these people are more likely to be members of relatively disadvantaged groups.

With income-contingent loan repayments, however, the above difficulties are avoided. Imagine that the repayment rule is 12 per cent of income when monthly incomes are more than $3000, and zero otherwise. In the above example, the former student pays $600 a month of her debt in the first year, but is not required to pay anything in the second year. That is, income-contingent loan schemes offer insurance against consumption hardship, and this is because they are based on capacity to pay, not time, as is the case with a bank-style loan.

An Important Administrative Concern

In Australia and other countries in which an income-contingent loan system has been introduced, this has turned out to be a relatively simple matter from an administrative point of view. The reasons for this are that the public administration systems of these countries feature a strong legal framework, a universal and transparent regime of income taxation and/or social security collection, and an efficient repayment mechanism. The last involves computerised record keeping of residents' vital financial particulars and, very importantly, a universal system of unique identifiers (often accompanied by an identity card).

Under these circumstances it is not complicated to identify and track individual citizens and their incomes over time and space. It is not expensive, moreover, to tack onto some existing tax-collection mechanism an additional function: the collection of payments from ex-students on the basis of a fixed proportion of income. In the developing world, however, the preconditions to allow income-contingent loans are often lacking.

Chapman and Nicholls (2004) argue that the minimum conditions for a successful income-contingent loan (Chapman 2006) seem to be

1. accurate record keeping of the accruing liabilities of students

2. a collection mechanism with a sound and, if possible, computerised record-keeping system

3. an efficient way of determining with accuracy, over time, the actual incomes of former students.

Some would argue that a further basic requirement for the introduction of an income-contingent loan is a strong legal framework and functional judicial system. Indeed, it is hard, from a developed-world perspective, to imagine implementing a workable scheme outside this context.

It is worth emphasising that of the three conditions noted above for the implementation of an income-contingent loan, two apply also to the collection of any kind of loan. The exception involves determining with accuracy, over time, the actual incomes of former students. This seems to require an effective income tax system including a reliable—preferably universal—system of unique identifiers; accordingly, this particular criterion is likely to be the most difficult institutional barrier to reform in developing countries.

Australia's Experience with HECS[6]

At the time of the introduction of HECS, close to nothing was known about the effects of income-contingent loans, because the scheme was the first of its kind. This section describes and evaluates the Australian higher education experience under this financing mechanism.

HECS Revenue, Changes in the Size of the System and Administration Costs

As illustrated in Figure 5.1, HECS has been associated with considerable increases in revenue for the government—of the order of about A\$13 billion in total, with annual receipts currently in the order of A\$1.2 billion. In lieu of a real rate of interest, the policy involves a discount for up-front payments (currently of 10 per cent), and it is clear from the figure that this feature has contributed quite significantly to total annual revenue. Essentially, governments have used the revenue both to increase the size of the sector and to reduce considerably the proportion of the financing that is funded by taxpayers.

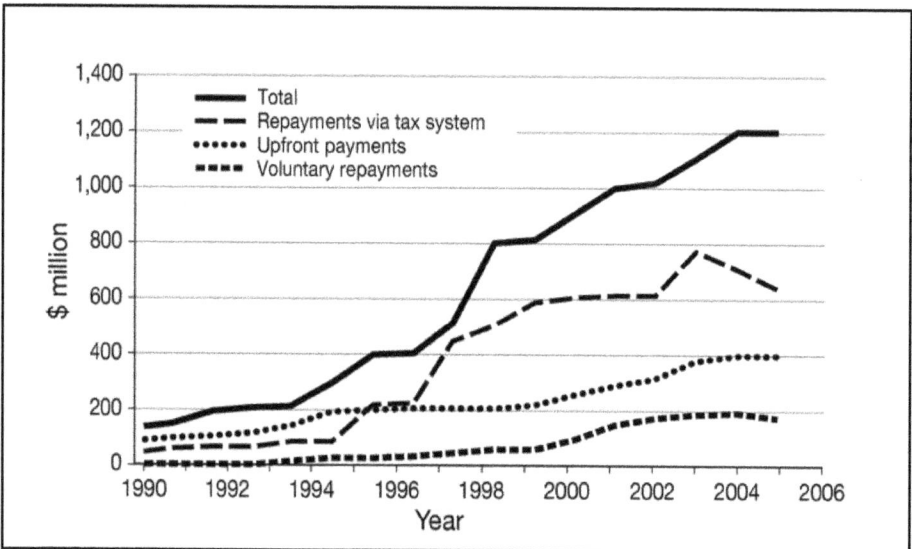

Figure 5.1 HECS revenue, 1989–90 to 2005 (A\$)

Note: The figure for 2005–06 is a government estimate. Up-front payments are based on annual figures from 1989 through to 2005, rather than financial-year amounts.

Source: Commonwealth Department of Education, Science and Technology, as reported in *Higher Education Report 2005*.

---

6   Some of the analysis of this section follows discussion in Chapman (2006).

Arguably, a major consequence of the substantial revenue received from HECS is that the government increased the number of places available, with the number of domestic students being shown for the period 1988–2000 in Figure 5.2. The data show a very large increase in the total number of domestic students since the introduction of HECS in 1989. In 12 years, female numbers had grown by 63 per cent from 208 309 to 337 981, with the male figures increasing by 35 per cent, from 194 334 to 261 897.

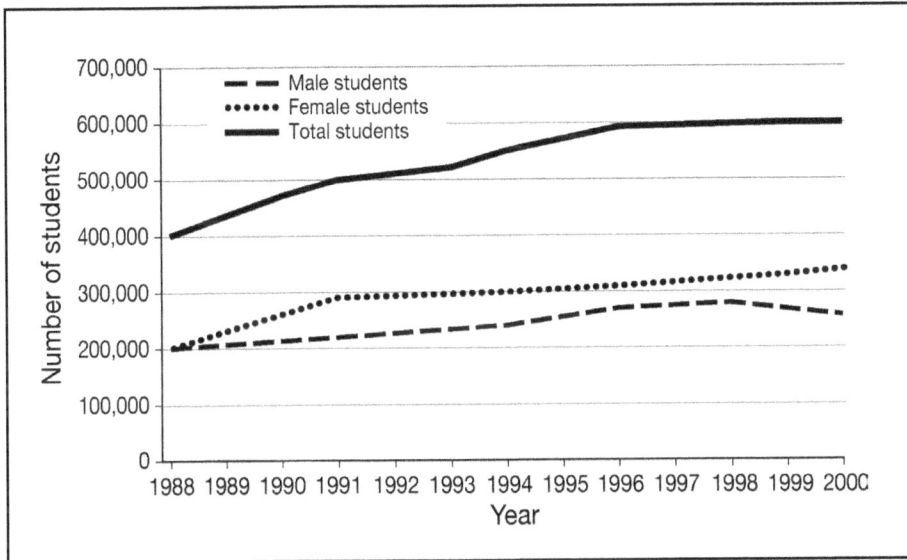

Figure 5.2 Student numbers (full-time equivalent), 1988–2000

Source: Commonwealth Department of Education, Science and Technology, Students (2000–2005) [Full Year]: Selected Higher Education Student Statistics; and Selected Higher Education Student Statistics 1999 and 1997.

In administrative terms, the costs of running HECS, for the Australian Taxation Office and the universities together, have been estimated by Chapman (2006) to be of the order of A$60 million per annum, which is less than 5 per cent of the annual receipts from the scheme.

Studies of the Participation of Disadvantaged Groups

The biggest policy and political concern with respect to the introduction of HECS was whether or not imposing a charge on students to be repaid in this way would have adverse consequences for the participation of poor prospective students. In the two instances in which the policy was changed after 1989—that is, in both 1997 and 2005—the same issue has arisen. There have been a large number of different investigations into this matter.

For example, Aungles et al. (2002) used the local area socioeconomic averages concerning education and occupation, as did Andrews (1999), to explore the possibility of there being an effect on commencements of the relatively disadvantaged from the very significant increases in HECS changes in 1997. In general, they found that the share of university commencements of students from low socioeconomic backgrounds did not change. There was, however, apparently an effect of differential HECS on subject choice, with a decrease in enrolments of low socioeconomic status males in courses in which the HECS charge increased most. The actual numbers involved were very small (less than 200 people) and these individuals were not discouraged from attending university per se; they simply changed their course choice. Chapman and Ryan (2005) report a similar effect in direction for this group using a measure of family wealth, but it was not found to be statistically significant.

Other studies have used individually based socioeconomic status measures in analyses of Australian higher education participation. Long et al. (1999) and Marks et al. (2000) used four and five panels of longitudinal data respectively to identify how education participation changed in Australia from the 1980s to the late 1990s. Long et al. (1999) used parental education and occupation to identify differences in education participation by socioeconomic status, as well as an indirect wealth index constructed from responses by individuals to questions about the presence of material possessions in their houses. They found no apparent effect of HECS on the access of the poor.

Chapman (1997) analysed university participation among eighteen-year-olds in the last two cohorts analysed by Long et al. (1999) and also concluded that the introduction of HECS had not affected university participation by students from disadvantaged backgrounds. Chapman's approach had the advantage of measuring university participation in 1988 for the third cohort, prior to the introduction of HECS. Not everyone aged eighteen in these data had, however, completed school when surveyed in the relevant years, so the estimates understated university participation among young Australians.

Marks et al. (2000) measured participation by the proportion of individuals in higher education in 1999 who had been in year nine in 1995. This measure differed from that used for the earlier cohorts by Long et al. (1999). The wealth measure used by Marks et al. (2000) for the last panel also differed from the earlier ones. This research confirmed the positive impact of wealth on higher education participation. In general, however, their results suggested that socioeconomic status was less important in determining higher education participation in the 1999 data than had been the case in the earlier panels.

Marks and McMillan (2006) analyse university participation within ranges of the entrance scores used by universities to select students for undergraduate courses in 1999. They find that within these entrance score ranges, individuals whose parental occupational backgrounds are non-professional are as likely to participate in university as those whose parental occupational backgrounds are professional. They conclude that since occupational origins have little influence on university participation once entrance scores are taken into account, HECS has not deterred students from less-privileged backgrounds from attending university.

Cardak and Ryan (2006) produced similar results. They found that students from the most disadvantaged social backgrounds entered university at similar rates to those from the most advantaged backgrounds who had the same university entrance scores as them. Their university participation rates were much lower than those from the most advantaged backgrounds because they were less likely to obtain an entrance score and obtained a much lower one on average when they did. Among students with the same levels of school achievement in year nine, those from more advantaged backgrounds were able to convert that achievement into substantially higher university entrance scores by the end of their schooling than otherwise similar students from poorer backgrounds.

Chapman and Ryan (2005) analyse the access effects of HECS using three of the longitudinal panels of data used in the Long et al. (1999) and Marks et al. (2000) studies. They use a consistent definition of university participation across these three cohorts. Chapman and Ryan (2005) analyse the participation in higher education of eighteen-year-olds in the first year they could potentially attend university. Thus, for the first two cohorts, they estimated the participation in higher education in 1988 and 1993 of individuals who should have reached year 12 in 1987 and 1992 respectively. For the 1999 cohort analysed in Marks et al. (2000), Chapman and Ryan analysed higher education participation among eighteen-year-olds.

Chapman and Ryan concluded that the introduction of HECS did not affect the access of the disadvantaged, in terms of enrolments. They found that the socioeconomic composition of the higher education student body changed somewhat between 1988 and 1993 in Australia, with the main change being the relative increase in participation by individuals in the middle of the wealth distribution.

In the period after significant modifications to HECS, all socioeconomic groups experienced the same proportionate increases in participation. Further, while there was an across-the-board decrease in the intentions of secondary students concerning university participation in 1996 after the announcement of the changes, in the next year (for all socioeconomic groups), enrolment intentions rebounded to their previous levels. Finally, for those who had not intended to participate in university, no differences associated with socioeconomic background were found in the proportion who eventually did participate.

More generally, Chapman and Ryan (2005) concluded that changes in overall university participation appeared to reflect different behaviour across genders rather than across socioeconomic groups, with the exception that growth was highest among the middle of the wealth distribution.

The conclusions from the Australian research with respect to socioeconomic mix and access are as follows.

1. The relatively disadvantaged in Australia were less likely to attend university even when there were no student fees. This provides further support for the view that a no-charge public university system (that is, financed by all taxpayers) is regressive.

2. The introduction of HECS was associated with aggregate increases in higher education enrolments.

3. HECS was associated with decreases in the participation of prospective students from relatively poor families (although the percentage point increases were higher for less-disadvantaged students, especially in the middle of the wealth distribution).

4. There was a small decrease in the aggregate number of applications after the 1997 changes, but no apparent decreases in commencements of members of low socioeconomic groups, except perhaps for a small number of males into courses with the highest charges.

5. The significant changes to HECS introduced in 1997 were associated generally with increases in the participation of individuals to 1999, irrespective of their family wealth. Even so, the growth in participation has slowed since then.

It appears that there have been few consequences for the accessibility to higher education for students from relatively disadvantaged backgrounds, at least as represented by enrolments. Broadly speaking, the socioeconomic make-up of the higher education student body was about the same in the late 1990s and early 2000s as it was before HECS was introduced. This might have also happened with other financing approaches, of course.

A Caveat

A qualification to the above conclusions is warranted. It is that the findings with respect to revenue, the number of places and student access cannot be traced directly to the fact that HECS is an income-contingent loan per se. Much of the 1989–2007 Australian higher education experience might well have resulted from the introduction of charges financed in other ways, such as up-front fees with scholarships or bank loans. As well, before it is decided that income-contingent loans constitute a broad panacea for higher education financing, it is critical to reinforce that the institutional and administrative arrangements need to be appropriate to allow such schemes to be implemented, and in many developing countries this will not be the case.

A Comment on the Form of the HECS Interest Rate

A proper understanding of the way HECS operates is to note that after it is incurred a HECS debt is adjusted only for changes in the consumer price index (CPI), implying that the real rate of interest is zero. This is not, however, in reality the case—a point now explained. The nature of the rate of interest on the charge is important. HECS has a form of a real rate of interest, but it is rarely reported as such. This comes from the 20 per cent discount for the up-front payment, meaning that those who choose to pay later are initially in debt to the tune of 25 per cent more than those who take the discount.

Calculations from Chapman and Kiananan (2008) reveal that (assuming a real discount rate of 3 per cent) there is very little interest rate subsidy associated with this form of a real rate of interest when it comes to the sizes of debts typically incurred in public-sector undergraduate courses. The story is very different when the scheme is transferred to the private sector, however, and it is in this context that the current form of the real interest rate on HECS needs to be revisited.

HECS Repayments and Consumption Smoothing

This section examines issues associated with the repayment of HECS. With the use of cross-sectional age–earnings profiles, the time paths and length of HECS repayments are shown for hypothetical male and female graduates working full-time, and these are compared with the repayment of an equivalent bank loan under typical arrangements. In terms of the welfare of borrowers, it is shown that there is a close similarity between the two types of loans for full-time workers, as represented by the proportion of earnings required to repay the different debts.

Through the construction of a hypothetical graduate who experiences substantial variation in earnings, however, the differences in the effects of the two types of loans become very clear. This exercise highlights the critical importance with income-contingent loans of the feature of consumption smoothing.

HECS Repayments for Full-Time Workers

To illustrate typical repayment scenarios for HECS debtors, three things are required

1. information concerning the HECS repayment rates
2. the construction of a hypothetical study, debt and working path
3. data concerning graduate earnings by age and sex.

Table 5.1 presents the repayment rates in operation in 2004–05.

Table 5.1 HECS income thresholds and repayment rates, 2004–05

HECS repayment incomes in the range (A$ p.a.)	Percentage of income applied to repayment
Below 35 000	Nil
35 001–38 987	4.0
38 988–42 972	4.5
42 973–45 232	5.0
45 233–48 621	5.5
48 622–52 657	6.0
52 658–55 429	6.5
55 430–60 971	7.0
60 972–64 999	7.5
65 000 and above	8.0

Source: Australian Taxation Office, *Repaying Your HECS Debt 2004–05*, Commonwealth Government, Canberra.

The information available in Table 5.1 should be interpreted in the follow context. When students incur a debt, it is recorded in conjunction with their unique tax file numbers in the Australian Tax Office. From Table 5.1, in 2004–05, no repayments were required if the income of the former student fell below $35 000 per annum, and above this level progressive proportions of income are subtracted from income until the debt is paid in full. For example, in a year in which the graduate earns $43 000, she will pay 0.05 x $43 000 = $2150 off her debt.

It is instructive to illustrate the effect of these charge levels and repayment parameters on the after-tax incomes of graduates by age. In what follows, the 2004–05 HECS repayment parameters have been applied for male and female students, assuming: they begin a four-year science degree at age eighteen, which incurs an annual charge of $5367 (or $21 468 in total), graduating at age twenty-two; and, after graduation, they take a full-time job earning the average income by age of graduates of their sex. The income data are taken from earnings functions estimated from the 2003 Household, Income and Labour Dynamics of Australia (HILDA) survey, updated to 2004–05 dollars, and as reported in Chapman (2006).

The results for males and females respectively are shown in Figures 5.3 and 5.4, which present taxable incomes before and after HECS repayments for the higher education investment scenarios described above. The data show that both male and female science graduates earning average graduate incomes for full-time workers will repay their total HECS debt about 10 years after graduating, or at about age thirty-one for our hypothetical students.

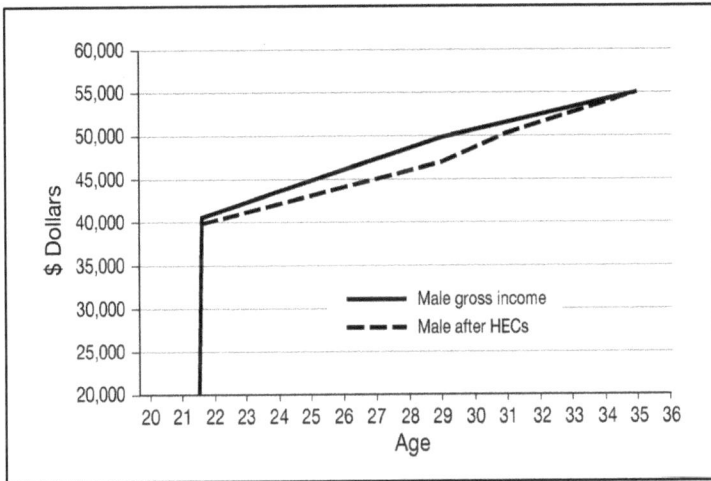

Figure 5.3 Earnings before and after HECS: males (A$ 2004)

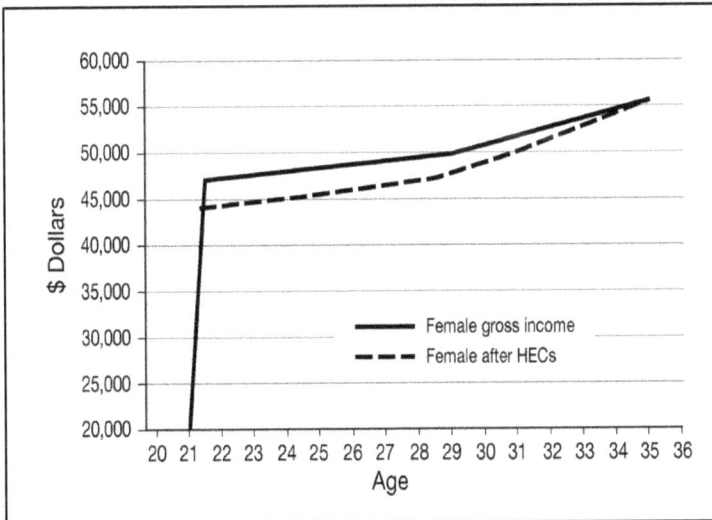

Figure 5.4 Earnings before and after HECS: females (A$ 2004)

To help motivate the important discussion below concerning the consequences of income-contingent loans with respect to consumption smoothing, it is instructive to compare the HECS repayment experience illustrated above for full-time earnings with what would have been the case with a bank loan of the same amount repaid on the basis of time.[7] In what now follows, we compare these repayments with what would be forthcoming from a bank loan of the same amount, repaid over 10 years. The dollar amounts by age and sex are illustrated in Figure 5.5.

The data from Figure 5.5 suggest that in absolute dollar terms the payment of bank loans and HECS per annum are roughly the same for both men and women: just more than $2000 per annum for 10 years with the bank loan, and about $2500 per annum for HECS payments for eight–nine years.

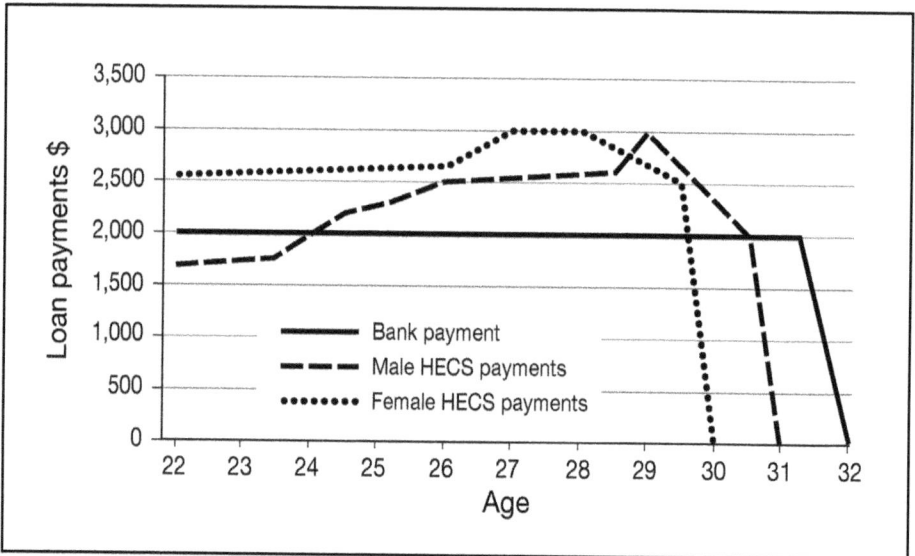

Figure 5.5 HECS payments and bank payments with full-time employment

Again, to further help motivate the consumption-smoothing discussion, we can express these repayments as a proportion of earnings for male and female graduates expecting to earn the average salaries for full-time workers. The data are shown in Figures 5.6 and 5.7.

The results are as follows. For both male and female graduates expecting to earn the average salaries of graduates of their sex, there is little difference between the borrowing regimes. With the bank loan, male and female graduates pay about 4 to 5 per cent of incomes per annum for 10 years, and for HECS the proportions are 4.5 to 6 per cent per annum for eight–nine years; it would be fair to describe these differences as minimal. In what now follows, the critical issue of consumption smoothing is explored in an earnings context quite different to that illustrated above.

---

7 For details of the hypothetical bank-loan arrangement, see Chapman (2006).

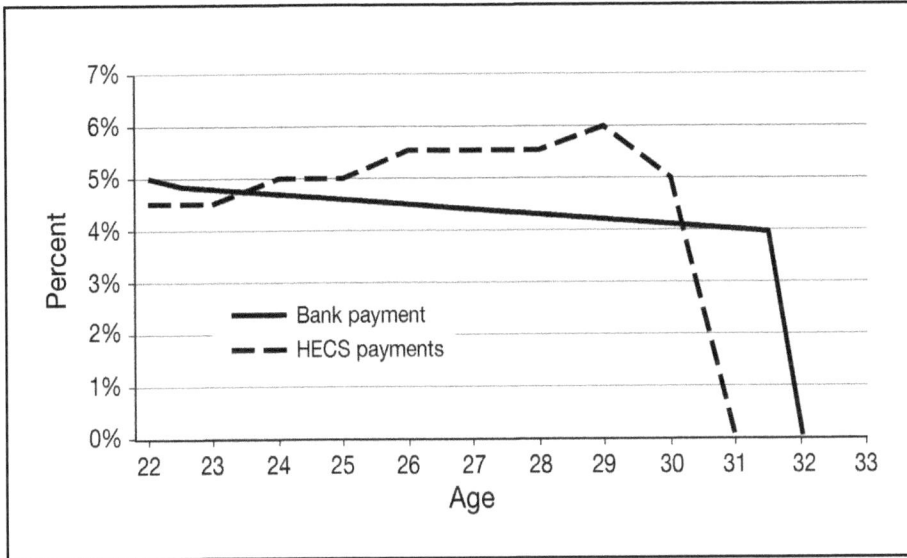

Figure 5.6 Debt repayments as a proportion of taxable income: full-time male graduate workers

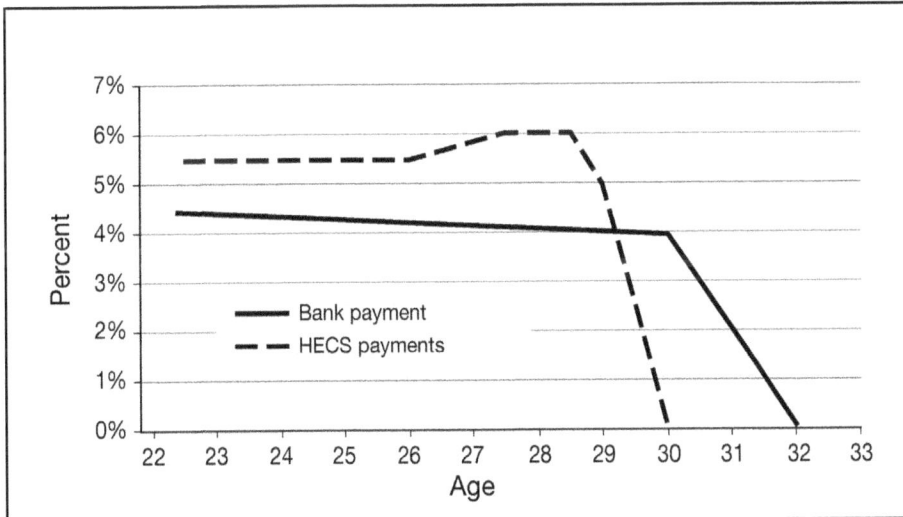

Figure 5.7 Debt repayments as a proportion of taxable income: full-time female graduate workers

HECS and Consumption Smoothing

In many cases, HECS repayments will be significantly different to those illustrated above, and comparisons of the effects of the different loan arrangements become much more interesting when graduate incomes are assumed to change markedly over time. This can be illustrated through the construction of the following scenario. Imagine our graduates have a serious accident at age twenty-five, which leads to job loss and a period of welfare dependency until they are aged twenty-eight. At age twenty-nine, it is assumed that they are sufficiently recovered to work part-time until age thirty-two, when part-time work is assumed to be half the hours and thus half the earnings of a full-time worker. At age thirty-two, they are fully recovered and resume full-time work, earning the same income as an average graduate with their level of full-time labour-market experience. The assumed income streams are shown in Figure 5.8 and Figure 5.9—again, taken from wage estimations using the HILDA survey and reported in Chapman (2006).

The above income streams will then be associated with substantially different loan repayments for HECS than was the case for the scenarios reported above for full-time workers. This raises the very obvious likelihood that compared with the bank loan considered above there will be a very different experience in terms of repayment hardships for members of the groups with highly variable incomes. To illustrate the importance of the consumption-smoothing point, we begin with an illustration of the structure of repayments of both men and women graduates for each type of loan in absolute dollar terms—now shown in Figure 5.10.

The data from Figure 5.10 show that, because repayments are fixed over time, the dollar level of bank-loan repayments does not change year to year, and is just more than $2000 per annum. Things are very different, however, for the income-contingent loan since in periods in which the graduate's income falls below $35 000 there are no HECS payments. Thus, in our example, the periods in which the graduate is either on welfare or working part-time are associated with no loan-related decreases in disposable income. Instead, the borrower is required to repay the loan for additional years.

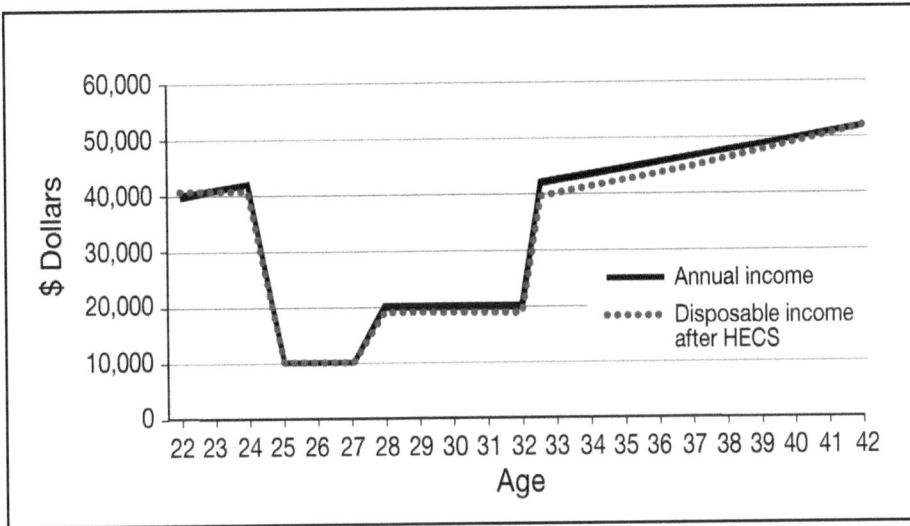

Figure 5.8 Earnings before and after HECS: graduate males experiencing unemployment and part-time work (A$ 2004)

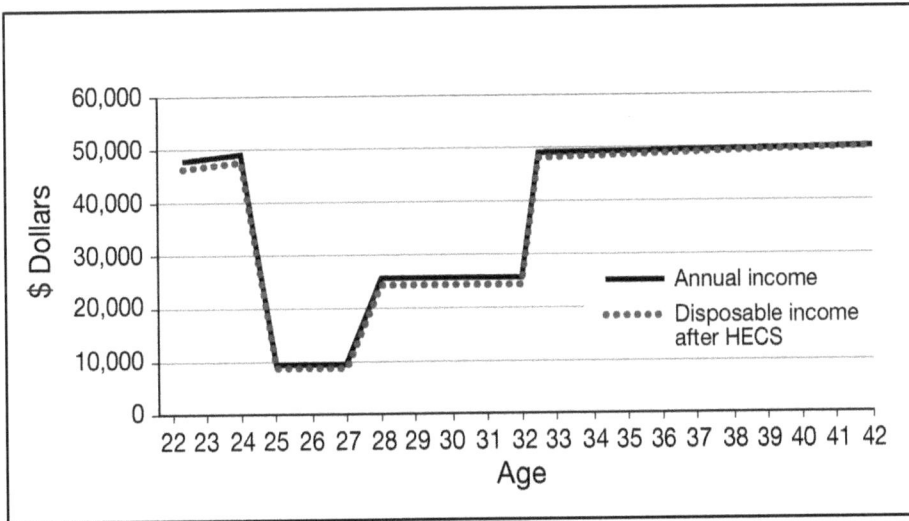

Figure 5.9 Earnings before and after HECS: graduate females experiencing unemployment and part-time work (A$ 2004)

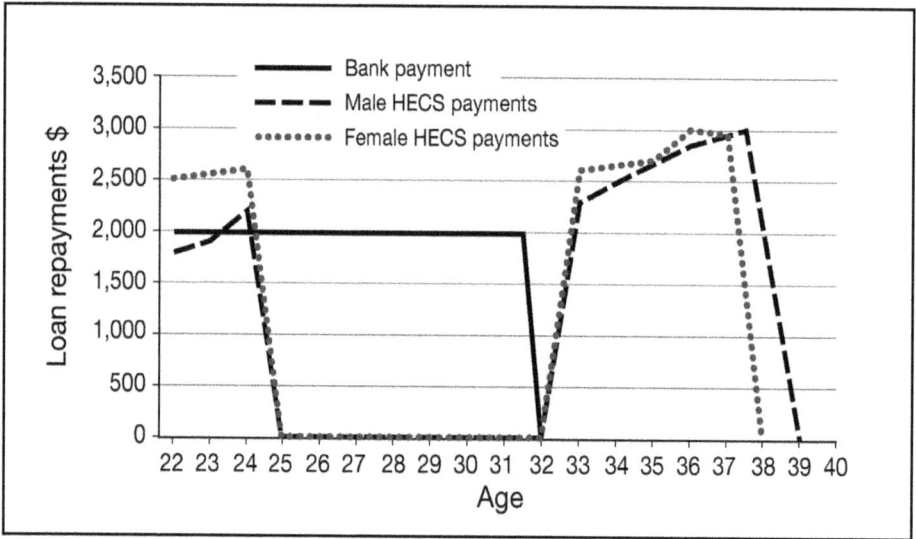

Figure 5.10 HECS payments and bank payments with unemployment and part-time work

That is, there are now payments of between $2500 and $3000 per annum from age thirty-three to age thirty-eight when incomes have risen to their full-time equivalents. Thus, both male and female graduates experiencing low salaries from ages twenty-five to thirty-one pay considerably more for a bank loan in periods of low earnings than is the case for the repayment of the HECS debt. With the latter there are no repayments when incomes are low, thus reflecting the critical benefit of an income-contingent loan. What this means in terms of proportions of taxable incomes is illustrated in Figures 5.11 and 5.12.

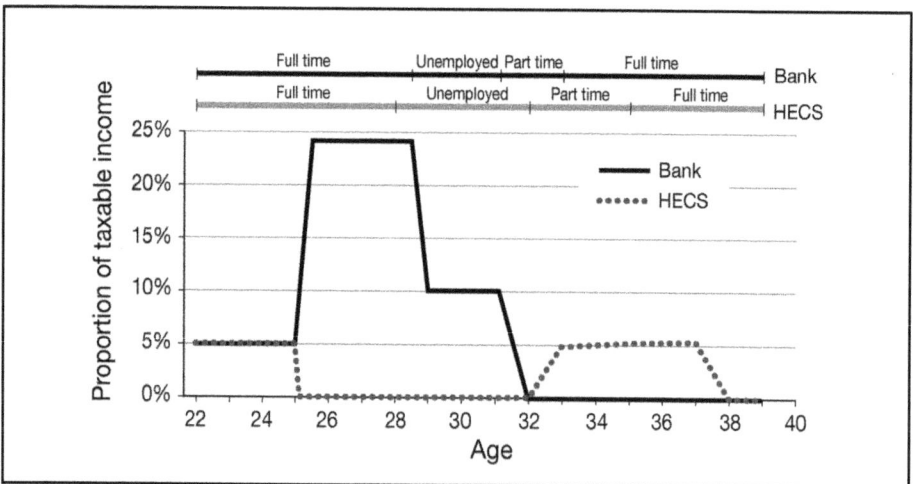

Figure 5.11 Debt repayments as a proportion of taxable income with unemployment and part-time work: graduate males

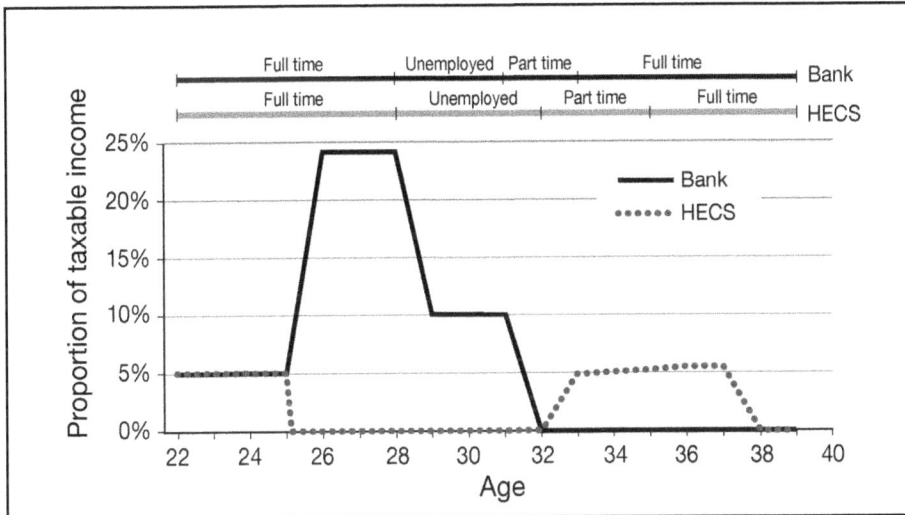

Figure 5.12 Debt repayments as a proportion of taxable income with unemployment and part-time work: graduate females

Modelling the consequences of HECS under various future income streams highlights the clear disadvantage of the bank loan. Repayment obligations of the latter, as a proportion of income, fluctuate between 5 and nearly 25 per cent, but HECS repayments do not exceed 6 per cent of taxable income at any stage.

The extreme situation is for the period in which the graduate is jobless and receiving only unemployment benefits. In those years, the bank loan takes about 24 per cent of taxable income for both males and females. As well, when graduates are working half-time, the proportion of income going to repay the bank debt is still almost 10 per cent. In contrast, HECS payments are zero in the periods of low incomes, and are not more than 6 per cent even when graduate incomes recover. The consequence for HECS debtors, of course, is that while the bank loan is repaid fully in 10 years (at age thirty-one), graduates experiencing periods of low income take until age thirty-eight to repay their HECS debts.

In summary, the exercises reveal that compared with the repayment of a bank loan, HECS delivers important potential consumption-smoothing benefits. For situations in which former students experience very low incomes, the repayment of normal loans results in very high proportions of incomes being obliged to pay debt, and thus being unavailable for consumption. HECS has no such implication, and this is a critical benefit of an income-contingent loan.

Conclusion

The Australian higher education financing system incorporated an income-contingent loan for the payment of tuition in 1989 through the income tax system, and this was the first time that such an approach to student financing had been used internationally. This chapter has: analysed the rationale for income-contingent loans; documented Australia's experience with HECS; and illustrated the major benefits of consumption smoothing of income-contingent loans.

The two major points are as follows. One, even though HECS meant that students would now be paying for some part of higher education, extensive research into the implications of the scheme for the access of the poor to universities reveals that there have been no discernible effects. Two, through a hypothetical exercise using the HECS rules and contemporary Australian data, it is shown that for those graduates receiving low incomes at some part of their lives there is a considerable potential for the system to provide consumption smoothing.

As noted at the beginning, and reinforced in the discussion concerning the administrative bases required for the institution of an income-contingent loan, the main policy conclusions of the chapter need to be handled with care. This is because in some countries the institutional framework might be currently inappropriate to allow efficient, even workable, collection of income-contingent loans. If this is the case, fruitful policy reform would seem to involve improvements in public-sector management.

References

Aungles, P., Buchanan, I., Karmel, T. and MacLachlan, M. 2002, *HECS and Opportunities in Higher Education*, Research, Analysis and Evaluation Group, Commonwealth Department of Education, Science and Training, Canberra.

Andrews, L. 1999, *The effect of HECS on access*, Research Report, Department of Education, Employment, Training and Youth Affairs, Canberra.

Barr, N. 2001, *The Welfare State as Piggy Bank*, Cambridge University Press, UK.

Beer, G. and Chapman, B. 2004, 'HECS system changes: impact on students', *Agenda*, vol. 11, no. 2, pp. 157–74.

Cardak, B. and Ryan, C. 2006, *Why are high ability individuals from poor backgrounds under-represented at university?*, La Trobe School of Business Discussion Paper A06.04, La Trobe University, Melbourne.

Chapman, B. 1997, 'Conceptual issues and the Australian experience with income contingent charges for higher education', *The Economic Journal*, vol. 107, no. 442, pp. 738–51.

Chapman, B. 2006, *Government Managing Risk: Income contingent loans for social and economic progress*, Routledge, London.

Chapman, B. and Nicholls, J. 2004, *Income Contingent Loans for Higher Education: Implementation issues for developing countries*, The World Bank, Washington, DC.

Chapman, B. and Ryan, C. 2002, 'Income contingent financing of student charges for higher education: assessing the Australian innovation', *Welsh Journal of Education*, vol. 11, no. 1, pp. 45–63.

Chapman, B. and Ryan, C. 2005, 'The access implications of income related charges for higher education: lessons from Australia', *Economics of Education Review*, vol. 24, no. 5, pp. 491–512.

Chapman, B., Rodrigues, M. and Ryan, C. 2007, *HECS for TAFE: the case for extending income contingent loans to the vocational education and training sector*, Treasury Working Paper 2007–2, April, Commonwealth Treasury, Canberra.

Edwards, M., Howard, C. and Miller, R. 2001, *Social Policy, Public Policy*, Allen & Unwin, Sydney.

Harrison, M. 1995, 'Default in guaranteed student loan programs', *Journal of Student Financial Aid*, vol. 25, pp. 25–42.

Long, M., Carpenter, P. and Hayden, M. 1999, *Participation in education and training: 1980–1994*, Longitudinal Surveys of Australian Youth Research Report No. 13, Australian Council for Educational Research, Melbourne.

Marks, G. and McMillan, J. 2007, 'Australia: changes in socioeconomic inequalities in university participation', in Y. Shavit, R. Arum and A. Gamoran (eds), *Stratification in Higher Education: A comparative study*, Stanford University Press, Calif.

Marks, G., Fleming, N., Long, M. and McMillan, J. 2000, *Patterns of participation in year 12 and higher education in Australia: trends and issues*, Longitudinal Surveys of Australian Youth Research Report No. 17, Australian Council for Educational Research, Melbourne.

Ryan, C. 2002, *Individual Returns to Vocational Education and Training Qualifications: Their implications for lifelong learning*, National Centre for Vocational Education Research, South Australia.

6. Higher Education Policies and Development: Approaches to funding higher education in Japan

Motohisa Kaneko
The University of Tokyo

Introduction

Japan's higher education system is similar to those in many East Asian counties in the sense that it comprises both public and private sectors. The public sector consists of the national universities, which are established by the national government, and local public universities, which are established by prefectures and other local governments. While the private institutions enrol three-quarters of undergraduates, the national institutions play significant roles in research and graduate education.

With the advent of globalisation and 'the knowledge society' on the one hand and the increasing pressure of financial stringency on the other, both national and private institutions are faced with pressures for change. Private institutions will have to respond to the challenge of the declining number of eighteen-year-olds. Meanwhile, from the perspective of the restructuring of the Japanese economy and society for the coming ages, reshaping higher education certainly assumes particular importance.

It is for these reasons that over the past decade the national government has set out radical changes for the institutional basis of higher education. The Ministry of Education, Culture, Sports, Science and Technology (MEXT) sought to change the nature of national universities. The Law for Incorporation of National University was enacted in 2004, thus transforming the legal status of the national universities as a kind of governmental facility with an independent legal entity. The new legal form, 'Kokuritsu Daigaku Hojin', can be roughly translated as 'National University Corporation'.

The private institutions have experienced a radical shift of governmental subsidies, with their weight shifted from the mandatory current-cost subsidy to discretionary subsidies. For 2007, the current-cost subsidy fell from the previous year for the first time in 30 years. The government also revised the Private School Law to enhance accountability in the governance and financing of private institutions.

Yet, reforms are incomplete. There are various political initiatives to bring in further changes in the higher education system. In this sense, the future of Japan's higher education is still open. How is Japanese higher education constructed? What are its major consequences for the society and the economy? How is the Japanese government trying to change the system, and what are the major issues in this context?

In order to answer these questions, this chapter describes the outline of the higher education system and its socioeconomic contexts, describes the scheme of incorporated national universities and its problems, examines policies on private institutions in the context of declining demands, and summarises current policy debates over the level of higher education expenditure in the national economy.

Outline of the System and Socioeconomic Contexts

The Higher Education System and Enrolment

At the post-secondary level there are three types of institutions. First, technical colleges (*Koto Senmon Gakko*) admit graduates from junior high schools and require five years for completion, implying two years at post-secondary level (total enrolment in this type of institution is minor, making up less than 1 per cent of total enrolments at post-secondary level). Second, miscellaneous schools (*Kakushu Gakko*) include various types of schools—mostly private—offering a wide range of education and training. The entrance requirement varies, from completion of compulsory education to high-school completion, or even higher. Third, special training schools (*Senshu Gakko*), which require a high-school diploma for admission, provide occupational or technical training lasting usually two years. They constitute the second-largest segment of the higher education system. In most cases, these institutions had originally been proprietary schools offering various types of occupational training before they received charter from the MEXT.

Two types of institutions offer higher education: universities and colleges (both called *daigaku*, and referred to as universities hereafter), which in most cases require four years for completion, except in the cases of departments of medicine and dentistry, which require six years. Of these institutions, about two-thirds offer graduate courses, in which 99 000 students are studying for a Master's or Doctor's degree. Junior colleges resemble universities in the basic structure of their curriculum, but require two years for completion. With student bodies predominantly female (90 per cent), most of these institutions offer terminal education in non-technical subjects such as literature and home economics. Unlike the case of the community college in the United States, here, transfer from a two-year to a four-year institution is exceptional.

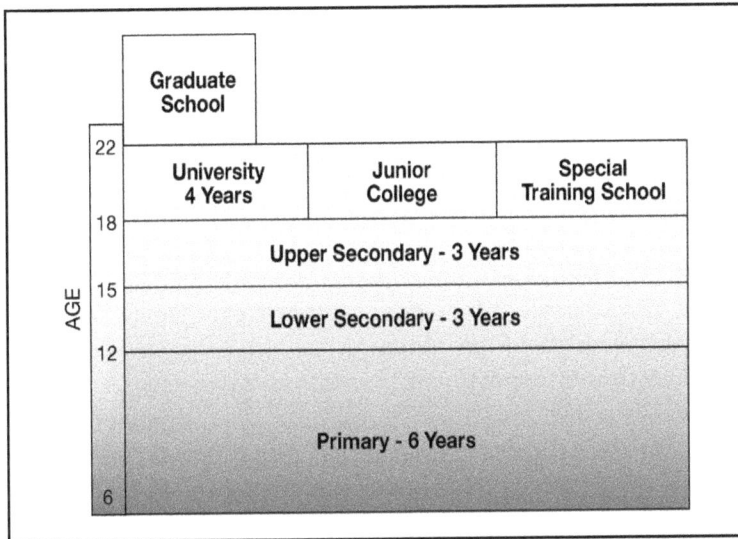

Figure 6.1 The school system

Recent statistics show that more than 70 per cent of eighteen-year-olds advanced to some form of post-secondary and higher education in 2007. Of those, more than half (about 37 per cent) went to four-year institutions. The distribution across different types of post-secondary education differed considerably by gender. Girls tended to go to junior colleges, but the difference has been diminishing in recent years. The shares of those entering the post-secondary courses at special training schools are similar between males and females.

Table 6.1 Size of enrolment, 2007

	Total	National	Local public	Private
Number of institutions				
Four-year institutions	756	87	89	580
Two-year institutions	434	2	34	398
Special training schools	2995	11	202	2782
Number of institutions (5)				
Graduate	262 113	153 900	14 471	93 742
Undergraduate	2 566 595	473 502	115 121	1 977 972
Two-year institutions	186 667	184	10 815	175 660
Special training schools	663 349	765	27 281	635 303
Number of students (%)				
Graduate	100.0	58.7	5.5	35.8
Undergraduate	100.0	18.4	4.5	77.1
Two-year institutions	100.0	0.1	5.8	94.1
Special training schools	100.0	0.1	4.1	95.8

Source: School Basic Survey 2007.

Legal Framework

The legal framework in which Japan's education is set is rather complex, because it comprises both public and private institutions. These differ significantly from each other with respect to the relationship with the government.

National Institutions

National universities play the most important role in developing academic research, in training researchers and in providing postgraduate education. Located almost evenly throughout the country, national universities have supported the infrastructure of regional education, culture and industry, and provided opportunities for higher education that are less dependent than others on students' economic situations. The national policy agenda, including the provision of certain professional courses and the promotion of science and technology, has been reflected more in funding of national universities than in that of private universities.

There was a major change in the legal definition of national universities in 2004. Under the old system, the national universities—established by the National School Establishment Law—were part of the government's administrative structure. The assets—including land and buildings—for the use of national universities are owned by the state. Their staff, including academic, administrative and technical staff, are civil servants. Under the National University Corporation (NUC) Law, implemented on 1 April 2004, the national universities were incorporated. Through incorporation, each of the former national universities was assigned a legal personality to become a 'National University Corporation'. The land and buildings of the universities are owned by the National University Corporations. Staff are no longer civil servants.

Private Institutions

To be officially qualified as a 'private school', an institution has to be established by a 'School Judiciary Person'. Usually, one school has its own Judiciary Person, but sometimes a few schools are established by a single Legal Person. The Board of Governors governs the Legal Person. The School Judiciary Person is a legal entity who can act similarly to regular judiciary persons such as in private enterprises; they may borrow funds from private financial agencies. They are, however, subject to government regulation.

Finances are not directly audited by the Ministry of Education, but by a certified public accountant. The regulation on finances has evolved over the years. In principle, School Judiciary Persons are not allowed to make a profit. Moreover, the present regulation allows transfers from the annual budget only for building and maintenance of the facility. In other words, they are not allowed to accumulate what would be called capital in business corporations. This is intended to ensure that the contribution from the present student body has to be returned in the form of service to that body.

Financial Flow

The national government, through the MEXT, contributes to the finances of higher education institutions through several channels, including institutional and non-institutional funding. Public expenditure on higher education is provided chiefly by the MEXT. In the national budget, its contributions to the finances of higher education are channelled mainly through the following three expenditure items: 1) transfer to the National Schools Special Account; 2) current-costs subsidy to private schools; and 3) non-institutional subsidy including grants-in-aid for science research and lending to the Japan Scholarship Foundation.

1) Subsidy to National University Corporations

The National Schools Special Account (NSSA) collectively financed the expenditure on national institutions of higher education before their incorporation. Transfer from the national government to the account was the major means for the national government to support these institutions. It is also the largest item of public expenditure on higher education.

The National University Corporations are a markedly different funding mechanism from the present one. After the reform, the new National University Corporation remains basically 'national' in the sense that the state remains responsible for its function, providing the major part of the funds needed. Their personnel and other operational costs will be covered by 'operational grants' from the government. The grants will be 'block grants', which may be used at the discretion of each university without designated applications. It will be possible also to carry the grants over to subsequent years. The costs necessary for construction of new facilities will be funded separately.

In the budget for 2008, as much as ¥1181 billion was allocated to this item. It accounted for 60 per cent of total government expenditure on higher education.

2) Current-Cost Subsidy to Private Institutions

The total amount of this subsidy was ¥428 billion for 2008—or 22 per cent of the total expenditure on higher education.

The government subsidy to the current expenditures on private universities and colleges accounted for more than 20 per cent in 1980. The proportion has declined since then—down to 10 per cent. The subsidy is channelled, together with the subsidies to private institutions at lower levels, through the Japan Private School Promotion Foundation.

Substantial national subsidies to private institutions for their current expenditures started in 1970. In 1975, the Private Schools Promotion and Assistance Law was enacted to allow the government to contribute to private institutions of higher education the amount not exceeding half of the current expenditure. Since the provision did not specify any obligation on the part of the government, the actual amount allocated to the subsidy fund is determined by the government every year.

In the actual process of distribution, the Japan Private Promotion Foundation first estimates, according to a predetermined formula, the total current expenditures of the applying private institutions. At the same time, the educational condition of the institution is measured with one or two simple indices, such as the size of actual relative to standard enrolment, or the size of the full-time faculty relative to actual enrolment. Based on the indices, a proper value is found in a table of 'coefficients' that represents the proportion of the current costs to be subsidised. The amount of subsidy is obtained through multiplying the estimated total current cost by the particular value of coefficient. The table of multiplication coefficients thus functions as an incentive system to encourage changes desired by the Ministry of Education. The table is also adjusted to account for the total amount of government appropriations.

3) Non-Institutional Subsidies

Two types of government expenditure do not go directly to either public or private institutions. One is the Scientific Research Subsidy, which is given to a group of researchers in academic institutions. The other is the subsidy to the Japan Scholarship Foundation, which in turn will become the basis for loans to students in various types of schools. These indirect expenditures account for a relatively small proportion of the whole expenditure.

Grants-in-Aid for Scientific Research (Science Research Grants) constitute the major vehicle for the national government to provide financial support for research activities in addition to direct institutional support. In 2008, the total government expenditure for this purpose amounted to ¥193 billion, or 10 per cent of the total national expenditure on higher education. It should be noted that this amount does not include the direct expenditure on various types of research institutions supported by the Ministry of Education or by other branches of the national government.

These grants are given primarily to the research projects undertaken in institutions of higher education or in academic research institutions. Qualified researchers may apply to the Ministry of Education for grants. A typical grant would encompass one to three years. The applications are reviewed by appropriate selection committees, whose members are nominated partly by the

Science Council of Japan. The selected projects are then administered by the Ministry of Education. The awarded grant is in principle administered by the institution to which the researcher belongs, and is subject to auditing by the Ministry of Education and by the governmental Board of Audit.

Government Loans

The government provides loans through the Japan Scholarship Foundation. There are two categories of loans: one without any interest, and the other with a subsidised interest rate of about 2 per cent per annum. For 2008, the government earmarked ¥152 billion—or 8 per cent of the total expenditure—for this purpose.

The government contribution accounts for only 16 per cent of the revenue of the Japan Scholarship Foundation. Borrowing in various forms constitutes as much as 58 per cent of revenue. The repayment of loans from past recipients provides another 26 per cent of revenue.

Socioeconomic Contexts

Background: Mass participation and its legacies

In the postwar period, various post-secondary institutions were integrated to form new national universities and colleges. Since most of these institutions lacked adequate facilities, the priority in higher education finance has been their development. In order to secure enough resources for this purpose, the finances of the national institutions were standardised, and the budgets for each institution were allocated according to standardised units. The mechanism still constitutes the basis for financing the national institutions, and has been attracting criticism for its inflexibility.

In the 1960s, policies continued to concentrate the limited resources available for higher education upon the upgrading of existing national universities and colleges, rather than upon increasing their number. Popular demands for higher education, however, led to an expansion of enrolment in private-sector institutions. By the end of the 1960s, the private sector accounted for three-quarters of total enrolments. At the same time, since most of the private institutions were financially dependent solely upon tuition fees, they had to charge considerably higher fees, and yet offered less favourable educational conditions than the public institutions. The quantitative predominance of the private institutions, together with qualitative disparities between the public and the private sectors, thus created one of the most basic characteristics of the Japanese higher education system.

Number of Institutions	Total	National	Public	Private
Four year institutions	756	87	89	580
Two year institutions	434	2	34	398
Special Training school	2995	11	202	2782
Number of Institutions (%)				
Four year institutions	100	11.5	11.8	76.7
Two year institutions	100	0.5	7.8	91.7
Special training school	100	0.4	6.7	92.9
Number of Students				
Graduate	262.113	153900	14471	93742
Undergraduate	2566595	473502	115121	1977972
Two year institutions	186667	184	10815	175668
Special Training school	663349	765	27281	635303
Number of students (%)				
Graduate	100	58.7	5.5	35.8
Undergraduate	100	18.4	4.5	77.1
Two year institutions	100	0.1	5.8	84.1
Special Training school	100	0.1	4.1	95.8

Figure 6.2 Change in participation rates

Source: School Basic Survey, various years.

Equity

Japanese society deems equity in educational opportunities among the highest priorities in the public sphere. Any incidence of mistreatment in entrance examinations causes a major social reaction. There is strong social resistance to raising tuition fees—not only in national institutions but also in private institutions. Japanese families have tended to sacrifice their wellbeing to send their offspring to university.

Indeed, various surveys and studies have shown that the chance of advancing to higher education is determined by academic achievement at high school to a much higher degree than by economic factors. If a student demonstrates a high level of academic achievement, their chances of participating in higher education are likely to be very high, irrespective of the family's income.

Nonetheless, there are significant differences in participation rates across family income levels. Figure 6.3 summarises the estimated participation rate in higher education among high-school graduates by family-income quintile class.

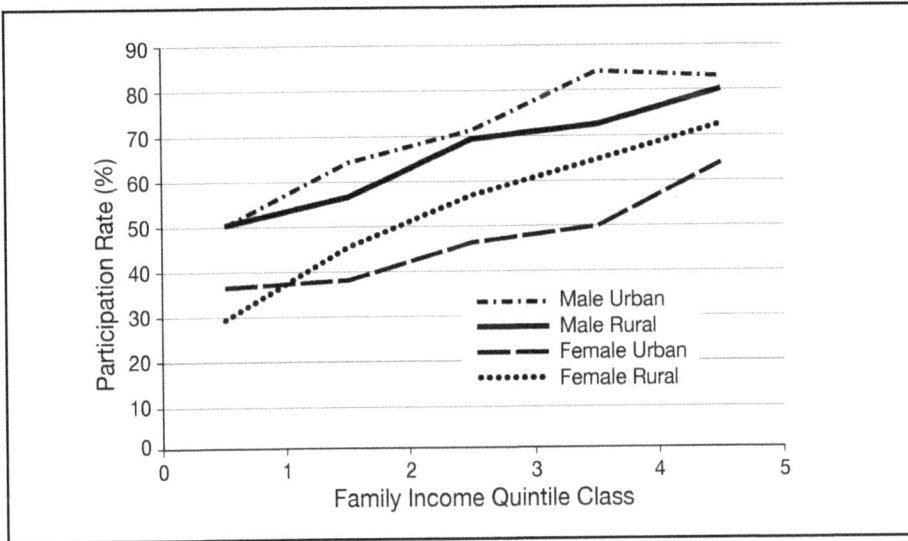

Figure 6.3 Participation rates by family income

Source: 2007 Tracer Survey on High School Students, University of Tokyo Center for Research in University Management and Policy Studies.

From the figure, it is apparent that the participation rate is as high as 50 per cent for males even in the lowest quintile class. Nonetheless, it is apparent that there are distinct differences in participation rates by family-income class. The elasticity of the participation rate with respect to family income tends to be greater with females and with students in rural areas.

It should be noted that a substantial part of these differences by family income rises from the indirect effect through academic achievement: the children from low-income families tend to achieve less academically in high school, and this causes the major hindrance to participation in higher education. Nonetheless, there are distinct direct effects of family income, and these tend to be strongest with female and rural residents.

Another dimension of the equity issue is the sharp hierarchy among the institutions with respect to selectivity, which implies that it is not whether you ever enter university, but which university you enter, that really matters. It is also known that students at prestigious universities tend to have family backgrounds characterised by the higher educational and occupational status of their fathers. It is likely that the indirect influences of the parents on their offspring are routed through non-school investment. If it were true, the non-school expenditure could be significant in reproducing social inequality. Yet, researchers have not found conclusive evidence that such expenditures in fact affected achievements in examinations.

Policy Environment

At the same time as Japan is struggling to rectify the negative consequences and confusion arising from the legacies of past expansion, it is faced with similar challenges to those experienced in other countries.

One such current is the coming of what might be called the 'knowledge society', in which knowledge assumes an increasingly central role. That such trends are becoming salient will be apparent to many. Fierce competition and rapid innovation have made it inevitable that research and development become critically important in producing competitive consumption goods.

Another important trend is the move away from the predominance of the government and towards the utilisation of market mechanisms. Some argue that these moves are a reflection of financial crises brought about by exponential increases in social spending. Others argue that such moves reflect more fundamental shifts in the mode and direction of social development. Since the increased diversity and complexity of the modern society and its needs necessarily have made centralised decision and control obsolete, it is argued that market mechanisms will be the only way to deal with the diversified and multidimensional changes.

In this context, Japanese higher education is faced with serious challenges. Among them there are three major issues with significant implications for the future of higher education. The first is the incorporation of national universities, which will significantly alter not only the nature of national universities and colleges, but also the structure of higher education finance. Second is the restructuring of the private sector of higher education due to the decrease in the size of the college-going population. The third is the current debate over the size of expenditure on higher education in the national economy, which presumes a particular importance in envisaging the new stage of development of higher education in Japan.

Each of these three issues will be examined in the following sections.

Incorporation of National Universities

National universities were transformed into National University Corporations in 2004.

Background

The idea of transition from the old national universities to the new model can be summarised as in Figure 6.4. In the old concept, the national university had two sides. On one hand, it was part of the government organisation. Its budget was specified in the national budget, and the purpose of the expenditure was specified in the budget details. The faculty members and administrators were government employees. The facilities were the property of the government. On the other hand, the academic side of the operation was governed by the faculty members.

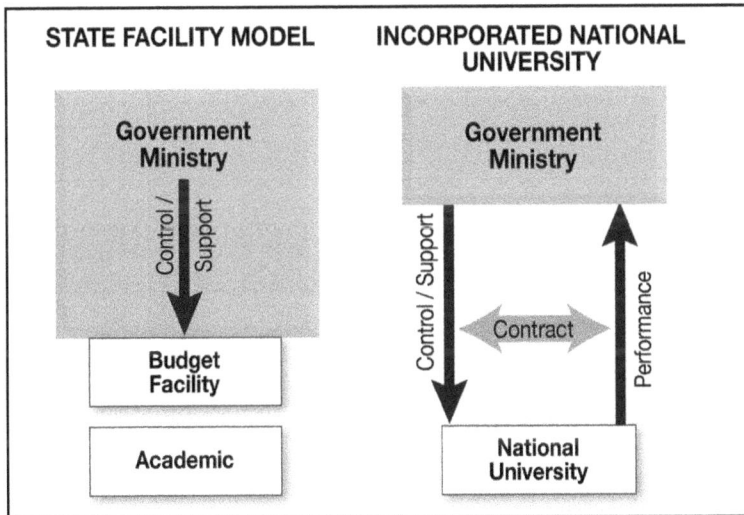

Figure 6.4 The relationship between the government and the university

In the new model, the government and the university are two separate legal entities. This raises two questions. First, how should the national university be governed as an independent entity? Second, how should the relationship between the government and the university be regulated? Obviously, the government loses its direct power to control the university, yet the government provides support to the university. The support and the performance of the university have to be balanced, and proper incentives for efficient use of resources should be built into this regulation. In a way, it is a contract between the government and the university.

These questions show that incorporation of national universities is critically dependent upon the design of the governance of the institution and the device of a latent or overt contract between the government and the university.

While the creation of the NUC scheme was a direct product of many political and economic factors, the design of the scheme was based on a body of logic. Basically, it was influenced by the 'New Public Management' or institutional economics that has gained momentum in the past two decades. At the core of that thought are the relationship between the 'principal' and the 'agent', and the explicit contract between the two. The scheme of the independent administrative institution is built on this concept: the government as the principal commissions an independent administrative agency to achieve a public purpose. The terms are specified in the mid-term goals and plan; subsequently, the level of achievement will be evaluated, the result of which will lead to consequences including financial rewards or punishment, or even discontinuation of the contract.

It is argued that by separating the principal and the agent, the agent will gain efficiency. The agent—free from the strict and minute control by the government—has to face competition with other agents, and is able to exploit local knowledge and initiate innovation. Moreover, it is given an incentive to gain efficiency through explicit goals. Provided with these mechanisms, the government is able to gain efficiency in the provision of its services and become more accountable.

In order to realise the assumed function, it is imperative that the contract should be clearly set out with an instrument to measure the level of achievement. It is also necessary that the chief executive of the agent should be designated as personally responsible for the contract, although the institution as a whole functions as an agent of the government. The chief executive then directs the whole organisation towards achievement of the set goal, and the members of the executive board assist the chief executive.

The same argument should be applied as the justification for the construction of the NUCs, as one of the variations of the independent administrative agency. From this perspective, it is natural that the mid-term goals and plans, and the corresponding evaluation, should assume the core of the new relationship between the government and the NUC. It is also understandable that the president of the NUC has to be given unusually strong powers. There are arguments that the theoretical framework cannot be simply applied to universities, which encompass a very wide range of objectives, and rely on the spontaneous intellectual activities among the members.

Legal Status and Governance

The basic framework of the NUC is outlined in the NUC Law of 2004.

Legal Status

Under the NUC Law, each NUC constitutes a legal person under the Civil Law. As a legal person, it is able to sue other legal entities and can possibly be sued by others. It owns its own assets, which are called the capital of the corporation, comprising mainly the buildings and land that were contributed from the government at the time of incorporation. In principle, it is supposed to be able to borrow funds, issue bonds or invest in other entities, but the government maintains strict conditions and restrictions.

Governance

By stipulations of the law, each NUC has a president, an executive board, an academic senate, a management council and auditors. The relations among these bodies are presented in Figure 6.5. In this scheme, the president assumes the ultimate power and responsibility for decision making and execution, while important decisions have to go through deliberation of the executive board. The academic council, upon request by the president, deliberates on academic matters and reports to the executive council and the president. Meanwhile, the management council—more than half of the members of which should be selected from outside the university—gives advice to the president. The auditors are selected by the university, but appointed by the Minister of Education and report directly to the minister.

The president—who was elected by the academic senate under the old system— is now elected by the committee for selection of the president. The committee consists of equal numbers of representatives from the management council and the academic senate; the president and the members of the executive board may join as members. The person elected is, in principle, appointed by the Minister of Education as the president. The length of term and the exact procedure taken for election are to be decided by each university. The committee also has the power to relieve the president of duty through a procedure similar to the election.

The scheme of incorporation does not necessarily require a change in the status of the workers from government employees. The cabinet, however, which was politically committed to the restructuring plan of the government organisations, pushed forcefully to change the employment status. Meanwhile, resistance from the national universities failed to gain momentum. Consequently, all the academic and administrative members of the NUCs changed their status from government employees to employees belonging to one of the NUCs. The pension and healthcare funds, however, remain practically a part of those for government employees.

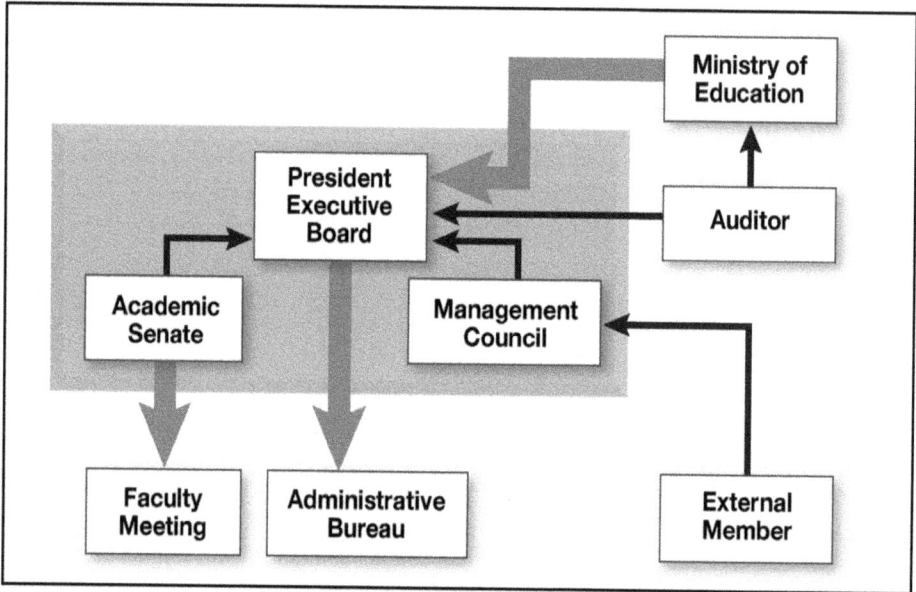

Figure 6.5 Governance structure of the National University Corporation

Because of the strong power given to the president, their selection process bears not only symbolic but also practical significance to the governance of the NUC. While the NUC Law required that the president should be selected by a presidential selection committee consisting of equal numbers of representatives from the academic and management councils, it does not stipulate the details for the procedure. Depending on the design of the procedure, it could lead to a significant departure from the tradition of participatory governance.

As it turned out, most NUCs bypassed this problem by implanting the participation of faculty members in the new selection process. In most cases, the presidential selection committee decided to include a 'reference ballot', in which individual faculty members cast a vote for their preferred candidate. The details of selection of the candidates and the specific rules for the reference ballot differed substantially by institution.

Nonetheless, a few NUCs started considering alternative schemes. The Board of Directors of Tohoku University—one of the seven former imperial universities—decided in early 2005 that the next president would be elected by the presidential selection committee itself, and direct involvement of the faculty members would not be allowed. It remains to be seen if this practice will be diffused to other NUCs.

Governance Structure

For each NUC, the first task for transition was to organise the basic governance structure. According to the NUC Law described above, each NUC organised an executive board, academic council and management council.

The number of members of the executive board is stipulated by an ordinance issued by the government basically according to the size of the institution. Various surveys showed that by far the majority of the board members were recruited from the professoriate—most of them former vice-presidents and faculty deans. In many NUCs—mostly those of large size—the boards included a non-academic, who was assigned to oversee managerial and financial matters. Many board members carried the title of vice-president.

The academic board—as the NUC Law stipulates—consists mainly of faculty members. In most universities, the size of the board, while not stipulated by any ordinance, tended to be smaller than the former university council it replaced. In most universities, the members were elected in the faculty meetings. The new council practically retained the conventions and procedures taken in the old council.

The size of the management council was subject to the discretion of each NUC. In most cases, they included executives in local businesses. It was common to include a member of the local mass media. Some NUCs appointed former government officials.

In most NUCs, each executive board member was assigned to a specific area of administration such as education, research or financial management. The board members were designated to direct the particular administrative section corresponding with his/her assigned function. There were differences among NUCs with respect to the secretary of the university, who had been practically nominated by the Ministry of Education. In some NUCs, the secretary was appointed to be one of the board members, and the title was abolished. In others, the title and the position were retained.

1. OLD SCHEME

General Account

Borrowing

NATIONAL SCHOOLS SPECIAL ACCOUNT

Revenue

University A   University B   University C

Tuition / Hospital Revenue   Expenditure

Tuition /Hospital Revenue   Expenditure

Tuition / Hospital Revenue   Expenditure

1. NATIONAL UNIVERSITY CORPORATION

General Account

Borrowing

University A   University B   University C

Expenditure   Tuition / Hospital Revenue

Expenditure   Tuition / Hospital Revenue

Expenditure   Tuition / Hospital Revenue

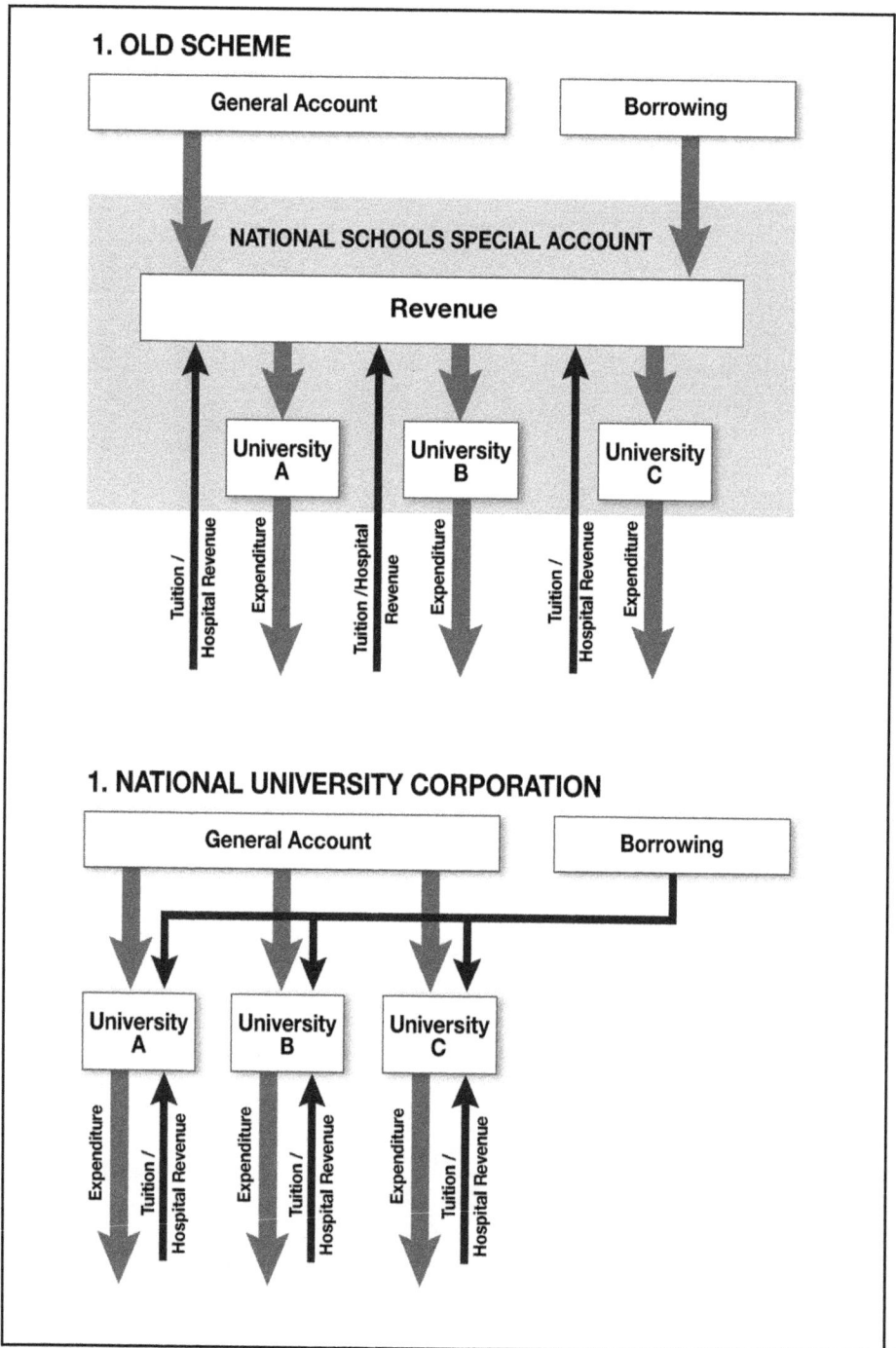

Figure 6.6 Old and new schemes of financing national universities

Finances

In the old system, the finances of national universities were constituted as part of the government budget; they were classified into separate lines, and the expenditure had to be made for the designated purpose of each line. Tuition fees collected at the national universities were treated as revenue for the national treasury. On the expenditure side, the national universities had to follow the budget and various government regulations in spending the funds. Moreover, the number of personnel was under the strict control of the government. On the other hand, necessary costs for the operation of the university were, in principle, assumed to be borne by the government.

The NUC Law stipulates that the NUCs are financially autonomous entities with their own budgets. After incorporation, the government subsidy was given to each university as a lump sum, without any division by line item. The NUC was, in principle, given basic autonomy over the expenditure of the budget.

With the enactment of the NUC Law, the government contributed most of the facilities, land and buildings to the NUCs. The evaluated prices of those facilities constituted the capital fund of each NUC. In contrast with the old system, in which the budget for a fiscal year had to be executed in the designated year and accounted for within the fiscal year, in the new system, the NUCs were allowed to carry the balance to the next accounting period. Within a limit, each university is free to make investments: it may borrow money either from government or from commercial banks; it also may issue a bond with the permission of the government.

At the same time, the NUC Law stipulates that the finances of NUCs will be accounted for according to the NUC Accounting Standards, which are similar to the accounting standards required for business corporations. In the old system, the budget was divided into line items, and the accounting procedure simply implied executing the budget accordingly without any infringement of governmental regulations. In the new system, accounting takes the form of double-entry bookkeeping. The financial report should include a balance sheet, profit-and-loss statement, cash-flow statement and other necessary statements.

One of the critical issues in this reform was, naturally, the level of government contribution to the NUCs. While the law does not provide for specific mechanisms to determine the level of government contribution to the NUCs, the 2003 *Report of the Expert Committee for Incorporation of National Universities* outlined the basic principle. First, the necessary amount of total costs was calculated for individual areas of study employing a formula that involves such indices as the number of students and teachers and other expenses and their corresponding unit costs. From the required amount, the institution's revenue is subtracted to derive the necessary amount of government subsidy. In other words, this method assumed the basic principle that the government had the responsibility to secure the necessary level of funding for each institution.

The last, and probably most significant, aspect is finance. While the NUC Law stipulates the framework of the NUCs and their relationship with the government, it does not specify the financial obligation on the part of the government to support the NUCs. As a result, there is a substantial range of alternatives in the level and methods for government financial support. That, however, will be a decisive factor for the nature of the NUC in significant aspects. There are three sets of important issues revealed in the process of implementation.

Government Subsidy

It was stated above that the original design laid out in the 2003 *Report of the Expert Committee for Incorporation of National Universities* assumed that the government remained responsible for securing necessary levels of revenue, calculated on a formula, for each institution. In other words, the government would maintain the 'compensation principle'—implying that the government will fully compensate for the gap between the calculated cost and the actual income of each university. This principle had to undergo a series of significant alterations in the following periods.

In the autumn of 2003, when the NUC Law had been enacted and the national universities started preparation for incorporation, the Ministry of Finance released its own plan for funding the NUCs. This plan did not follow the expert committee that proposed a set of formulas to derive the amount of government contribution to each institution. Instead, the Ministry of Finance indicated that each NUC would be given the amount that the institution received in the previous year irrespective of any change in the numbers of students and faculty members. A fixed rate of across-the-board reduction in government expenditures would apply to the allocated amount. In the case of NUCs, the rate will be 1 or 2 per cent. The Ministry of Education, in a political climate of government restructuring, had no alternative but to oblige.

In the short run, this might not make much difference to the original design with respect to the amount of subsidy, but it implied a significant shift in the principle of government contribution—not only were any prospects for increasing the allocated budget closed, but also the compensation principle was abandoned.

Government Regulations

Meanwhile, the Ministry of Education retained a substantial number of regulations on finances. Even though the government subsidy is allocated in a lump sum including wage costs, the ministry enforces NUCs to limit the numbers of academic and administrative employees to the level specified in the mid-term plan. This in effect allowed the ministry to maintain a significant level of control over the management of NUCs. Also, each NUC has to get approval from the Ministry of Education to record either a surplus or a deficit for a given fiscal year, to borrow funds from banks, to issue bonds, or to make investments. In each of these cases, the NUC has to satisfy rigorous conditions.

Under these circumstances, the NUCs are left in a situation where they have to seek to survive with gradually decreasing funds under still heavy government control. Over time, it is likely that these regulations will be gradually reduced to allow increased levels of financial autonomy to the NUCs. On the other hand, that would necessitate a new set of instruments for the ministry to oversee management. How such arrangements should be made is still unclear.

Financial Management and Accounting

Prior to the reform, each national university was given the budget separated into line items. Because the formula to calculate the allocated budget was known, it was clear how much each faculty received in the budget. Under these conditions, the faculties had a strong basis for demanding allocation. On the other hand, the university administration was given little room in which to manoeuvre.

With the transformation to NUCs—which receive government subsidies in a lump sum—the university administrators are given a considerable degree of arbitration. In distributing the funds to faculties and other constituent units, most universities set the basis as the previous year and then deduce institutional funds by applying the same rate across the board. Through this measure, most institutions increased the resources at the discretion of the institutional level. Some institutions introduced redistribution schemes to provide incentives related to achievements in research. These reforms appear to indicate that management at the institutional level is increasing resources at their discretion.

Meanwhile, the disappearance of line items implies that each institution has to have sufficient ability in financial management in order to gain efficiency on the one hand and to avoid risks on the other. The Accounting Standards for NUCs were designated exactly for that purpose. For most of the administrative sections, however, it was difficult to introduce the new bookkeeping system. Moreover, the organisation of universities is extremely complex, with numerous sub-units cutting across each other. It is, in a sense, a nightmare for cost accounting. Moreover, each unit has its own source of income through research funding.

It will take time to use the new accounting system for strategic financial management. This implies that the financial mechanism of NUCs, as it currently stands, is not only incapable of leading to appreciative gains in efficiency, it also involves substantial risks.

Relations with the Government

The relationship between the government and each NUC—which is legally independent of the government—is regulated mainly by mid-term (six-year) goals and the corresponding mid-term plan, which is in effect a contract between the two. Figure 6.7 presents the basic framework.

Mid-Term Goals and Plan

As the law stipulates, the Ministry of Education assigns each NUC mid-term goals that specify the goals to be achieved within six years in enhancing the level of education and research, in improving efficiency of management of the institution, and in other areas. Based on these goals, the university should prepare a mid-term plan to achieve the specified goals, which should be approved by the government. Reflecting criticism that this clause will give the government overwhelming power over the NUCs, both Houses of Parliament passed attached resolutions that required the government to respect the autonomy of the NUCs. In practice, the Ministry of Education asked each NUC to draft its mid-term goals, and then approved them without substantive changes.

Evaluation

Towards the end of the six-year period, the newly established Council for Evaluation of NUCs will evaluate the levels of achievement of the goals with the assistance of the National Institute for Academic Degrees. The law states that, depending on the results of evaluation, the government will examine the need for continuation of the institution and necessary actions to be taken by the institutions. The last clause implies that the results might be related to government subsidy to the institution. The attached resolutions of both Houses of Parliament again draw attention to the possibility that this mechanism could lead to encroachment on academic freedom, and request the government to take precautions. Further details in either the method of evaluation or the consequences of evaluation have not yet been worked out.

As stated above, each NUC is, in principle, an independent organisation under the Public Law, implying that the finances are completely separated from the government even though it may receive subsidies from the government.

The above discussion indicates that the backbone of the scheme of the NUC lies in the cycle encompassing goal–evaluation–reward. That is, the success of the scheme is critically dependent on the power of the evaluation methods as the key of the cycle.

The Independent Administration Agency Law stipulates that the government may take a range of actions, including discontinuation, against the institution after deliberation on the results of evaluation. This principle applies to NUCs. The report of the experts committee under the Ministry of Education indicated that evaluation results in a mid-term period would be reflected in the mid-term goals, and, as a consequence, the level of government subsidy, for the following period. Exactly how they are related was not specified in the report, leaving the issue to be solved after the new scheme is implemented.

The process involves a wide range of practical questions. The central problem is that the mid-term goals, and accordingly the corresponding process of evaluation, have to cover the whole activity of a university. At the same time, the results of evaluation should be given a reasonable level of reliability. Since the results entail significant consequences for the NUCs, including budget allocation, the lack of reliability should lead to a number of problems including with the credibility of the scheme as a whole and the collapse of the incentive system that the scheme was supposed to create.

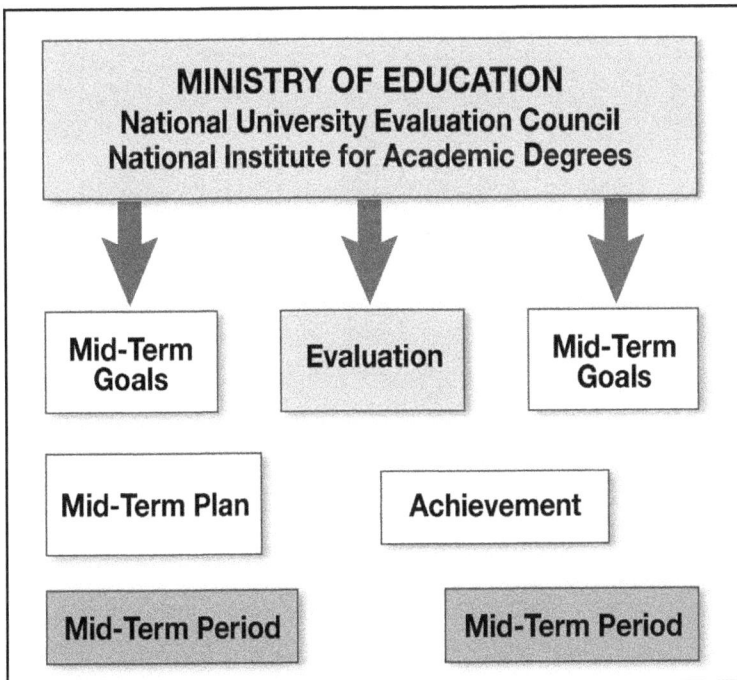

Figure 6.7 Mid-term goals and plan cycle

Reactions and Problems in the Future

It is beyond the scope of this chapter to describe the complex process of evaluation. This is probably the most comprehensive and the most ambitious scheme of evaluation in the world. It is comprehensive in three ways.

First, it involves both judgment on achieving the goals specified in the mid-term plan on one hand and evaluation of the absolute levels of education and research on the other. While the logical construct of incorporation requires only the judgment of whether the mid-term goals have been achieved, it does not necessarily demand judgment on the absolute levels of academic abilities. The government and the National Institution for Academic Degrees (NIAD) argued, however, that in order to make judgments on goal attainment, one needs the basis of evaluation on the levels.

Second, it requires both self-evaluation by the university and objective evaluation by NIAD. The Incorporation Law requires that the incorporated universities not be subject to arbitrary control by the Ministry of Education. In other words, the mid-term goals are set as an agreement between the ministry and individual universities. This principle applies to the evaluation procedure. Self-evaluation is also indispensable for practical reasons. Since the evaluation has to be undertaken for all 80 NUCs at the same time, NIAD is not able to start gathering information by itself.

Third, its scope covers both education and research—at the institutional as well as the school level. Even though evaluation of research is difficult, it might still be feasible if enough time and resources are provided. In contrast, evaluation of education raises more serious problems. One might remember that in the United Kingdom, where research assessment exercises have been undertaken for some time, assessment of education has not been implemented even though it was persistently proposed by the government. In the case of the incorporation scheme in Japan, evaluation of the mid-term goals, which play the role of a comprehensive contract between the government and the university, has to cover the whole scope of those goals including education.

These issues point to the fundamental assumptions of the scheme built on contract and evaluation. If the contract covers a single or very small number of objectives, it is likely that the results can be easily evaluated and translated into rewards or punishment. That could lead to higher levels of accountability and efficiency. On the other hand, to the extent that the contract covers a wider range of objectives, and for longer periods, the evaluation could become technically involved and difficult.

It is evident that such a comprehensive evaluation entails an enormous amount of costs, if it is feasible at all. A more serious problem is how the results will be connected to the next mid-term goals. This critical point is still unclear.

It should be evident from the discussion above that incorporation in fact introduced a range of radical changes in the ways the national universities operate. How was it received by the universities, and where are the problems?

In 2006, two years after incorporation, a survey was undertaken to ask the opinions of the presidents of NUCs about the consequences of incorporation (Figure 6.8). The results show that, so far, the presidents believe incorporation has, on the whole, had positive effects. They particularly thought the reforms made management easier and activities more efficient. It is, in a way, a reflection of the frustration they harboured under the old system.

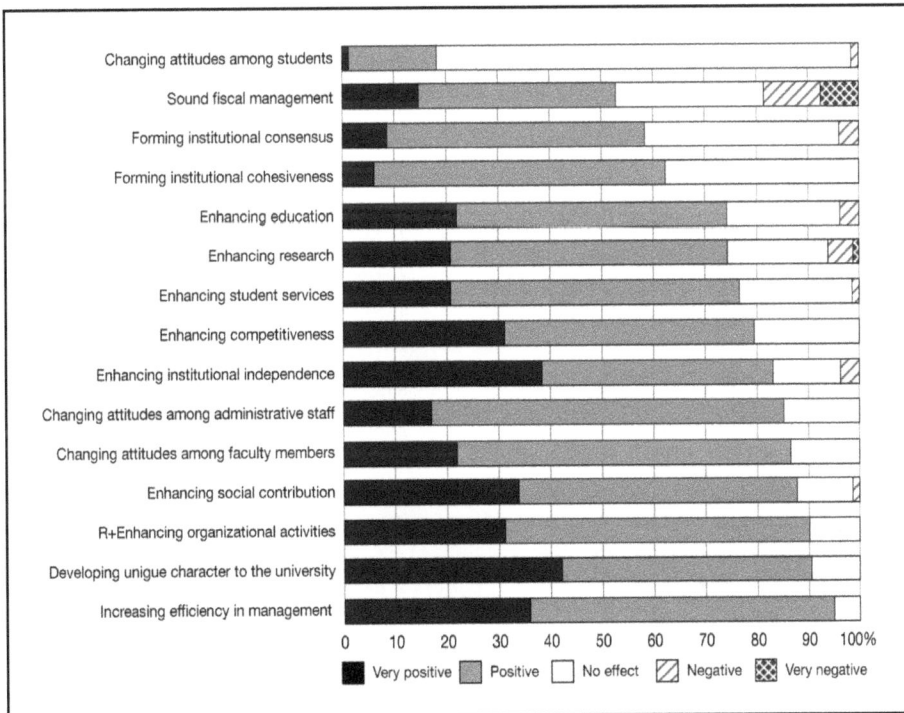

Figure 6.8 Presidents' opinions of the consequences of incorporation

Source: Center for National University Finance and Management (2007:Appendix).

The ultimate judgment, therefore, should be given after the cycle of the first mid-term is completed—that is, after the scheme of evaluation is implemented and the next mid-term goals are set.

The uniqueness of the NUC model derives from its direct application of the theoretical scheme based on the principal–agent relation with contract–

evaluation sequence. Even though such concepts are used in the analyses of the existing economic institutions, the Japanese NUC system is probably the first case to apply it to the design of public institutions. As discussed above, such a construct engendered a number of contradictions and ambiguities. At present, the factors of the state facility model still remain strong, and they function as an adhesive to prevent the contractions from creating real problems. Remaining regulations from the Ministry of Education, academic participation in the election of the president, and inertia among administrators are among such factors.

Over time, however, such compromises will have to be replaced with a more realistic scheme for the relationship between the government and the NUCs and the internal governance and finance in each NUC. Such a scheme will include a regime of government monitoring and partial evaluation, together with stronger capacity in financial management. One thing that is clear is that, for the time being, the reform has created among a substantial proportion of academics an atmosphere that each national university has to seek its own way to realise its wishes.

Moreover, the current political climate, moving towards radical restructuring of the government organisation and reduction of government outlays, has started to threaten the basis on which the original design of the NUC scheme was built. If things move further in that direction, the NUC scheme could lose its original characteristics and shift to become a different entity.

Between the innate problems in details of the original design on one hand, and the political climate shifting towards further radical restructuring of the government on the other, NUCs will keep exploring their destination for some years to come.

Financial Crisis Among Private Institutions

The second issue is the decline in the demand for higher education as a consequence of the diminishing size of the population of eighteen-year-olds.

Demographic Shift and Private Institutions

Japan's higher education sector experienced a major rise in participation rates until the mid-1970s. Since then, the momentum of expansion has been rather contained, due to the policy of restraint of the Ministry of Education on the establishment of new institutions and the expansion of existing institutions. The policy was concomitant with a new government subsidy to private institutions. Through these schemes, the Ministry of Education regained the power to control the total enrolments in the private sector of higher education. Through this power, the ministry has been able to sustain the quality of higher education by limiting the proportion of high-school graduates entering college. At the same time, existing private institutions have been able to enjoy a practical monopoly in the market for higher education at the undergraduate level. Such a situation had to change due to the decreases in the college-going population.

The size of the college-going population reached its second peak after World War II when the second baby-boom generation reached eighteen years of age in about 1990 (Figure 6.9). The growth of the population under limited expansion of supply resulted in a decrease in the participation rate. The following cohort, however, started shrinking rapidly. The size of the eighteen-year-old cohort, after reaching the two-million level, shrank to about 1.5 million by 2000. Since then, the decline has become slower, but it is continuing steadily. It is envisaged that the population of eighteen-year-olds will drop to about 1.2 million in 2010. The population will remain at that level for the foreseeable future.

Until recently, the participation rate had been steadily increasing—to cancel out the effect of the decrease in the number of eighteen-year-olds. In fact, the participation rate, which was less than 25 per cent in the early 1990s, grew to 46 per cent in the spring of 1998.

Nonetheless, it is unlikely that the participation rate will keep growing at the same pace as before. The decline of the number of eighteen-year-olds will create redundant enrolment capacity in universities, and the supply–demand gap will disappear. The selection of students will undergo significant changes, and it is likely that the economic benefits of a university education will decline at least for some students. Moreover, some private institutions have begun to face the possibility of insufficient applicants for admission, and hence the chance of closure.

In fact, many institutions—most of them with a relatively short history and small in scale—are faced with the effects of demographic shift already.

The direct consequence of the shrinking market will be the prospect of institutional closure. Some institutions are already facing a decline in applicants, and, in a number of cases, the freshman class failed to fill the legal sitting capacity. The situation will be further aggravated towards the next decade. It should be noted that the effect of the demographic shift is not the same across the institutions. In general, those institutions at the higher tiers in the institutional hierarchy are least affected by this change. On the other hand, those at the bottom will be hit hardest. Most of these institutions are new and small—the newcomers among the entrepreneurial type of institution. Because the average size of enrolment is small, the number of institutions affected will be large for a given size of total reduction in demand.

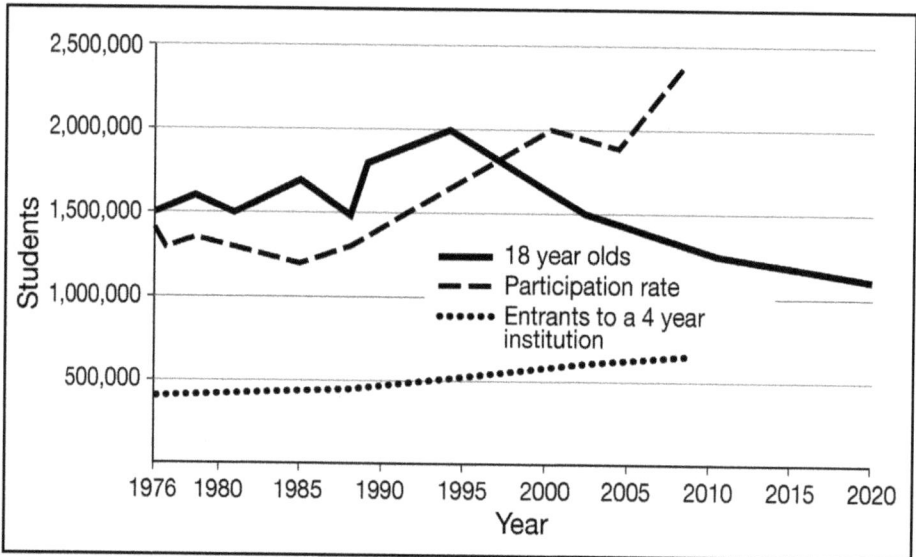

Figure 6.9 Number of eighteen-year-olds

The reduction in the size of enrolment will inevitably affect the financial health of the institutions, in some cases leading to closure of the institution. In a sense, such a crisis has already started. The risk of closure can be measured by two indices

- *fulfillment rate*: (number of entrants)/(enrolment capacity)
- *application rate*: (number of applications for enrolment)/(enrolment capacity).

The 'enrolment capacity' is prescribed by the National Council on University Establishment for each institution. Even though the government does not have authority to enforce the capacity, admission of students significantly above this capacity will result in reduction in, or in severe cases cancellation of, the Current-Cost Subsidy from the government. On the other hand, if the institution is enrolling less than the capacity (and therefore the fulfilment rate falls significantly below 1.00), the institution will not be able to collect sufficient tuition income to support its operations.

Meanwhile, some of those institutions admitting capacity might be very selective in accepting students. Those institutions are receiving fewer students than the capacity to maintain the academic standard for admission as dictated by their policy. From this perspective, the application rate is an important source of information.

The two indices for the year 2004, derived from the data made available for 493 institutions, or about 90 per cent of the total number of private institutions, are presented in Figure 6.10. Each institution is represented by the dots in the space where the vertical axis stands for the fulfilment rate, while the horizontal axis for the application rate is in logarithmic scale.

The space is further divided by two lines. The horizontal line represents the fulfilment rate of 0.9, implying that the institutions below this line are admitting less than 90 per cent of capacity. The vertical line indicates the application rate of 1.0, signifying that the institutions to the left of this line are receiving less applications than the capacity. By combining these lines, the institutions can be divided into three groups: 1) low-risk institutions accepting more than 90 per cent of capacity; 2) medium-risk institutions, which are receiving less than 90 per cent of capacity, but for whom the application rate is higher than 1.0; and 3) high-risk institutions that are located in the lower-left quadrant, receiving fewer than 90 per cent of capacity and for whom the number of applying students does not reach capacity.

The figure shows that more than 100 institutions belong to the medium and high-risk categories thus defined. There are 44 institutions, or 9 per cent of the total, that belong to the high-risk group. Most of the institutions in the high-risk group are small and relatively new. This implies that their financial basis tends to be weak.

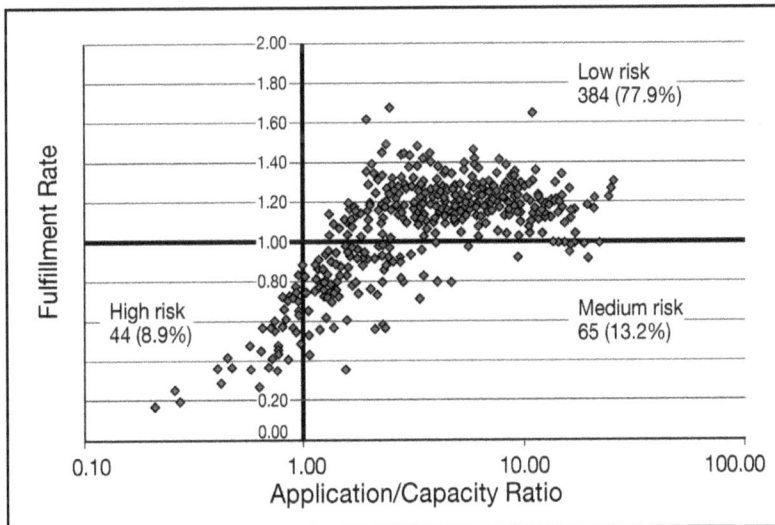

Figure 6.10 Distribution of private institutions by fulfilment rate and application/capacity ratio

Viability of Institutions

Despite the large number of institutions in the high and medium-risk groups, there have been very few cases of closure as a consequence of genuinely fiscal reasons. Many institutions appear to have sizeable margins in their current revenue over costs. Some of them have succeeded in slashing costs by either decreasing the number of employees or cutting wage levels. Nonetheless, the prospect of closure is definitely looming. How many, and when, institutions will have to close depends on many factors and remains uncertain at this point.

What will happen if an institution is faced with financial difficulty? There are a few scenarios. In the most peaceful case, the institution might seek financial help from an individual or an organisation. Or, another institution might try to acquire the university in difficulty to take them under its wing. If the prospect for such a solution is small then the institution can declare bankruptcy: the students will be transferred to neighbouring institutions. In the worst case, the School Juristic Person (SJP) may stop operations, and, even after liquidation, significant debt and unpaid salary for the employees might remain. Not only might the employees and creditors not be able to recover their losses, the students might have to move to another institution and pay for tuition again (MEXT 2005).

Social attitudes towards the prospect of closure remain ambiguous. The media has been reporting the likelihood of closure with a tone that suggests such incidences are inevitable. Some social critiques are arguing that such natural selection is healthy and useful for improving the efficiency of higher education. Nonetheless, in the event massive closures take place, the public's attitude might change quickly.

As a consequence of these changes, private institutions appear to be increasingly polarised in their interests. Accordingly, they will seek very different directions towards the future.

On one hand, there are a number of institutions that are positioned at the higher echelon of the market and therefore are faced with less acute risk in the market. These institutions tend to be large or medium sized, and are either the voluntary or the sponsored type. Their strategic goals are to enhance their market position and to increase competitiveness not only against their peers but also against the national institutions.

If these institutions wish to achieve these goals, they have to achieve certain conditions. They tend to be less attached to the Current-Cost Subsidy. They are also less persistent in following the financial scheme of the Accounting Standards. They are already receiving subsidies competitive with those of primary institutions. They might welcome the shift from institutional subsidies to individual subsidies through either a direct grant to students or some form of voucher.

A more significant issue will be how donations to private institutions are treated in the tax system. Under the current system, donations to private institutions may be deducted from taxable income (income deduction) to an extent, but not from the amount of tax itself (tax amount deduction). The institutions will have to seek the tax-deduction status in order to become competitive with public institutions. This change should, however, require corresponding changes in governance. Being given tax-amount deduction status implies that the organisation is permitted to accumulate public funds as assets. The asset should be owned by a group of responsible persons who cannot get any benefit from the operation of the university. The decision making by the membership group, or the practice of participatory management, might have to be seriously questioned.

On the other hand, there are a number of institutions that are faced with the pressure of reduction in demand. Many of these institutions are striving to strengthen their competitiveness in their segment of the market and survive the struggle. From this standpoint, the provision of the Current-Cost Subsidy is indispensable not only for its value as a source of stable income, but also as a sign of recognition by the national government of their function as an educational institution. They would also be opposed to the further disclosure of finances, on the ground that such disclosure could generate misinformation. The entrepreneurial-type institutions particularly are unlikely to change their governance and management. In that sense, they would not expel the element of private ownership. In this sense, they might take the direction of entrenchment as far as it is possible.

Ironically, the entrenchment strategy could be challenged by an unexpected competitor: for-profit institutions currently allowed on a trial basis. The proponents of the for-profits argue that the present private institutions established under the School Juristic Person are in fact generating interests for the people engaged in management. At the same time, it is likely that some of the bankrupt universities might be purchased by the enterprises that wish to build for-profit institutions. In this sense, some part of the private sector is moving towards the private domain.

The discussion above indicates that the private higher education sector in Japan has been changing—and it will keep changing towards the future. There has been a wide variation among private institutions, and this will continue—albeit in a different way—in the future. Such variation and changes are created by the dynamism of the market forces in higher education together with the shifts in demographic, social and political factors.

National Expenditure on Higher Education

The most fundamental issue in the financing of higher education is the level of expenditure on higher education in the national economy. Recently, there have been public debates concerning this issue.

Higher Education Expenditure in the National Economy

One of the outstanding characteristics of Japan with respect to higher education finance is the low level of government expenditure on higher education relative to the size of the total economy. According to the statistics of the Organisation for Economic Cooperation and Development (OECD), government expenditure on higher education in Japan as a proportion of GDP stands at 0.5 per cent, compared with the OECD average of 1 per cent. In fact, Japan, along with Korea, is ranked at the bottom among the OECD countries in this respect. On the other hand, the higher education system is heavily dependent on private contributions. The OECD statistics show that private expenditure on higher education stands at 0.8 per cent of GDP, compared with the OECD average of 0.4 per cent. Indeed, this level ranks third among OECD nations, after the United States (1.9 per cent) and Korea (1.8 per cent). The high level of private contributions is a reflection of the high share of private institutions in enrolment and their dependence on tuition revenue. This pattern of dependence on private contributions is not unique to Japan in the East Asian region.

In Japan, this characteristic derives from the unique path along which the country's higher education system has developed. As indicated earlier, the demands for higher education in Japan started growing at relatively early stages of its economic development. As the government still lacked the financial resources to supply sufficient rooms in public institutions, the excess demand had to be met by expanding the private sector of higher education. After Japan went through a period of rapid economic development, it shifted towards a welfare society by promptly raising the levels of social expenditure, including on higher education. The government started the Current-Cost Subsidy in 1975, which was intended to substantially increase the level of public expenditure on higher education. This development was, however, short-lived. By the end of the 1980s, a rising budget deficit became apparent and the government turned to a stringent fiscal policy. This shift had to be accelerated even further in the later period by the explosive increases in expenditure on national pensions and health plans on one hand, and the economic recession after the boom on the other.

There have been persistent demands for greater government expenditure on higher education, and one of the grounds for the argument is Japan's low standing in international comparisons. The voices advocating this argument have been loudest among the associations of national and private institutions of higher education and the Central Education Council under MEXT. On the other hand, there have been strong criticisms of this argument from the Ministry of Finance and various economic advisory committees. It is claimed that the low level of government expenditure is not the main issue; after all, government expenditure is financed by tax revenues, one of the main sources of which are taxes on individuals. Japan's higher education tends to be financed through direct contributions from households, not through tax and government expenditure. The latter argument gained even greater momentum in the context of fiscal stringency and the popularity of marketisation orientation.

Quality Shift and Funding

A new dimension has been added recently to this debate. A few members of the Central Education Council issued a statement claiming that, having reached the stage of universalisation of higher education after 50 years of quantitative expansion, Japanese higher education should initiate a new drive for restructuring towards qualitative upgrading. On one hand, such a shift is critical in responding to the challenges created by globalisation and the fierce economic competition that requires high competencies among college graduates. On the other hand, it is necessitated by the changing behaviours and values among youth.

The group claimed further that such a shift towards a qualitative leap was impossible without substantial increases in expenditure on higher education. One of the grounds for this argument is, again, an international comparison.

Figure 6.11 presents the distribution of OECD countries with respect to unit costs of higher education institutions (vertical axis) and the level of per capita GDP (horizontal axis). The two indices are expressed in equivalent US dollars converted using purchasing power parity (PPP). It is shown that, in general, the unit cost increases as per capita GDP rises. The difference by country, however, is substantial, especially among more wealthy countries.

Particularly striking is the high level of unit costs among a few countries, including the United States, Switzerland and Canada. Especially in the first two countries, the unit costs lie in the range of $25 000. On the other hand, a large group of OECD countries—including Finland, Denmark, the Netherlands, the United Kingdom, Germany, France, Australia and Japan—is located in the range between $10 000 and $15 000.

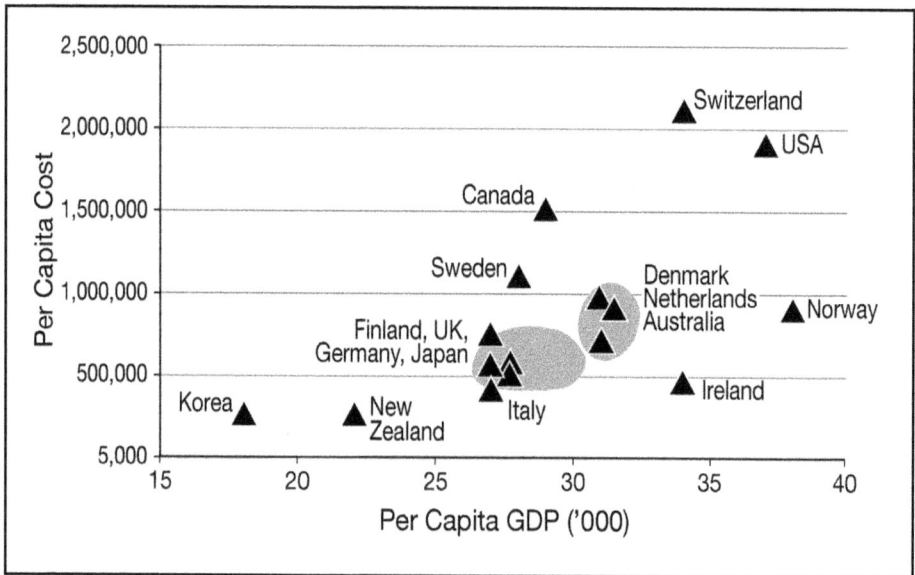

Figure 6.11 International comparison in per capita costs

Source: *OECD Education at a Glance 2006*.

Obviously, the figures should be interpreted with caution for there are substantial problems with international comparison of unit costs due to the difference in the range of higher education institutions and other factors. Nevertheless, it seems to be true that there are substantial differences among the OECD countries with respect to the unit cost of higher education institutions.

It should be noted that the differences among the OECD countries have developed in the past two decades. In particular, the present high level of unit costs in the United States is the result of the steady increase in unit costs since the end of 1980s.

The rapid rise in unit costs in the United States was not necessarily induced by explicit government policies either at the federal or the state level. In fact, there have been strong criticisms of higher education institutions for the sharp increases in tuition fees that partly financed the increase in unit costs. Rather, the increase was induced by the leading universities increasing spending on education, which was then followed by other institutions.

Nonetheless, the shift in development appears to have corresponded with the economic strategy that the United States has been pursuing. Threatened by the rise in productivity of the manufacturing sector in such countries as Japan, the US economy had to assume its hegemony by strengthening its power in the global economy. It required a number of talented college graduates who could handle the particular demands required in the multinational enterprises. And this had to be the area where the United States had the advantage (Reich 1991). From this perspective, the increasing investment in higher education constitutes a significant part of the strategy for fortifying the strength of the United States in the globalised economy.

If Japan is to remain competitive in this environment, it can no longer rely entirely on the high productivity on its factory floors. The competence of regular white-collar workers and engineers should be the critical factor for competitiveness, and higher education is expected to contribute to enhancing it. Arguably, that will not be possible without radical reformation of higher education through increased investment.

It is interesting to note that, recently, an EU committee made a statement to the same effect.

Benchmarking with the United States

Even if the above argument for the necessity of increased spending is accepted, there remain a number of issues to be considered. Who should pay, how should it be delivered and who should receive the spending? From this perspective, it will be informative to compare closely the components of higher education expenditure in Japan with those in the United States.

Figure 6.12 presents the results of a benchmarking exercise to estimate national expenditure on higher education by different forms (direct government subsidy to higher education institutions, government funding for research on a competitive basis, tuition fees and donations to higher education institutions). These amounts are further divided into revenues to public institutions and those to private institutions. Observations from this figure can be summarised in the following three points.

First, the contributions from households through tuition fees are similar in the two countries—about 0.7 per cent of GDP. The distributions by public and private sectors are different, reflecting the relative sizes of the two sectors in the two countries. The difference in total expenditure on higher education between the two countries arises from the differences in the other three sources of funding.

Second, the major source of difference between the two countries comes from government expenditure. Direct institutional subsidies amount to 0.8 per cent of GDP in the United States compared with less than 0.5 per cent in Japan. Funding for research activities through competition stands at 0.2 per cent of GDP in the United States compared with less than 0.1 per cent in Japan.

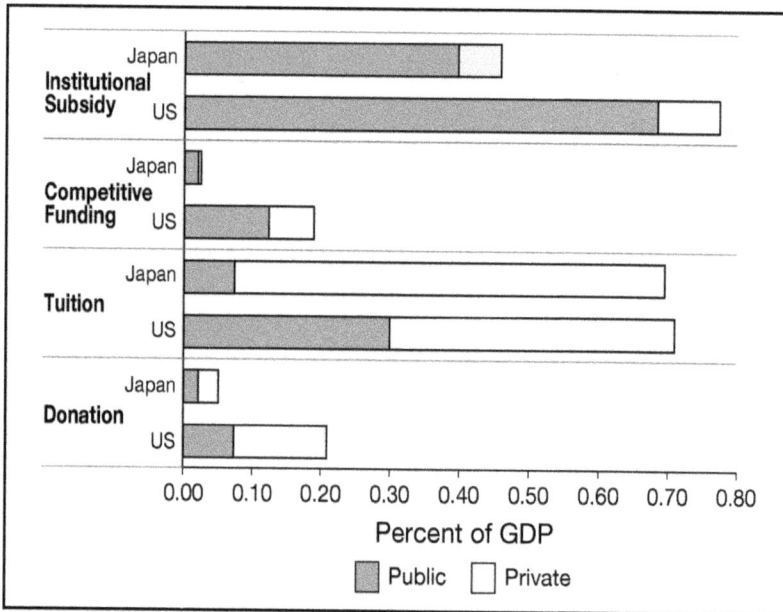

Figure 6.12 Components of national expenditure on higher education: Japan and the United States, 2003

Source: Author's estimations from various sources.

Third, there is a substantial difference in private contributions in the form of donations. In the United States, this source stands at 0.2 per cent of GDP, compared with about 0.05 per cent in Japan. This is particularly important for private institutions.

These results do not necessarily imply that Japan will inevitably have to follow the United States in its pattern of expenditure if it is to increase the total amount of expenditure. It is also unrealistic, because it implies a doubling of the present level of government expenditure. Private donations will be welcome, but it could take a while to foster the culture for voluntary contributions to social causes. More realistically, significant increases in tuition fees will be inevitable if Japan is to raise the level of expenditure on higher education.

Nonetheless, the exercise does seem to indicate that the further increases in expenditure will necessitate, along with tuition revenues, at least a marginal increase in government expenditure on higher education in the form of various incentives for qualitative improvement and a reorganisation of the national student loan system. Whether that option is viable in the present political climate remains to be seen.

Conclusions

After a half-century of robust expansion, higher education in Japan is clearly at a crossroad. In order to respond to the new challenges, it has to undergo a significant transformation in which changes in financing assume the critical role.

Some of the changes have already been translated into concrete policies—most prominent of which is the incorporation of national universities that took place in 2004. The other changes are about to take place, as in the case of reconfiguration of the private sector of higher education. There are also debates taking place about the macroscopic basis of higher education expenditure.

All of these developments involve a number of issues about which there are significant differences of opinion. In this sense, Japanese society is struggling to find a definite direction for higher education financing towards the future.

References

Center for National University Finance and Management 2007, *Kokuritu Daigaku Hojin no Zaimu Keiei ni Kansuru Jittaichosa* [*Report of the Survey on Finance and Management of National University Corporations*], Center for National University Finance and Management, Tokyo.

Durea, E. D. 2000, *The Academic Corporation—A history of college and university governing boards*, Falmer Press, New York.

Kaneko, M. 1987, 'Public and private sectors in Japanese higher education', in *Public and Private Sectors in Asian Higher Education Systems*, Research Institute for Higher Education, Hiroshima University, Japan, pp. 21–34.

Kaneko, M. 1989, *Financing Higher Education in Japan*, Research Institute for Higher Education, Hiroshima University, Japan.

Kaneko, M. 2004, 'Japan's higher education: the past, its legacies and the future', in P. Altbach and T. Umakoshi (eds), *Past and Future of Asian Higher Education*, The Johns Hopkins Press, Baltimore.

Kaneko, M. 2005, 'Marketization of higher education: trends, issues and prospects', *Proceedings of the International Seminar on University Management and Higher Education Policies, held in Tokyo, 19–20 September 2005*, Center for University Management and Policies, University of Tokyo, Japan.

Kaneko, M., Yamamoto, K. and Omori, F. 2004, *On the Edge: Securing a sustainable future for higher education—national study, Japan*, Organisation for Economic Cooperation and Development, Paris.

Reich, R. 1991, *The Wealth of Nations*, Knopf, New York.

US Department of Commerce 1987, *Statistical Abstract of the United States 1987*, US Government Printing Office, Washington, DC.

US Department of Education 1987, *Digest of Education Statistics 1987*, US Government Printing Office, Washington, DC.

Part 3. Experience in East Asia

7. Student Loan Reform in China: Problems and challenges

Wei Jianguo and Wang Rong
China Institute for Educational Finance Research,
Peking University

Development of Student Loans in China

The development of student loans in China accompanies China's higher education 'massification'. In 1999, the Chinese government launched a policy onhigher education expansion. Since then, Chinese higher education has shifted rapidly from elite education to mass education. In 2002, China's gross enrolment rate in higher education increased to 15 per cent from 9.8 per cent in 1998—meeting the minimum standards of mass higher education defined by Professor Martin Trow. The rate increased to 23 per cent in 2007. In the process of promoting mass higher education, the Chinese government has also reformed the previous free tuition policies. Starting in 1997, all students who are enrolled at public higher education institutions (HEIs) are required to pay for tuition. According to the latest statistics, revenue from tuition and fees in 2007 accounted for 33.66 per cent of the total expenditure of Chinese ordinary HEIs (Ministry of Education 2008:28). The introduction of these macro-policies brought about a real problem: how to help the growing number of needy students to successfully complete their higher education.

Many countries have adopted student loan schemes to share the cost of higher education. To resolve the above-mentioned problem, China has also launched a student loan policy.[1] So far, four patterns of student loan programs have developed in China: commercial bank loans from an agency in the HEI's region;[2]

---

1 In addition to student loans, financial assistance to Chinese students includes: grants, national incentive scholarships, work–study programs, tuition waivers and reductions, subsidies for needy students, 'one-stop student assistance stations for financially needy students', and so on.
2 The student loans originated by commercial banks—that is, state-subsidised student loans, which will be mentioned below.

rural credit cooperative[3] loans from an agency in the household's region; a China Development Bank[4] loan from an agency in the HEI's region; and a China Development Bank loan from an agency in household's region.[5]

In 1999, state-subsidised student loans were experimented with in HEIs controlled by the relevant ministries of the State Council in eight pilot cities, and the Industrial and Commercial Bank of China (ICBC) was the bank that handled the matter. In 2000, the program expanded across the country, and its administering bank expanded from the ICBC to also include the Agricultural Bank of China, the Bank of China and the China Construction Bank.[6]

When the state-subsidised student loan program was implemented nationally, some provinces startedinstitutional innovations in student loans. In July 2001, Zhejiang Province launched a Rural Credit Cooperative loan from an agency in the household region, which was the first in China. At present, this pattern of student loans is carried out in many other areas.

In 2003, the origination of state-subsidised student loans encountered obstacles. As the program has the features of large quantities, high cost and high risk, commercial banks do not want to get involved. The provision of state-subsidised student loans stopped in nearly all parts of the country. In order to promote state-subsidised student loans, the Ministry of Education, the Ministry of Finance, the People's Bank of China and the China Banking Regulatory Commission jointly issued 'Several Opinions on Further Improving the Work on the State-Subsidised Students Loans' in June 2004—reforming previous policies of the program. During the same period, the China Development Bank distributed student loans in some provinces. This program originated in Henan Province, so it is also known as the 'Henan Pattern'. After the adjustment of the state-subsidised student loan policies in 2004, student loans in Henan have not been provided completely. In December 2004, the country's only pilot province, Henan, cooperated with the China Development Bank (Henan Branch) in student loan business. Afterwards Qinghai Province followed suit. At present, that pattern has also been adopted in Shanxi, Hunan, Guangdong, Inner Mongolia, and other places.

---

3 Rural credit cooperatives are rural financial institutions providing financial services for their members. They are set up with the approval of the People's Bank of China. Their shares come from their members and therefore are under democratic administration. At present, rural credit cooperatives are undergoing reform and some have shifted to become rural cooperative banks.

4 The China Development Bank is different from the commercial banks mentioned previously. It was established in 1994 and is a policy financial institution controlled directly by the State Council. Its funds come mainly from the domestic and foreign bond markets. At present, reform of the China Development Bank is also under way.

5 The HEI's region refers to the location of the HEI at which the student studies; the household region refers to the place where the home of the student is located.

6 These banks are operated in accordance with the Law of the People's Republic of China on Commercial Banks.

In 2007, the State Council issued the 'Opinions on Establishing and Improving the Policies for Subsidising Students in Universities of Regular Undergraduate Education, Post-Secondary Vocational Schools and Secondary Vocational Schools from Families with Financial Difficulties', making a major adjustment to the student-assistance system, which is also the biggest step since the higher education expansion. The document also suggested the China Development Bank loan from an agency in the household region and experimented with this in Jiangsu, Hubei, Chongqing, Shaanxi and Gansu.

Comparison of Four Patterns of Student Loan Programs in China

Below we provide a comparison of China's four types of student loan programs from aspects of the principal provider, the borrower's eligibility, loan size, loan origination, interest subsidy, risk-sharing, repayment conditions, loan collection, and so on (see Table 7.1 for a summary).

Principal Provider

The principal of the current four types of Chinese student loans is provided by financial institutions and not directly by the government. The principal of the commercial bank loan from an agency in the HEI's region is provided by the commercial banks in the HEI's region. The principal of the rural credit cooperative loan from an agency in the household region is provided by the rural credit cooperatives in the student's household region.

Borrower's Eligibility

The borrowers of a commercial bank loan from an agency in the HEI's region should be full-time junior-college students, undergraduate students, second bachelor'sdegree students or graduate students from public ordinary colleges and universities. For a rural credit cooperative loan from an agency in the household region, it is more complicated. In some provinces, the students themselves apply for loans, but in others, parents apply instead; in some areas, loans are not granted to students in private HEIs and independent colleges,[7] and in others they are accessible to all; some loans are given to second bachelor's degree students and graduate students, but other loans are given

---

7 Independent college results from China's higher education reform; they are set up by ordinary universities under the new mechanism and models. They are not public institutions of higher education. Enterprises, institutions, social groups or individuals may serve as partners and provide the necessary conditions and facilities for operating the colleges and participating in their management and supervision. The colleges independently enrol, grant certificates and conduct financial accounting. They have legal personality and bear civil liability.

only to ordinary junior-college students and undergraduate students. For the China Development Bank loan from an agency in the HEI's region, eligible borrowers are similar to those in the commercial bank loan from an agency in the HEI's region. For the China Development Bank loan from an agency in the household region, it is required that the borrowers be ordinary junior-college students or undergraduate students, excluding postgraduates and second bachelor's degree students. It is also required that students and their parents sign the loan contracts as co-borrowers. In addition, students in private HEIs and independent colleges may apply for the China Development Bank loan from an agency in the HEI's and the household's regions. Apart from the above requirements, applicants for all four types of student loans must be students from families with financial difficulties.

Loan Size

The loan size of all four patterns of student loan is generally limited to no more than RMB6000 each year.

Loan Origination

The originations of the four student loan patternsvary greatly. Under the commercial bank loan from an agency in the HEI's region, the loan origination is completed by HEIs and commercial banks. Under rural credit cooperative loans from an agency in the household's region, the rural credit cooperatives originate the loans themselves. For the China Development Bank loan from an agency in the HEI's region, HEIs are mainly responsible for loan origination. For the China Development Bank loan from an agency in the household's region, all counties or districtsin pilot provinces have been required to set up student-assistance management centres in charge of the loan's origination.

Interest Subsidy

It is the government that will subsidise the interest of all four patterns when the students are in school. Under a commercial bank loan from an agency in the HEI's region, the loan's interest is centrally controlled by the HEIs but is borne by the central government, and that of students in locally owned HEIs is borne by the local government. For rural credit cooperative loans from an agency in the household's region, the interest is borne by the provincial government sometimes, but otherwise is borne by the corresponding local government according to the affiliation of the HEIs. For the China Development Bank loan from an agency in the HEI's region, the interest is generally borne by the corresponding local government. For the China Development Bank loan from an agency in the household's region, the level of government that will bear the interest is determined by the affiliation and location of the HEI the student is enrolled in.

Risk-Sharing

A risk compensation fund is generally established to share risk in China's student loans. The system was introduced during the reform in 2004. The amount of risk compensation is equal to the loan amount multiplied by the ratio of the risk compensation fund. Under commercial bank loans from an agency in the HEI's region, the HEI and the government that the HEI is affiliated with each bears half of the risk compensation fund. The ratio of the risk compensation fund is determined when banks bid for the final selection of the administration of the student loan. It is more complicated for risk compensation funds in a rural credit cooperative loan from an agency in the household's region.[8] For example, the HEI and the local government each bears half in some provinces, but in others, the local government shouldersthe whole amount. For the China Development Bank loan from an agency in the HEI's region, the ratio is determined when negotiation between the provincial student assistance centre and the provincial branch of the China Development Bank is carried out and it is shared equally by the provincial government and the HEI. For the China Development Bank loan from an agency in the household's region, the ratio of risk compensation is 15 per cent, according to the policies governing pilot areas. Which level of government will bear the risk compensation fund is determined by the affiliation and location of the HEI the student is enrolled in.

Repayment Conditions

The interest on the loan incurred from the date of the student's graduation is paid by the student (or their parents). Under the commercial bank loan from an agency in the HEI's region, students may choose to repay the principal within one–two years after their graduation according to their employment and income. The principal and interest must be paid off within six years after graduation.[9] Under the rural credit cooperative loan from an agency in the household's region and the China Development Bank loan from an agency in the HEI's region, the principal and interest also must be paid off within six years after graduation. The loan-repayment term of the China Development Bank loan from an agency in the household's region is

---

8 In this type of student loan, in some provinces borrowers are also required to provide a guarantee.
9 The students who signed their loan contract before the reform in 2004 must pay off the principal and interest within four years after graduation.

determined in accordance with the full-time study period of junior college or university with an addition of 10-year limits, reaching a maximum of 14 years. The grace period is the time while students are studying at the HEI and two years after graduation. After that period, students and their parents must repay the principal in yearly instalments in accordance with their loan contracts. An undergraduate must pay off all the principal and interest within eight years after the grace period. In terms of the repayment mode, for both the China Development Bank and the rural credit cooperative loan from an agency in the household's region, in some provinces this is paid yearly, while the principal and interest of the commercial bank loan from an agency in the HEI's region may be paid by yearly, quarterly or monthly. All loans may be repaid ahead of schedule. Borrowers need to pay the actual interest only. Under the commercial bank loan from an agency in the HEI's region and the China Development Bank loan from an agency in the HEI's region, if a student borrower continues their postgraduate study, the banks will provide him with a loan-repayment extension. The government subsidises the interest at the corresponding level. In addition, if graduates from centrally controlled HEIs work in the grassroots units in the western regions or remote areas for three or more years, the central government will repay the loan's principal they receive in school and the interest incurred previously. Such a system has also been implemented in some provinces so that when graduates of provincially owned HEIs work in designated places, the provincial government will pay the principal and interest of student loans.

Loan Collection

Different loan types vary in their method of collection. Under the commercial bank loan from an agency in the HEI's region, HEIs and banks are responsible for collection.[10] Under the rural credit cooperative loan from an agency in the household's region, rural credit cooperatives themselves are responsible for collection. Under the China Development Bank loan from an agency in the HEI's region, HEIs are responsible for the collection. The final settlement of the risk compensation fund links to the HEIs' loan-collection performance. If the loans are collected well and the loan default amount is less than the risk compensation fund then the HEIs will be able to receive the remainder as rewards. Under the China Development Bank loan from an agency in the household's region, the student assistance centre at the county level is responsible for the loan recovery. If the loans are collected well, the student assistance centre at the county level is also correspondingly rewarded by the risk compensation fund as an incentive.

---

10   As the commercial banks are reluctant to offer student loans, generally, HEIs are responsible for loan collection in practice, so as to motivate commercial banks.

Table 7.1 Main features of four types of student loans in China

	Commercial bank loan from agency in HEI's region	Rural credit cooperative loan from agency in household's region	China Development Bank loan from agency in HEI's region	China Development Bank loan from agency in household's region
Principal provision	Commercial banks	Rural credit cooperatives	China Development Bank	China Development Bank
Borrower's eligibility	Borrowers are students: full-time junior-college students, undergraduate students, second bachelor's degree students and graduate students from public ordinary colleges and universities	Borrowers are students or their parents—it varies in different places	Borrowers are students: full-time junior-college students, undergraduate students, second bachelor's degree students and graduate students from ordinary colleges and universities	Students and their parents are co-borrowers; only granted to junior-college students and undergraduates and excluding postgraduates and second bachelor's degree students
Loan size	Not exceeding RMB6000 per school year per person	Not exceeding RMB6000 per school year per person	Not exceeding RMB6000 per school year per person	Not exceeding RMB6000 per school year per person
Loan origination	HEIs and commercial banks	Rural credit cooperatives	Mainly in the charge of HEIs	Mainly in the charge of county-level student assistance management centres
Interest subsidy	Borne by the government at the corresponding level according to the affiliation of HEIs	In some provinces, it is borne by the provincial government, but in other provinces, it is borne by the local government at the corresponding level according to the affiliation of HEIs	It is usually borne by the local government at the corresponding level according to the affiliation of HEIs	Which level of government bears it depends on the affiliation and location of the HEI at which the student is enrolled
Risk-sharing	Risk compensation fund: the government and HEI each shares half of the risk compensation fund; the part borne by the government is determined according to the affiliation of HEIs	Risk compensation fund: it varies in different provinces. Guarantee: in some provinces it is required that the borrowers provide a guarantee	Risk compensation fund: the government and HEI each shares half of the risk compensation fund	Risk compensation fund: which level of government bears it depends on the affiliation and location of the HEI at which the student is enrolled
Repayment conditions	The principal and interest must be paid off within six years after graduation yearly, quarterly or monthly	It is generally required that the principal and interest be paid off yearly within six years after graduation	It is required that the principal and interest be paid off yearly within six years after graduation	It is generally required that the principal and interest be paid off yearly within 10 years after graduation
Loan collection	Both HEIs and commercial banks are responsible for loan collection	Rural credit cooperatives are responsible for loan collection	HEIs are responsible for loan collection	The county-level student assistance centres are responsible for loan collection

Problems and Challenges Confronting Chinese Student Loan Reform

The four types of student loans play an important role in helping needy students successfully complete their studies. It is noteworthy that none of the current four types is perfect. At the national level, as an important part of the student-assistance system, student loans have not yet functioned to their full extent. The development of Chinese student loansis facing many problems and challenges.

1. Some students are not yet eligible to apply for student loans. There are restrictions on the eligibility of applicants from private HEIs and independent colleges. Some loans are not accessible to graduate students.

2. The loan size fails to meet the needs of some students. At present, the maximum amount of all loan types is RMB6000 per annum. According to the study of Song Yingquan, however, the private educational expenditure of a student in a locally owned HEI, on average, is more than RMB10 000 (Yingquan n.d.), including tuition and fees, accommodation, board expenses, and transportation fees. In addition, the tuition fees for medicine and art majors are higher than for other majors. Generally, the tuition fees of private HEIs and independent colleges are more than RMB10 000. As a result, for students with nogrant or other form of financial assistance, the current loan size is not enough to pay for their higher education costs.

3. The distribution of student loans cannot fully meet the needs of the students. According unpublished data from the Ministry of Education,[11] since the adjustment of student loan policies in 2004 (see Table 7.2), there is still a wide gap between the number of students receiving student loans and the number of applicants. In addition, according to a survey we conducted in 2007,[12] the success rate of applications for loans is not high. Of the 8120 students in the sample survey, a total of 1434 applied for student loans, accounting for 18.54 per cent of valid samples; 6312 did not apply; and 374 students did not provide any information. Of the 1434 students who applied for student loans, only 961 eventually received a loan. The success rate of applications for student loans is 67.02 per cent. These data show that the loan requirements for students from families with financial difficulties have not been met.

---

11 The summary data include data for all types of student loans.
12 The survey was conducted in 30 HEIs in Zhejiang, Jiangsu, Hubei, Sichuan, Qinghai and Ningxia provinces and autonomous regions. A total of 8152 student questionnaires were handed out and 8120 valid, completed questionnaires were returned.

Table 7.2 Statistics of distribution of student loans nationwide, 2004–06

	2004	2005	2006
The total number of on-campus students (10 000 people)	1350	1387	1849
The number of loan applicants (10 000 people)	70.32	118.31	190.00
The number of students receiving loans (10 000 people)	36.73	91.61	85.50
The success rate of loan applications	52.23%	77.43%	44.74%

Source: Ministry of Education, unpublished data.

4.   The student loan coverage varies in different colleges and universities. The coverage in centrally controlled HEIs is higher than in locally owned HEIs. In 2004, the student loan coverage of HEIs controlled by the Ministry of Education, those controlled by other ministries and locally owned HEIs was 9.04 per cent, 7.13 per cent and 1.60 per cent, respectively. In 2005, the corresponding coverage was 7.11 per cent, 7.55 per cent and 6.50 per cent (see Tables 7.3 and 7.4). In addition, the situation in locally owned vocational colleges is not as good as in regular undergraduate colleges and universities. According to a survey carried out in 2007, we can see the differences of coverage between locally owned regular undergraduate colleges and universities and vocational colleges. In locally owned regular undergraduate colleges and universities, 391 of the 2349 students in our sample survey received student loans—accounting for 18.55 per cent. In the case of locally owned vocational colleges, 459 of the 4213 students in our sample survey received student loans—accounting for 12.16 per cent. In addition, there are no considerable differences between the tuition fees of vocational colleges and regular undergraduate colleges and universities. Moreover, the family economic situations of students in vocational colleges are even worse (Yingquan n.d.). These factors make it more difficult for vocational-college students to pay for higher education. In addition, compared with students in public HEIs, students from private HEIs and independent colleges face more difficulties in receiving student loans. Though the rural credit cooperative loan from an agency in the household's region and the two types of China Development Bank loans allow students from these two types of colleges to apply for loans in some provinces, they do not enjoyequal treatment with those from public HEIs. According to the 2007 survey mentioned previously, 114 of the 1652 sample students from private HEIs and independent colleges received student loans—accounting for only 7.7 per cent, which is much lower than the percentage of students from locally owned ordinary colleges and universities in the survey.

Table 7.3 Statistics of student loans in various HEIs nationwide, 2004

	HEIs controlled by the Ministry of Education	HEIs controlled by other central ministries	Locally owned HEIs
The total number of on-campus students (10 000 people)	162.52	42.71	1145.00
The number of loan applicants (10 000 people)	17.20	3.80	49.30
The number of students receiving loans (10 000 people)	14.69	3.04	18.98
Loan coverage	9.04%	7.13%	1.60%

Source: Ministry of Education, unpublished data.

Table 7.4 Statistics of student loans in various HEIs nationwide, 2005

	HEIs controlled by the Ministry of Education	HEIs controlled by other central ministries	Locally owned HEIs
The total number of on-campus students (10 000 people)	168.03	41.22	1177.95
The number of loan applicants (10 000 people)	16.07	4.20	98.05
The number of students receiving loans (10 000 people)	11.95	3.11	76.56
Loan coverage	7.11%	7.55%	6.50%

Source: Ministry of Education, unpublished data.

5. It is difficult to identify a student's family's financial conditions. All types of student loan programs offer loans with a government financial subsidy to needy students. When a loan application is examined, the student's family's economic situation will be identified. Since there is no strict and sound individual income tax declaration system in China and many taxpayers cannot meet the current standard of individual income tax deduction expenses, it is impossible to collect the information on all the students' families' economic situations.

6. There is no sound risk-sharing mechanism. As mentioned previously, instead of providing guarantees, the Chinese government shares and controls the risks of student loans by way of a risk compensation fund. This risk-sharing approach is not sound. Its main problems are as follows. HEIs bear half of the risk of the compensation fund. The number of students receiving loans will affect the amount of risk of the compensation fund the HEI bears. Unfairness could arise among different HEIs. More importantly, is it reasonable to require HEIs to bear the risk of the compensation fund? The specific meaning of the risk compensation fund is not the same for different types of loans. Under the commercial bank loan from an agency in the HEI's region and the rural credit cooperative loan from an agency in the household's region, the risk compensation fund is derived from income for the current period. No matter what the loan repayment is in the future, banks may receive a fixed amount of the risk compensation fund. This institutional arrangement will not solve the possible future risk-control problems. After getting the risk compensation fund, financial institutions will bear all the losses arising from loan defaults in the future. The financial institutions' worries about the future uncertainties have not been completely resolved. Under the China Development Bank loan from an agency in the HEI's and the household's regions, the risk compensation fund is not the bank's income for the current period. The final settlement depends on the collection performance. There is a loss-sharing system that defines that the China Development Bank, HEIs and provincial student assistance centres (or the China Development Bank and county-level government) share the loss together when the loan default amount is bigger than the risk compensation fund. This institutional arrangement defines the control and sharing mechanism of the future uncertain risks and there is also an incentive mechanism. There are, however, also problems in this system. With regard to incentives, the motivation chain is too long. The final settlement is after the expired repaymentdate. During this period, there could be many changes in personnel of the various agencies. There are no efficient indicators to give them day-to-day, real-time incentives. The reason is not strong enough for HEIs and county-level governments to bear the losses. As with bearing the risk compensation fund mentioned above, it is risky to require colleges and universities to share the loss. That the losses

of loan defaults are borne by the county-level governments is not sufficient since students work in all parts of the country after graduation.

7. There are disadvantages with the repayment options. The repayment period for all types of student loans is six years, except for the China Development Bank loan from an agency in the household's region (its repayment period is 10 years for undergraduates). The repayment period of six years seems too short whether in comparison with international student loans or in consideration of the repayment burden of Chinese student loans. None of the four patterns takes into consideration all the exceptions when designing the repayment period, such as unemployment, low income, major diseases, emergencies, and so on. Regarding the forgiveness of student loans, the current policies of some provinces support only the student borrowers from the locally owned HEIs who work in designated areas of the same province, but do not support the above-mentioned students who work in poor areas of other provinces. Therefore, the issue of forgiveness will be considered from the central government's point of view. In addition, there is an extension system for postgraduates only for the commercial bank loan from an agency in the HEI's region and the China Development Bank loan from an agency in the HEI's region. Improvements to the other loan types should be made in a timely manner. The interest subsidy in loan-repayment extension is a very complicated issue. Local governments are reluctant to continue to subsidise the loan interest for locally owned HEI graduates who pursue their Master's degrees in other provinces. Like the forgiveness mentioned above, this issue will also be considered from the central government's point of view.

8. The coexistence and competition of the US Federal Family Education Loan (FFEL) and Federal Direct Loan (DL) give us positive inspiration (Galloway and Wilson 2005). Since none of the Chinese student loan patterns has obvious advantages, the strategy of coexistence and competition of various loan types should be adopted. The disadvantages mentioned above exist in basically all the student loan types. At present, the commercial bank loan from an agency in the HEI's region is applied across the country with regard to the policy coverage. But in some areas this pattern has stopped or has not been carried out at all. A rural credit cooperative loan from an agency in the household's region, the China Development Bank loan from an agency in the HEI's region and the China Development Bank loan from an agency in the household's region are offered in some areas.The feasible option for the future is to allow the coexistence and competition of a variety of student loan types, rather than choosing a single type, so as to find the most suitable type for each place through practice. This might offer friendly conditions for the formation of more mature patterns of student loans.

References

Galloway, F. and Wilson, H. 2005, *Reframing the Student Loan Costing Debate: The benefits of competition*, Educational Policy Institute, Washington, DC, viewed 10 September 2008, <http://www.educationalpolicy.org/pdf/loandebate.pdf>

Ministry of Education 2008, *Brief Information on National Education Expenditure Statistics*, Department of Finance Affairs, Ministry of Education, Beijing.

Yingquan, S. n.d., Rough estimation on the family income and educational cost of students of secondary vocational schools, vocational colleges and locally owned regular undergraduate colleges and universities, Unpublished draft ms.

8. Recent Developments in Higher Education in Indonesia: Issues and challenges

Teguh Yudo Wicaksono and Deni Friawan
Centre for Strategic and International Studies, Indonesia

Introduction

Secular higher education in Indonesia has a relatively short history. It began with the establishment by the Dutch colonialists of tertiary schools training indigenous people in medicine and engineering. Before the colonial education system, higher education was considered an Islamic institution. The growth in higher education post independence has, however, been very swift. Since the endorsement of the very first *Education Act* in 1961, Indonesian higher education has continuously experienced rapid expansion. The development of higher education grew during the period from the 1970s to the 1990s, when Indonesia was experiencing strong economic growth, fuelled by an oil-price boom and solid non-oil and gas export performance. Nizam (2006) recorded that the student population in higher education institutions (HEIs) increased from about 200 000 students in 1975 to 2.5 millions students in 1995. By 2005, there were nearly 2300 HEIs, consisting of 86 public HEIs and about 2200 private HEIs. More than 3.5 million students were educated in these HEIs.

Though this rosy trend gives a good signal, some observers addressed crucial problems behind the growing HEIs. Moeliodihardjo et al. (2000), for example, argue that the rapid expansion of HEIs has not been in parallel with appropriate planning and funding mechanisms. The higher education system has suffered internal inefficiency and poor initiatives due to a centralised education system. In addition, the bureaucratic dependency on a central authority has made HEIs (particularly public HEIs) unable to respond to external changes or receive appropriate support (Nizam 2006). Further, the public HEIs have lacked any sense of public accountability, as, according to a bureaucratic structure, they are part of the institution of government under the Ministry of National Education.

Consequently, the absence of any autonomy and the diminished sense of community in HEIs have resulted in a lack of accountability and responsibility to society (World Bank 1996). This has had an adverse impact on the quality, efficiency and relevance of higher education in Indonesia. The poor quality of higher education can be seen from the low levels of qualification of the teaching staff, inadequate laboratory facilities (especially in the private HEIs) and limited library holdings. Meanwhile, low efficiency is best demonstrated by the extended enrolment period in which a typical undergraduate—in both public and private HEIs—spends about five to six years completing their studies instead of the four years required. Low internal efficiency can also be seen from the low student–teacher ratios of about 12:1, limited utilisation of physical space, and the low number of student/staff contact hours.

As far as public financing is concerned, it has long been recognised that the government is facing strained resources to support higher education. Before the economic crises hit the country, higher education was not a top priority in education policy. This is understandable, as the country is still struggling to achieve its nine-year compulsory education policy (primary and junior high school), which consumes a large amount of resources. The financial crisis has aggravated critical conditions for HEIs, particularly public HEIs that rely mostly on the government for support. Public HEIs have to compete for public resources not only with primary education but also with other social sectors and issues such as health, poverty alleviation and social security.

This recent study is an attempt to outline the main characteristics of the higher education sector in Indonesia and review major policy developments affecting the financial mechanism and the delivery of tertiary education over the past few decades. It will pay particular attention to the effective roles of government-funding schemes and types of student loan arrangements in the broader policy setting.

This chapter will discuss the evolution of the structure of institutions of higher education in Indonesia. It focuses on the access to and equality of higher education services, and reviews several issues related to the financing mechanisms of higher education in Indonesia, including the general trend and composition of public expenditure, the sources of funds, and the impact of the economic crisis and decentralisation on the allocation of finances.

Overview of Higher Education in Indonesia: Structure, institution and type

The Evolution of the Structure of Institutions

Indonesian higher education witnessed a massive expansion in tertiary education post independence. In the colonial period, there were very few HEIs in the country. These institutions were designed to provide professional training to local people mainly in the areas of medicine and engineering. Academic and research programs were not established in this time. Due to the social stratification in colonial times, there were students only from elite groups enrolled in universities. It is estimated that only 200 students enrolled in universities in the colonial period (KJPP 2003). Post independence, the political climate and the national spirit have meant the country aspired to have at least one public university in each province. About 23 new HEIs were established during the 1960s, and these institutions covered almost 26 provinces in Indonesia (Nizam 2006). This policy has brought higher education to a mass scale.

Another important point in the 1960s was the enactment of the first education law—Law No. 15 of 1961—which detailed the structure for higher education. Under the law, universities have a standardised division of faculties and structure of governance (Buchori and Malik 2004). The law defines the mission of HEIs and details the 'Tri Dharma Perguruan Tinggi' (Three Pillars of National Higher Education): learning, research and community service. The law also encouraged diversification in higher education programs. Before the endorsement of the law, private HEIs were not recognised as part of the national education system. With the implementation of the law, private HEIs, along with public HEIs, were standardised and brought in as part of the national education system. This provision has encouraged private HEIs to flourish around the country.

The demand for education increased in the 1970s, which corresponded with a shift in the economy from the traditional sector to a more modernised one. Indonesia's economy experienced high economic growth thanks to an accelerating process of industrialisation in the export industry. This process led to mounting demand for skilled workers, particularly science and technology graduates. As the government could provide only limited support for higher education, in 1975, it made considerable changes to the higher education system.

In 1975, the Ministry of Education through the Directorate-General of Higher Education (DGHE) established a framework for the development of higher education. This framework worked as a basic guide to standardise the national higher education system. It covered the structure of academic programs (undergraduate and graduate), governance, and the roles and responsibilities of faculty members.

A dual system—academic and vocational—was also initiated in the same period. According to the framework, academic programs consist of a four-year undergraduate degree (strata 1-S1), two-year Master's level (strata 2, S2) and a three-year doctorate program (Strata 3-S3). Vocational programs offer one to four-year non-degree training places.

It could be argued that these considerable changes taken by the DGHE were influenced by the end of European or continental influence in Indonesia's higher education system. By the end of the 1970s, the government adopted the US-style system of including the accumulation of credit points in the curriculum.

A student of a three-year diploma program is required to complete 110 to 120 credit units. A student of an undergraduate degree (s1) has to complete 144 to 160 credit units. This significant change could be attributed to the large number of faculty members and bureaucrats who studied in the United States. The credit system is also more desirable as it monitors student performances easily and reduces the length of study. This shift in the education system sent a signal that the government valued the role of HEIs in creating skilled workers and responding to labour-market changes.

In 2003, the House of Representatives endorsed a new education law—Law No. 20 2003—which also outlines the structure and purpose of HEIs. The new law essentially adopts the same groundwork for the higher education system; however, it provides greater autonomy to HEIs than the previous law.

The Types of Higher Education in Indonesia

The higher education system cannot be analysed separately from Indonesia's entire education system. Figure 8.1 illustrates the organisational structure of the country's education system. Recently, the organisational structure of the school system was separated into two streams: the Islamic stream under the Ministry of Religious Affairs (public and private), and the secular stream under the Ministry of National Education (public and private). These two steams are separated over three levels of education: basic education, middle or secondary education, and higher education.

Children are not required to go to preschool, however, the government makes every effort to encourage parents to send their children to preschool before entering them into elementary schools. In May 1994, the President of the Republic of Indonesia affirmed that basic education in Indonesia included nine years of compulsory schooling. The basic education includes six years of elementary school and three years of junior secondary school. Middle or secondary education includes three years of general senior secondary school or vocational senior secondary school.

Higher education is an extension of secondary education. The Indonesian higher education system consists of academic and professional learning. Academic education is designed at mastering science, technology and research. Professional education is aimed at developing practical skills. The institutions providing higher education are categorised into universities, institutes, collages, academies, and polytechnics in both the public and the private sectors.

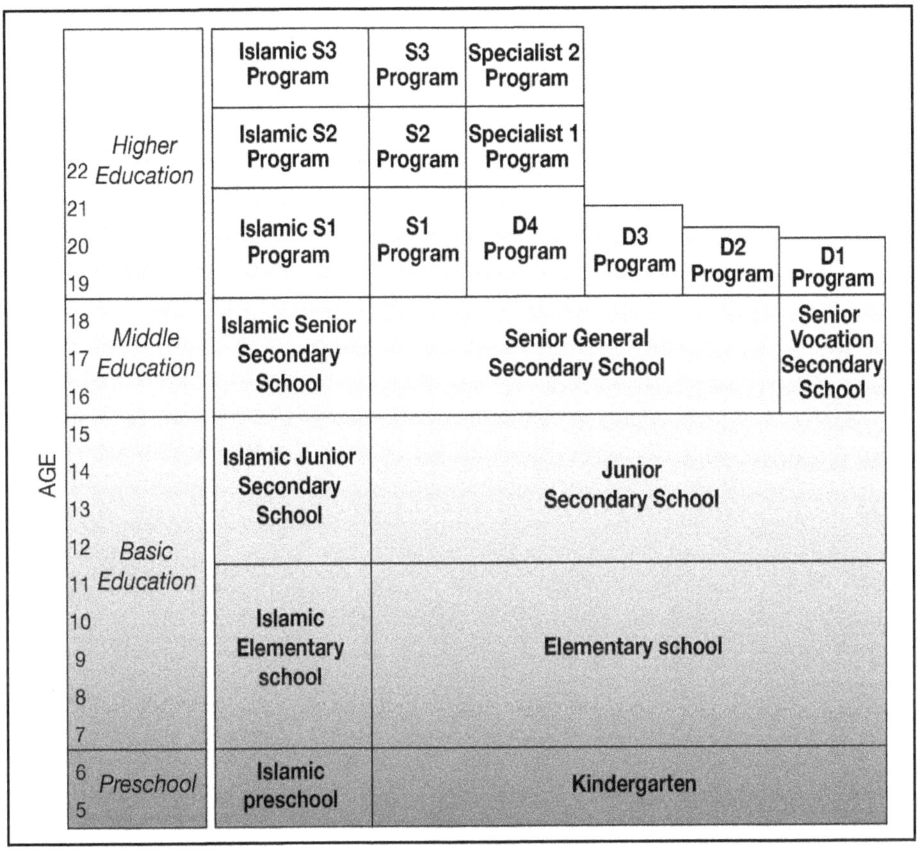

AGE	Level						
22	Higher Education	Islamic S3 Program	S3 Program	Specialist 2 Program			
21		Islamic S2 Program	S2 Program	Specialist 1 Program			
20		Islamic S1 Program	S1 Program	D4 Program	D3 Program	D2 Program	D1 Program
19							
18	Middle Education	Islamic Senior Secondary School	Senior General Secondary School				Senior Vocation Secondary School
17							
16							
15		Islamic Junior Secondary School	Junior Secondary School				
14							
13							
12	Basic Education						
11		Islamic Elementary school	Elementary school				
10							
9							
8							
7							
6	Preschool	Islamic preschool	Kindergarten				
5							

Figure 8.1 School system in Indonesia

Source: Mohandas (2004).

In addition, a university consists of several faculties conducting academic and/or professional education in several disciplines. An *institute* consists of faculties conducting academic and/or professional education in disciplines that align with a set profession. In comparison, a *college* conducts academic and professional education in one particular discipline. Meanwhile, an academy and a polytechnic are vocational HEIs that provide professional skills and diploma degrees.

Based on their status, the HEIs in Indonesia can be divided into two groups: the public HEIs and the private HEIs. The public HEIs are under the jurisdiction of the state treasury law, education system law and civil servant law and are treated as part of the ministry. Private HEIs are regulated under the Foundation and Education System Law, and are considered the business arm of the foundation. Brodjonegoro (2000) argues that, under these regulations, the HEIs have no independent means of carrying out their mission as a moral force and they become less accountable and less innovative.

There is also a difference in the admissions processes. The admission process in public HEIs is done through the national examination for higher education (*Seleksi Penerimaan Mahasiswa Baru*). As seats in public HEIs are limited, a prospective applicant has to compete nationally for a specific field. Usually the applicant submits for acceptance to two to three prospective programs. This system ensures that only those with the highest scores are admitted. Admission into private HEIs is considered to be less competitive. As several private HEIs have a very good reputation, admission to these institutions is, however, as competitive as it is for public HEIs.

The Recent Issues of Higher Education in Indonesia

Access and Equality

As in many places, in Indonesia, equality in education has become a hotly debated issue, particularly in regard to higher education. There are several reasons that could explain this. The first is due to a common perception that higher education is a public good. Second, the function of higher education is to train future elite groups who will be an important part of the country's development, which has led HEIs to be politico-imperative educational institutions. History shows that critical moments in Indonesia's political and economic progress were strongly linked to the roles of HEIs. Indonesia's independence movement, for example, was prompted mainly by well-educated young Indonesians. Political turbulence in the country was closely related to the political activities of university students. Therefore, graduates of HEIs carry high social status. The third reason for inequality in education is the expectation of graduates in the job market. Graduates are expected to enjoy well-paid jobs and work in the formal sector, whose members are considered better off than those in the informal sector. Therefore, there is a strong political aspiration to produce opportunities in higher education for all groups in society.

Although higher education has expanded rapidly in the post-independence era, the growth in supply of HEIs still does not meet the growing demand. Meanwhile, the government's ability to expand the supply of public HEIs is constrained by the budget, and the fact that the private sector has dominated the tertiary education market for the past 20 years. Most private HEIs, however, rely on student fees in running their institutions, which means they are quite expensive for those who come from a disadvantaged background. As such, participation rates in higher education have been low for years.

Recent data gathered by the National Socio-Economic Survey (*Survei Sosio-Ekonomi Nasional*; Susenas) of *Badan Pusat Statistik* (BPS; Central Statistics Agency) shows that the enrolment rate in higher education is quite low in Indonesia. It is worth noting, however, that Susenas data might underestimate the numbers enrolled in tertiary education in Indonesia. This might be due to the fact that a large proportion of students are from middle–high-income households, while those from an upper-class background are not included in the data.

Another issue with the data is demographic mobility. It is likely that Susenas does not sample students who are still living with their parents. Also, the sampling method of Susenas excludes students who live in boarding houses (off-campus and on-campus). This is due to the sampling guide of Susenas for which a person who lives in a boarding house, military barracks or prison will not be surveyed. Despite this, Susenas data are the best available considering the sample size and national coverage.

By 2006, the gross enrolment rate[1] (GER) in tertiary education reached only 12.16 per cent. Figure 8.2 illustrates that, during 1993–2003, the GER in higher education tended to stagnate. The economic crisis that hit the country in 1998 seemed to have no strong effect on the enrolment rate. Generally, a low participation rate indicates high inequality of access to HEIs. This presumption is confirmed by Figure 8.3.

According to Susenas, the GER of students from a low-income family background was about 0.63 per cent in 1993.[2] This was far lower than the enrolment rate of students from the top 20 per cent bracket of income per capita household (about 27.78 per cent in the same year). After more than a decade, the gap has not narrowed significantly. In 2006, the number of low-income students enrolled in tertiary education was 2.67 per cent. This number was still far lower than that for students from the top 20 per cent income bracket (about 33.9 per cent).

---

1 The GER of tertiary education is the ratio of all tertiary school students to all tertiary school-aged people (nineteen–twenty-four). The age range (nineteen–twenty-four years old) is based on BPS's definition. Even though this range covers only undergraduate-aged persons and ignores graduate-aged persons, this approach is still appropriate and convenient considering the very low number of people going in at graduate level.

2 Low income means the 40 per cent lowest expenditure per capita distribution. In this context, we assume that household expenditure will be a good proxy for household income. Regarding expenditure itself, it is the current household expenditure per capita of the student (total expenditure is divided by the number of household members regardless of the age of the members).

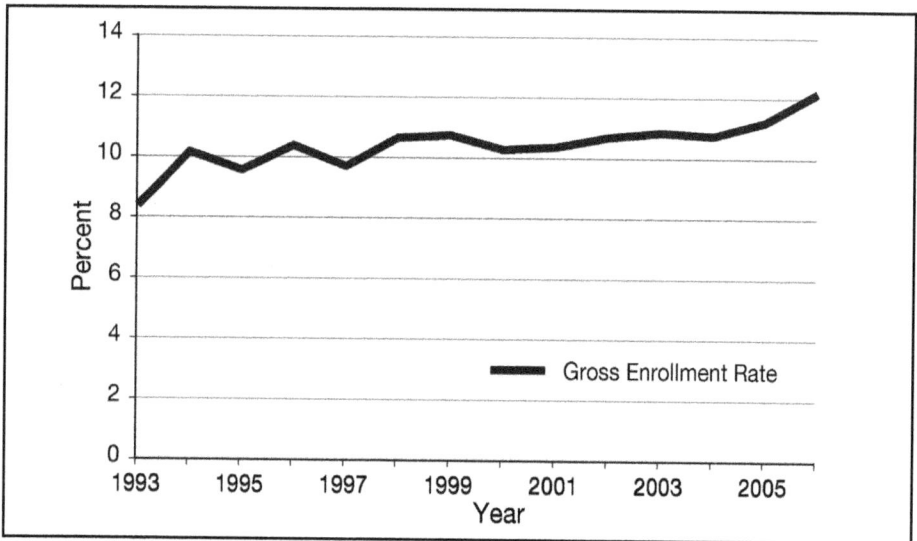

Figure 8.2 Gross enrolment rate in higher education

Source: National Socio-Economic Survey (Susenas) 1993–2006.

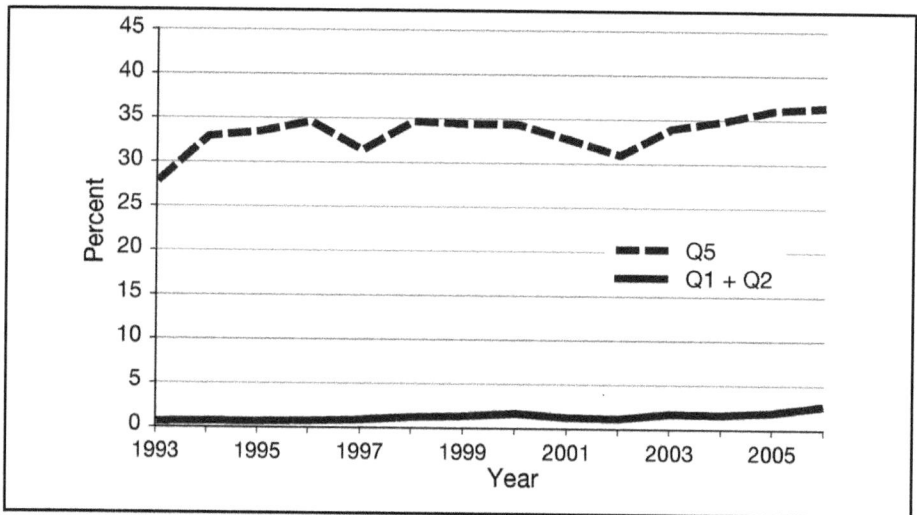

Figure 8.3 Gross enrolment rate in higher education by income group

Source: National Socio-Economic Survey (Susenas) 1993–2006.

We have found that the gender gap in tertiary education has tended to decline in recent years. The trend between 1993 and 2006 shows that the participation rate of females became closer to that of males at a relatively fast pace. In 1993, the female GER was 6.7 per cent and, by 2006, it reached 12.1 per cent—or, it increased proportionally by 81.17 per cent. Meanwhile, the male GER in the same period increased proportionally by only 18.9 per cent in 2006.

Interestingly, the gap between the sexes is relatively lower in the low-income group than in the high-income group. Figure 8.3 demonstrates that the average male enrolment rates from both the low-income and the high-income groups[3] are higher than the female enrolment rates. In terms of progress, however, female participation grew faster than male participation between 1993 and 2006. In 1993, the female GER from low-income families was very small: only 0.46 per cent. This was lower than the GER for males from the same family background, which was about 0.82 per cent. After a decade, female participation in this group had grown rapidly and, by 2006, there was a sixfold increase in the participation rate.

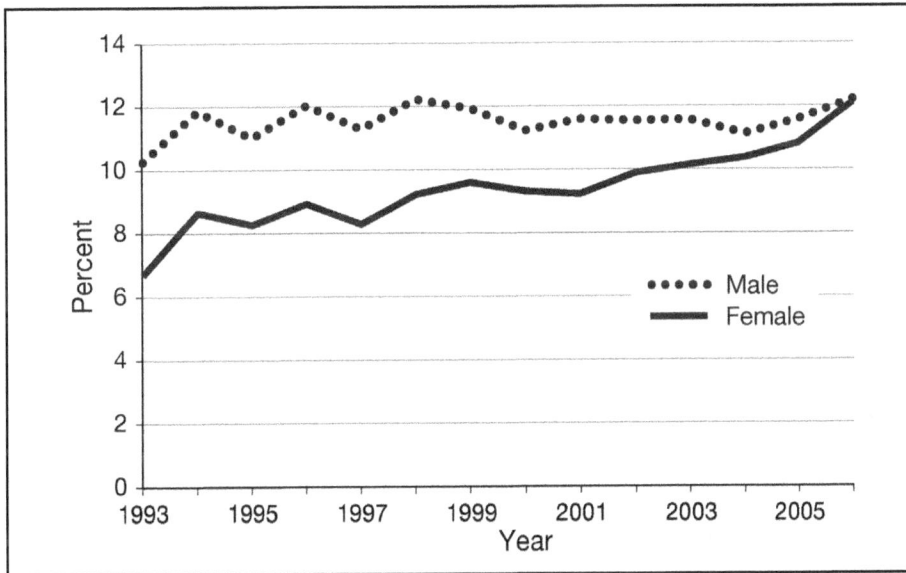

Figure 8.4 Gross enrolment rate in higher education by sex

Source: National Socio-Economic Survey (Susenas) 1993–2006.

Female students from a higher income group have also achieved rapid progress. Within more than a decade, the female GER from the high-income group increased, proportionally, by 49.3 per cent—from 22 per cent in 1993 to 32.8 per cent in 2006. Meanwhile, the male GER grew, proportionally, slower, with 16.6 per cent difference between 1993 and 2006. The relatively low gender gap in participation essentially supports studies arguing that parents rarely discriminate daughters over sons in getting an education, including at the tertiary level. In some cases, discrimination against women within the household can occur due to economic shocks (Oey-Gardiner 1997).

---

3   The low-income group is defined as the 40 per cent lowest expenditure per capita household; meanwhile, the high-income group is defined as the 20 per cent highest expenditure per capita household.

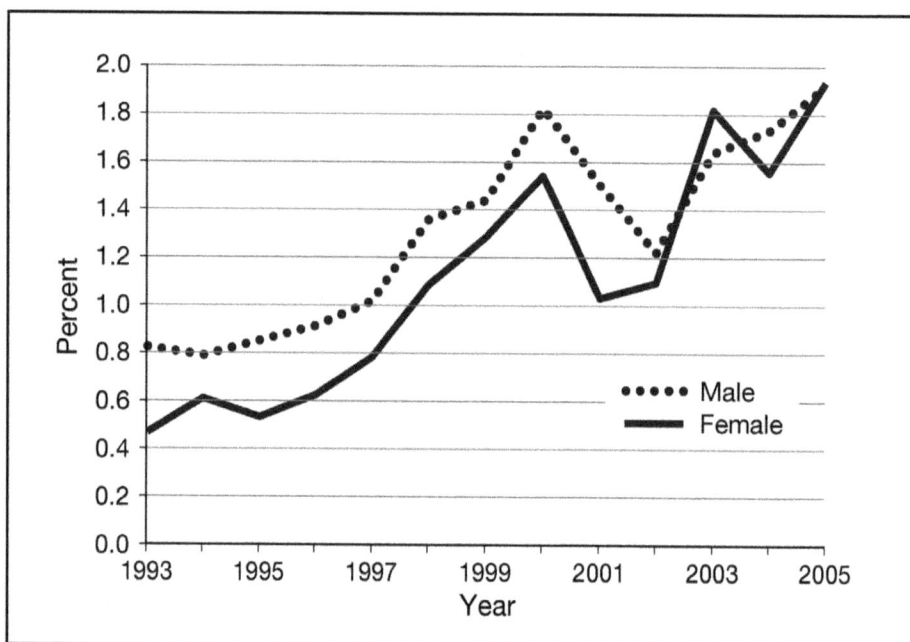

Figure 8.5 Gross enrolment rate: tertiary education of low-income students by sex

Source: National Socio-Economic Survey (Susenas) 1993–2006.

Some education observers argue that a low participation rate at the tertiary level is caused mainly by few HEIs relative to growing demand. Though this argument might sound reasonable, it must be taken with caution. Based on our findings, a low participation rate in higher education is not spurred by supply-side problems. A low participation rate in secondary education and a low continuation rate from secondary education to higher education are the main reasons for a low enrolment rate in tertiary-level education. This suggests that the policy to improve access to higher education cannot be separated from education policies aimed at other educational levels, particularly secondary education. Figure 8.7 shows that there was an upward trend in the GER of senior secondary education between 1993 and 2006. In addition, there was no significant gap in enrolment between males and females. Indeed, the female participation rate in secondary education tended to catch up with the male rate in recent years and this could explain the relatively swift increase of female participation in higher education.

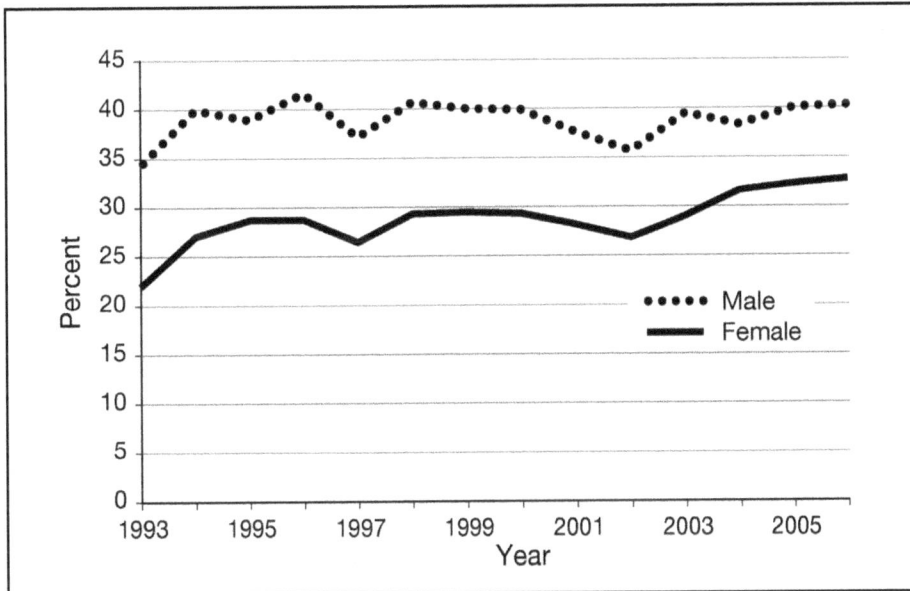

Figure 8.6 Gross enrolment rate: tertiary education of the 20 per cent richest students by sex

Source: National Socio-Economic Survey (Susenas) 1993–2006.

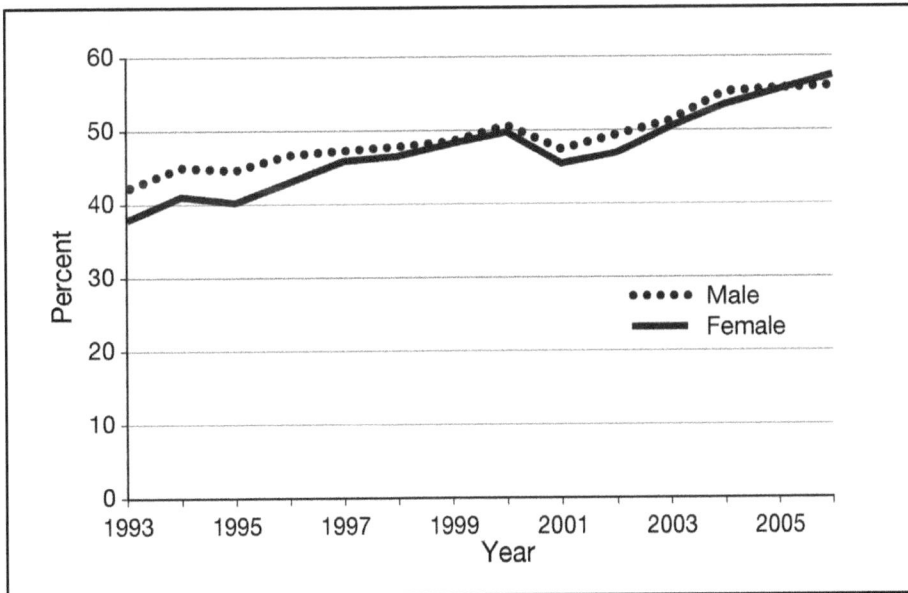

Figure 8.7 Gross enrolment rate in senior secondary education by gender

Source: National Socio-Economic Survey (Susenas) 1993–2006.

Accreditation, Quality Assurance and Research Capacity

The quality control of HEIs is run through an external and internal accreditation system in Indonesia. The internal accreditation system at some of the more established universities, such as the University of Indonesia and Gajah Mada University, was introduced in the late 1990s as part of a good-practice process within the universities. The quality assurance is run internally and aims to improve the quality of higher education services. Meanwhile, the external accreditation is carried out by the National Education Board for Higher Education (*Badan Akreditasi Nasional Perguruan Tinggi*; BAN-PT), which was establish in 1994 to conduct academic program assessments and evaluation for both public and private HEIs.

Mandated by the *National Education Act No. 2/1989* and *Government Regulation on Higher Education No. 60/1999*, the BAN-PT is the only accreditation body in Indonesia's higher education system and is based on Ministerial Decree 188/U/1998. The accreditation process was conducted for the first time in 1996, and all programs had to be accredited by BAN-PT by 2001.

The BAN-PT carries out several functions. The first is to monitor the quality and efficiency of HEIs through the accreditation process in all programs of every institution. The second is to ensure public confidence in the quality of higher education and to guarantee that the quality can be maintained and enhanced. The third is to give recommendations on how study programs can be improved. In order to carry out these functions, the BAN-PT conducts regular quality and efficiency assessment for all HEIs in Indonesia. The assessment covers many aspects: curriculum, the quality and quantity of lectures, student welfare, the institution's facilities and infrastructure, and the management administration. Through the accreditation process, undergraduate and diploma programs are categorised into four levels—from A (satisfactory) to D (unsatisfactory)—while postgraduate programs are categorised into three levels: U (excellent), B (good), and T (fair). Figure 8.8 describes the flow of the accreditation process carried out by BAN-PT.

According to BAN-PT's report, the quality of many HEIs is still poor. As reported by BAN-PT in 2002, of 6777 programs, 84 per cent were undergraduate programs, 85 per cent of which were categorised as B and C. About 15.73 per cent of public HEIs were accredited A, while only 5.26 per cent of private HEIs were accredited A. This result indicates that the public universities are considerably superior to private HEIs—further reflecting the role of public HEIs as quality leaders and private HEIs as expansion absorbers.

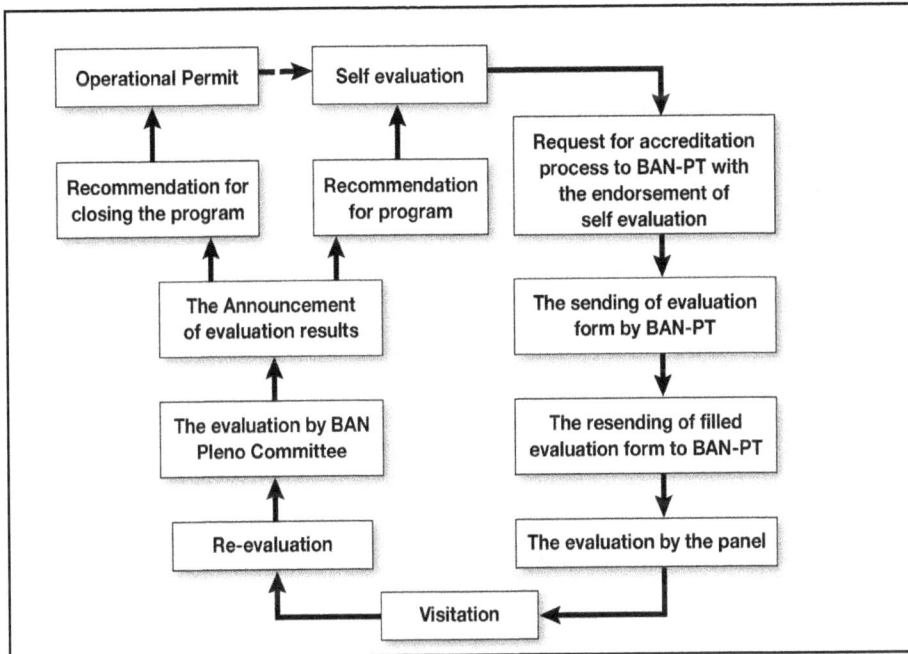

Figure 8.8 The flow of the accreditation process

Source: BAN-PT.

The low quality of HEIs in Indonesia is caused by the fact that the HEI system has grown so fast there has been no allowance for ensuring high standards for academic staff. As explained by Buchori and Malik (2004), many academic staff in Indonesia's public HEIs have not been well paid. This means that many faculty members at public HEIs dedicate their energy and time to off-campus work: managing or teaching at private HEIs. The conditions in the private HEIs are even worse, as there is a lower proportion of qualified and full-time staff.

In addition, the proportion of staff with higher degrees (Master's or PhD) varies significantly across the sectors. As explained by Nizam (2006), the extensive program of human resource development in the 1980s aimed to develop the research capacity of public universities. Prior to this, most university staff did not have the opportunity to be trained beyond undergraduate level. Mochtar and Buchori (2004) have illustrated that in public HEIs there is only 8.6 per cent of academic staff who hold a PhD and 29.2 per cent who possess a Master's-level qualification. These statistics are better for public HEIs than for private HEIs. In 2006, the World Bank showed that the difference was almost 300 per cent; only 11 per cent of academic staff in private HEIs were trained beyond their first degree, compared with 30 per cent in public HEIs. As argued by Welch (1997, 1998), this was due to few HEIs offering graduate programs and the fact of very low salaries in HEIs compared with other occupations where high-level degrees are needed.

Recently, the increased funding from the government for the development of human resources has directly generated an increased number of academic staff holding PhDs and Master's degrees. As shown in Figure 8.9, the number of PhDs and Master's from overseas and in-country universities increased in the past decade. During 1996–2000, for example, the number of PhDs and Master's from overseas increased by 32 per cent and 40 per cent, respectively, while the new in-country PhDs also grew significantly and even surpassed those from overseas in 1998. According to the 2000 *Directory of Doctors*—as seen in Table 8.1— about 75 per cent of registered PhDs worked in the four established public HEIs in Java (University of Indonesia, Institut Pertanian Bogor, Institut Teknologi Bandung and University of Gajah Mada). This shows a high disparity of staff qualification between universities on the most-populated island in Indonesia, Java, and outside Java. We need to also consider, however, that 74 per cent of total students in Indonesia are enrolled on Java.

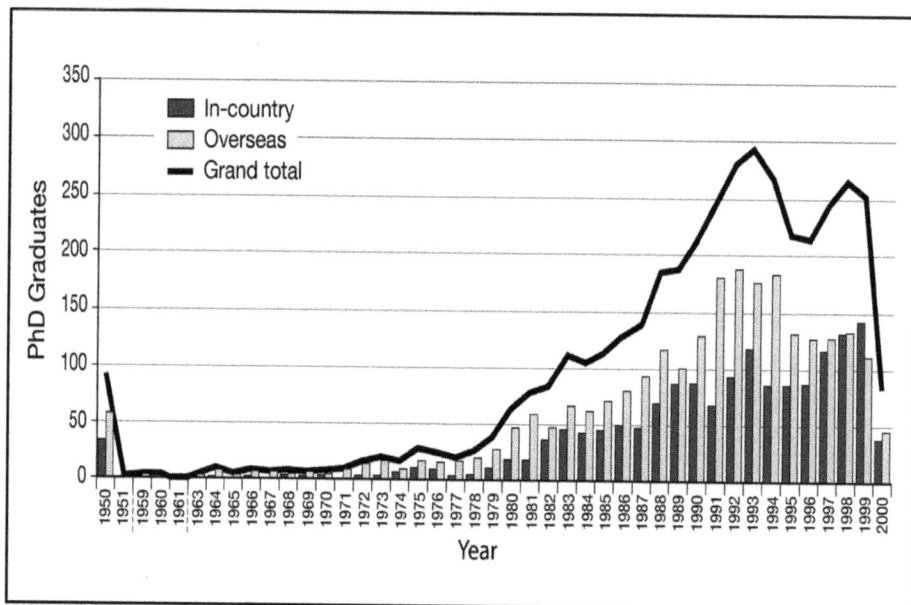

Figure 8.9 The number of new in-country and overseas PhD graduates

Sources: Nizam et al. (2003).

Table 8.1 Distribution of staff with PhDs, 2000

Location	Private	Public	Autonomous	Total
Java	333 (9%)	1054 (28%)	1420 (38%)	2807 (75%)
Outside Java	47 (1%)	891 (24%)		938 (25%)
Total	380 (10%)	1945 (52%)	1420 (38%)	3745 (100%)

Source: *Directory of Doctors*, 2000.

In addition to the poor quality of teaching staff, the HEIs lack a solid system to support high-quality study programs and research. The quality of Indonesian HEIs, particularly the private HEIs, is weakening due to low staff–student ratios. Welch (2006) shows that staff–student ratios deteriorated in the past few decades. The staff–student ratio decreased from 1:6.6 to 1:10.1 in 1980, to 1:12.4 in 1990, and to 1:13.7 in 1998. In the same vein, the quality of HEIs has been reduced due to low investment. Welch (2006) states that the levels of computer equipment and software are 'below the performance standard' for the number of students enrolled.

Trend and Composition of Public Expenditure on Education

Even though public expenditure on education (in terms of the absolute and the percentage of total national expenditure) increased in recent years, Indonesia's spending on education remains below 20 per cent of total national expenditure. The Constitution obliges the government to spend at least 20 per cent on education. Table 8.2 shows the national public expenditure during 2001–07. This table reveals that both the percentage of national education expenditure to GDP and the proportion of total education expenditure to total national expenditure remained low, despite recent improvements. In 2007, for example, the national education expenditure was only 3.8 per cent of GDP, while it accounted for about 17.2 per cent of total national expenditure.

Table 8.2 National public expenditure (central + province + district), 2001–07 (Rp trillion)

	2001	2002	2003	2004	2005	2006*	2007**
Nominal national education expenditure	40.5	48.2	64.8	61.8	74.0	118.2	135.4
National education expenditure (2001 prices)	40.5	43.1	54.3	48.8	52.9	74.9	80.7
Growth in real national education expenditure (%)	40.3	6.4	26.2	−10.2	8.4	41.6	7.8
Education expenditure (% total of national expenditure)	11.4	14.3	16.0	14.0	13.9	16.9	17.2
National education expenditure (% of GDP)	2.4	2.6	3.2	2.7	2.7	3.8	3.8
Total nominal national expenditure	353.6	337.6	405.4	441.8	531.7	698.2	785.4
Total real national expenditure (2001 prices)	353.6	301.8	340.0	348.9	380.0	442.4	468.3
Government size (total expenditure as % of GDP)	21.0	18.1	19.8	19.4	19.5	22.4	22.2

* preliminary realisation of APBN and estimates for sub-national spending

** central government budget (APBN) and estimates for sub-national government

Source: World Bank (2007).

Compared with its neighbouring countries, in Indonesia, total education expenditure is still relatively low. Table 8.3 illustrates public education expenditure in Indonesia and its neighbouring countries. This table shows how Indonesia's education expenditure is almost the same as other developing countries with a similar per capita income. The latest data from the World Bank's World Development Indicators (WDI) show that education expenditure as a percentage of total national expenditure in Indonesia, Malaysia and Thailand is 16.9 per cent, 27 per cent and 27 per cent, respectively.

Table 8.3 Education public expenditure in Indonesia and its neighbouring countries

	Highest		Lowest	
Education public expenditure as % of total expenditure	Malaysia 27.0	Thailand 27.0	Indonesia 16.9	Philippines 16.0
Education public expenditure as % of GDP	Malaysia 8.1	Thailand 4.6	Indonesia 3.8	Philippines 3.1
Total public expenditure as % of GDP (size of government sector)	Malaysia 29.7	Indonesia 22.4	Philippines 19.6	Thailand 16.8
GDP per capita (constant 2000 US$)	Malaysia 4290	Thailand 2356	Philippines 1085	Indonesia 906
Population	Indonesia 217.6	Philippines 81.6	Thailand 63.7	Malaysia 24.4
Percentage of population aged 0–14	Thailand 4.1	Indonesia 3.5	Malaysia 3.0	Philippines 2.8

Source: World Bank (2007).

In Indonesia, the allocation of money to public education has been dominated by the basic education level. A recent study by the World Bank demonstrates education spending per program and level of government (Figure 8.10). As shown in the diagram, tertiary education received less than 10 per cent of education spending, while primary education (preschool, primary school and junior secondary) and middle or secondary education obtained about 75 per cent and 15 per cent of the total education budget, respectively. In this respect, the government policy seems to focus on the provision of basic education for the masses.

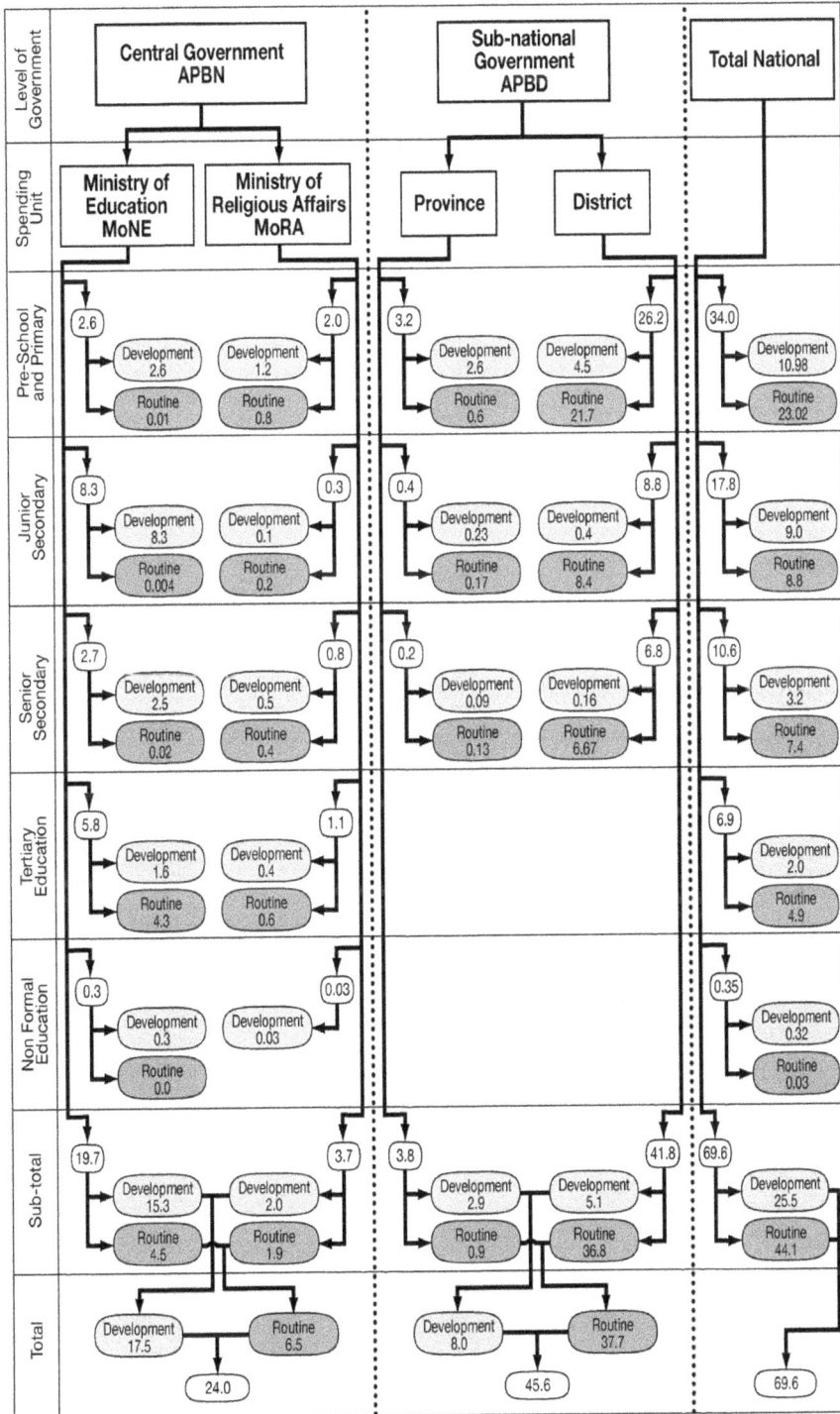

Figure 8.10 Education spending per program and level of government, 2004

Source: World Bank (2007).

Compared with other countries in the Asia-Pacific, in Indonesia, the resources allocated to tertiary education are roughly similar. Table 8.4 reveals the public expenditure on higher education of some countries in the Asia-Pacific. As seen in the table, although it is below Australia and United States, the proportion of expenditure for higher education in Indonesia is higher than in Japan, Republic of Korea, Mexico and India. Indonesia's public expenditure per pupil as a percentage of GDP per capita is, however, the second-lowest in the group.

Table 8.4 Public expenditure on higher education of some countries in the Asia-Pacific

	Australia	Indonesia	Japan	Malaysia	Korea	Mexico	United States	India
Public expenditure per pupil as % of GDP per capita	22.48	13.27	19.61	93.69	9.34	44.07	26.68	68.57
Education expenditure on tertiary education as % of total educational expenditure	23.92	23.16	16.80	34.99	13.60	16.86	26.25	20.09

Source: Fahmi (2007).

The largest part of the outlay of expenditure at the tertiary level goes to recurrent costs, such as salaries for academic and non-academic staff. Figure 8.11 illustrates the tertiary education expenditure by nature of spending during 2000–03. Based on this table, we can see that in that period, more than 80 per cent of tertiary education expenditure was spent for the current activities expenditure, while the remaining 20 per cent was used for capital expenditure. The capital expenditure consists of land acquisitions, university building development, and equipment purchases.

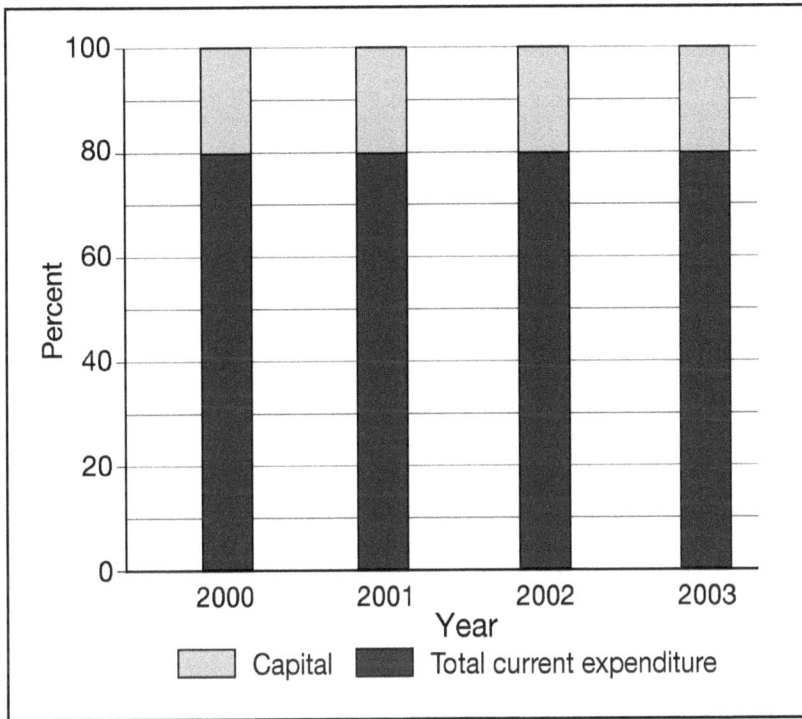

Figure 8.11 Tertiary education expenditure by nature of spending, 2000–03

Source: United Nations Educational, Scientific and Cultural Organisation.

Student Fees, Student Loans and Scholarships

Higher education expenses borne by parents and students vary greatly and depend on the degree taken, the study program, the status of the HEI and the location of the HEI. As a consequence of higher education reform, public HEIs may now set their own tuition fees, whereas they were previously set by the central government.

Table 8.5 illustrates the total higher education expenses borne by parents and students for undergraduate programs for the academic year 2004–05. The expenses for higher education cover not only tuition fees but also other items such as books, lodging, food, transportation and other personal expenses. In the academic year 2004–05, for example, the total cost carried by the parents and students of first degrees ranged from more than Rp6.8 million for the lower public HEIs to Rp20.8 million for the higher public HEIs, while it was about Rp31 million for private HEIs.

Table 8.5 Higher education expenses borne by parents and students for a first degree, academic year 2004–05 (rupiah converted to US$ by 2004 PPP estimate: $1 = Rp2255)

		Public		Private
		Low public	High public	High private
Instructional expenses	Special 'one-time' or 'up-front' fees			
	Tuition	Rp300 000 [$133]	Rp1 000 000 [$443]	Rp4 000 000 [$1773]
	Other fees			
	Books & other educational expenses	Rp900 000 [$400]	Rp1 350 000 [$598]	Rp2 250 000 [$997]
	Subtotal expenses of instruction	Rp1 200 000 [$532]	Rp2 350 000 [$1042]	Rp6 250 000 [$2770]
Student living expenses	Lodging	Rp900 000 [$400]	Rp9 000 000 [$3990]	Rp10 800 000 [$4790]
	Food	Rp3 600 000 [$1596]	Rp6 300 000 [$2 793]	Rp8 100 000 [$3592]
	Transportation	Rp315 000 [$140]	Rp450 000 $200]	Rp2 250 000 [$997]
	Other personal expenses	Rp800 000 [$354]	Rp2 700 000 [$1197]	Rp3 600 000 [$1,596]
	Subtotal expenses of student living	Rp5 615 000 [$2490]	Rp18 450 000 [$8180]	Rp24 750 000 [$10 975]
	Total cost to parent & student	Rp6 815 000 [$3022]	Rp20 800 000 [$9223]	Rp31 000 000 [$13 747]

Low public: low public tuition, living at home with parents.

High public: high public tuition, living as 'independent adult'.

High private: high private tuition, living in dormitory or shared apartment.

Source: Collected from web sites of Indonesian universities, 2005 (quoted from World Bank 2007).

This high level of expenses would have an adverse effect on students coming from a poor family background. To help disadvantaged students, the government works closely with HEIs to provide financial assistance schemes in the form of scholarships. Before the recent reform in higher education, scholarship programs allocated to students in private HEIs were relatively limited. Yet a recent policy change has increased the allocated funds for scholarships to private HEIs; however, students of public HEIs are still the larger beneficiaries. Based on our interview with a government official, about 25 per cent of the total government scholarship program is allocated to students at private HEIs. Instead of giving directly to private institutions, as the government does to public HEIs, the government allocates the funds to the *Koordinasi Perguruan Tinggi Swasta* (Kopertis; Coordination of Private Higher Education Institution), and the Kopertis authority then allocates the funds amongst its members. Kopertis itself is a network of private HEIs with only private HEIs as its members.

The government offers three types of scholarship: for student achievement in academic activities; a social safety net scholarship provided by compensation from the oil-subsidy reduction; and for student achievement in sport and cultural activities. In principle, all the scholarship schemes are targeted at disadvantaged students. The government has granted the universities a full set of criteria for recipient students and to manage the distribution of the funds. The amount of the scholarship itself is about Rp250 000 per month per student (US$25), which covers tuition fees and a living allowance, regardless of which HEI the student attends.

In addition, the universities cooperate with other institutions, such as private enterprises, foundations and alumni associations, to provide scholarships. Unlike scholarships from the government, scholarships from these other institutions vary regarding their schemes and criteria. These scholarship programs are given not only to disadvantaged students, but also to students who meet other criteria. Tanoto Foundation—which provides scholarships—targets its scholarships at intelligent students with potential leadership qualities but who face financial difficulties.

These scholarships are granted not only for undergraduates but also for graduate students. They cover tuition fees and an allowance. The scholarship may also be extended to research funding, though case-by-case criteria apply. For undergraduate students, the foundation granted Rp500 000 a month for a living allowance given directly to the individual student's bank account and up to Rp3 million a semester for tuition fees. About 300 undergraduate students and 50 graduate students have received scholarships from Tanoto Foundation. These students have been limited to only six public universities.

Parallel with scholarships, the government is now planning to create a student loan program and a voucher program for disadvantaged students that will cover their tuition costs. The Ministry of National Education introduced student loans in the early 1980s and what was called 'Kredit Mahasiswa Indonesia' (KMI; Indonesian Student Loan). The high default rate, however, made the student loan program unsustainable. According to our interview with several key people, the default rate reached 95 per cent. Unfortunately, there are no available data that can help evaluate this program. By the end of the 1980s, the government ended the student loan program.

The failure of the KMI was due to poor administration. Many recipient students did not repay their loan after finishing their studies. The banks giving the loan had poor administration, which failed to monitor and trace the graduates. The banks treated the student loans like grants since they thought it was part of the government's development program from the central bank, the Bank of Indonesia. This poor loan management was recorded as a non-performing loan and student loans have been perceived by the banking sector as a high-risk business. This has meant banks are reluctant to once again engage in this program.

By 2006, a private education foundation called Sampoerna Foundation redesigned the student loan program. In designing the program, the foundation cooperated with the International Finance Corporation (IFC) and Bank International Indonesia (BII) as creditors. The scheme essentially is a risk-sharing mechanism to leverage contributions from the foundation into a portfolio of student loans (IFC 2006). In this program, BII acts as an administrator of the program. According to an estimate, the total budget of the student loan program was almost US$20 million, with half of the fund supported by the IFC.

Based on our interview with a high-ranking manager of Sampoerna Foundation, the organisation previously focused only on the scholarship program, but it now designs the first private-supported student loan scheme. The decision to promote the student loan program was encouraged by the fact that many potential students who do not have long-term financial difficulties cannot go to college because of cash-flow problems. Their main financial problem usually is up-front fees, which are very large.

The loan is characterised as one without any collateral, although the student or their family members who act as guarantor are required to be 'bankable' (they must have a job and minimum earnings of Rp40 million a year). The loan cap provided by the foundation ranges from Rp10 million to Rp200 million, while the maximum loan that can be given is up to five times the student's or their family member's net income per month. The bank charges interest of 1.5 per cent a month, with a repayment period ranging from six months to three years.

This student loan program is different from a typical program in other countries, particularly regarding the payment method. The program is best described as a mortgage loan in which students, or the parents of the student, have to repay the loan every month after the first disbursement of the loan. Sampoerna Foundation helps students with short-term cash-flow problems.

Since the program's launch in 2007, the number of students receiving a loan is about 15, suggesting that the program covers very limited recipients. This limitation is due not only to the short period of program implementation, but also to the institutional or regulatory restrictions. From the institutional or regulatory aspect, banks still perceive student loans as very risky and there is no strong incentive given from the government or the central bank for banks to lend money to a student loan program.

Recent Major Policy: Higher education reform

Due to increasing globalisation and internationalisation pressures, the government has taken a number of measures in the past decades to improve the quality, efficiency and relevance of higher education in Indonesia. The first initiative started in 1994, when the government through the DGHE formed the Higher Education Strategy Task Force—assigned to develop a strategy for higher education in Indonesia for the next few decades. The task force introduced 'The New Paradigm' for higher education management based on quality, autonomy, accountability, accreditation and evaluation. This new paradigm has significantly altered the mode of individual HEI operation and the overall legal, regulatory and financial controls.

Structure and Institutional Reform

As part of the paradigm shift to strengthen institutional capacity at the centre as well as at individual universities, the DGHE established the Board of Higher Education (DPT), with three councils (education, research, and development) and the National Accreditation Board for Higher Education (BAN-PT). The DPT has responsibility to provide strategic recommendations and to act as the bridge between the DGHE and external funding bodies as well as between the DGHE and the universities that receive competitive grants. BAN-PT is mandated to independently arrange and conduct the accreditation of academic programs at private and public HEIs. BAN-PT aims to improve the transparency of the higher education system in Indonesia, to guide consumers, to guarantee accountability, and to strengthen incentives for individual universities to raise quality standards, efficiency and relevance. Based on the *National Education Act No. 2/1989* and *Government Regulation on Higher Education No. 60/1999*, BAN-PT is the only accreditation body in Indonesia's higher education system. BAN-PT, mandated by Ministerial Decree 188/U/1998, since 2001 has accredited all programs in HEIs, both public and private.

By 1999, the government also issued a new government regulation (PP 61/1999) that set out the mechanism to transform state/public HEIs into autonomous universities called 'State Legal Entity Universities' (*Universitas Badan Hukum Milik Negara*; BHMN). The government asked the four most established public HEIs (University of Indonesia, University of Gajah Mada, Institut Teknologi Bandung and Institut Pertanian Bogor) to pioneer the transformation. In December 2000—based on government regulations PP 152, 153, 154 and 155/2000—those four universities formally changed to become new public legal entity universities.

Since the transformation, the universities are no longer part of the government bureaucracy and, consequently, they are responsible more to the public rather than to the Ministry of National Education. Similar to reforms in Latin America, here, by creating a 'para-market relationship', the government provides the operational cost in the form of a block grant based on the performances of the HEIs. In addition, university management is structured more like a corporate system. In the university transition plans, all staff who used to be civil servants become university employees within 10 years. As argued by Susanto and Nizam (2004), however, the inadequate support for legal and financial measures has hindered the reform from effectively embedding into the entire system.

Competitive Funding Schemes

Along with the institutional and structural changes, the new paradigm has also changed financial aspects of HEIs. The new paradigm has given individual public HEIs the power and responsibility to work as if they were private-sector institutions. Individual public HEIs are required to conduct self-evaluation, prepare institutional development plans based on their own particular needs, and arrange budgets according to their projected resources and priority needs in order to receive investment funds from the central government. Supported by loans from the World Bank and the Asian Development Bank (ADB), the government also initiated several competitive funding schemes as a mechanism for allocating its funds to universities.

Before the government launched the new competitive fund scheme—which has opened opportunities for private HEIs to participate—there were large differences between the funding mechanisms of private and public HEIs. In the past, the government supported very limited funding for private institutions. The major cause of this is the very limited budget allocation from the state budget and the large publicly funded HEIs. Public HEIs have relied on their recurrent and development government budgets for their funding, while private HEIs relied on student fees and contributions from external sources. Bray and Thomas (1998) estimate that about 87.92 per cent of the government budget for higher education (about Rp1.3 billion) went to public HEIs in the period 1995–96. This allocation funded about 853 students enrolled in public HEIs. For the same period, only 3.8 per cent of funding from both the recurrent and the development budgets went to private HEIs, which enrolled 58 per cent of total students. The remainder of the allocation went to Islamic HEIs.

The competitive funding schemes were initially implemented by the introduction of the University Research for Graduate Education (URGE) project, in 1994. The project has, however, been limited to public HEIs. URGE was implemented through a competitive funding process to develop research capacity for the units conducting postgraduate programs.

In 1996, the DGHE introduced the first special competitive grants through the Development of Undergraduate Education (DUE) project, covering all disciplines, courses and study programs. This project aimed to advance the educational quality of undergraduate programs. It is targeted at 17 of the least-established public HEIs, which have not seen any major investment in the past five to 10 years. The funding for universities is granted on a competitive basis according to proposals from the universities. The funding was granted under a block-grant contract and the granted HEIs were required to match funds in the amount of 5 per cent of the total grant. The funds were distributed to a particular account of the institutions, in order to reduce the existing bureaucratic structures. Tadjudin (2007) explains that the evaluation of the DUE project was more complicated than those in the URGE projects since the evaluation of education projects involves more qualitative performance indicators compared with the evaluation of research projects. In addition, unlike in the evaluation of research projects, in education projects, there are many dimensions that need to be identified.

During 1998–2004, the DGHE introduced the second competitive funding program, called the Quality for Undergraduate Education (QUE) project—80 per cent of which was funded by a World Bank loan. Like the DUE project, this project aimed to enhance undergraduate education. Unlike the DUE project, however, which was open only to public HEIs, the QUE project was open to private HEIs as well. The QUE project was an open bidding process based on a proposal submitted by a study program, and the merit of the proposal was essential for success. The main performance indicators of this project covered the areas of leadership, relevance, academic atmosphere, institutional management, sustainability, efficiency and productivity (L-RAISE). Each grant was valued about US$1.8 million, which was provided for five-year institutional development programs. Nizam (2006) explains that the project was highly competitive and attracted many applicants, as illustrated in Table 8.6. Furthermore, he argues that this funding mechanism has been considered one of the most significant reforms in financing HEIs since it gives a sense of ownership and direct accountability to the recipient institutions.

Table 8.6 The Quality Undergraduate Education (QUE) funding project

	Pre-proposals submitted	Selected for full proposals	Selected for site visit	Funded
Batch 1 (1998)	317	45	25	16
Batch 2 (1999)	250	51	27	14
Batch 3 (2000)	249	61	26	16

Source: Nizam (2006).

Pursuing the success of the QUE project, the government adopted this model as a mechanism for transferring its funding to HEIs. As a consequence, the government has introduced several other competitive funding schemes, including the DUE-like project, the Semi-QUE project, and the Competitive Funding Program (PHK). These competitive funding schemes are directed towards achieving certain targets as measured by performance indicators that have been decided and made by the grantees. The DUE-like project was introduced in 1999. This project was analogous with the DUE project, except that the source of funding was government funds. In the same vein, the Semi-QUE project that was launched at the same time as the DUE-like project was financed wholly by government funds. This project was similar to the QUE project with more weight given to entrepreneurship development. Like the QUE project, here, the government used the L-RAISE criteria in selecting the proposal process for the funding. The PHK project was introduced in 2001, and was also funded by the government in order to continue the quality improvement of HEIs. The project was divided into four program categories: PHK-A1 focused on the advancement of management and organisational health for units involved in running educational programs; PHK-A2 emphasised the improvement of internal efficiency at the departmental level; PHK-A3 stressed the importance of enhancing a graduate's skills and competencies; and PHK-AB focused on the ability of departments to develop competitive programs.

In addition, the ADB adopted a similar competitive funding scheme in the region when it supported the Indonesian government to launch the Technological and Professional Skills Development Project (TPSDP) in 2001. This project used the same evaluation criteria as the QUE project, but with some additional criteria, including access and equity. This project aims mainly to improve the relevance of the learning outcomes and to advance the professionalism of graduates. The project was directed to both public and private institutions, except for autonomous universities. The loan from the ADB contributed about 80 per cent of funding, while the rest came from the government (12 per cent) and institutional matching funds from the HEIs (8 per cent).

The Reform and its Impact on Financing: HEI perspectives

The reform has brought significant changes in the financing mechanisms at the HEI level, particularly to public HEIs that relied a lot on government support. Recent findings show an adverse trend in which public HEIs are becoming more reliant upon student fees because of the reform. As a result, public universities have responded to the limited funds by offering professional and vocational programs. In these programs, they usually charge higher tuition fees compared with academic programs (Welch 2007). In the teaching activities, these institutions open less-demanding academic programs with high tuition fees, creating new professional and vocational programs. In non-teaching activities, they commercialise the institution's infrastructure. These institutions, as a result of reduced subsidies, have increased tuition fees and additional admission fees for regular academic students. For example, in the 1998–99 academic year, the tuition fee at the University of Indonesia—one of the HEIs involved in the project—was about Rp550 000. By the 2000–01 academic year, the tuition fee increased almost threefold for social sciences. An additional admission fee, even though voluntary, is asked for at the beginning of the academic year, particularly for medical and engineering schools.

The impact of the financing reform is now strongly felt by HEIs that have been involved in the pilot project of the reform. Those HEIs are the University of Indonesia (UI), Institut Pertanian Bogor (IPB), University of Gadjah Mada (UGM) and Institut Teknologi Bandung (ITB). After nearly a decade, these HEIs still seek the best formats and practices. Figure 8.12 illustrates significant changes in income sources for University of Indonesia—one of the most established public HEIs in Indonesia. There is a declining trend of government support for University of Indonesia. In 1994, income from the government accounted for about 81 per cent (28.5 per cent from the recurrent budget and 52.5 per cent from the development budget). In 1999, the trend was reversed: self-generated and external sources began to replace the government budget, which accounted for 46.7 per cent of total income. By 2006, income from the development budget shrank considerably—to only 2.7 per cent of the total; meanwhile, self-generated and external source contributions increased to 80.2 per cent .

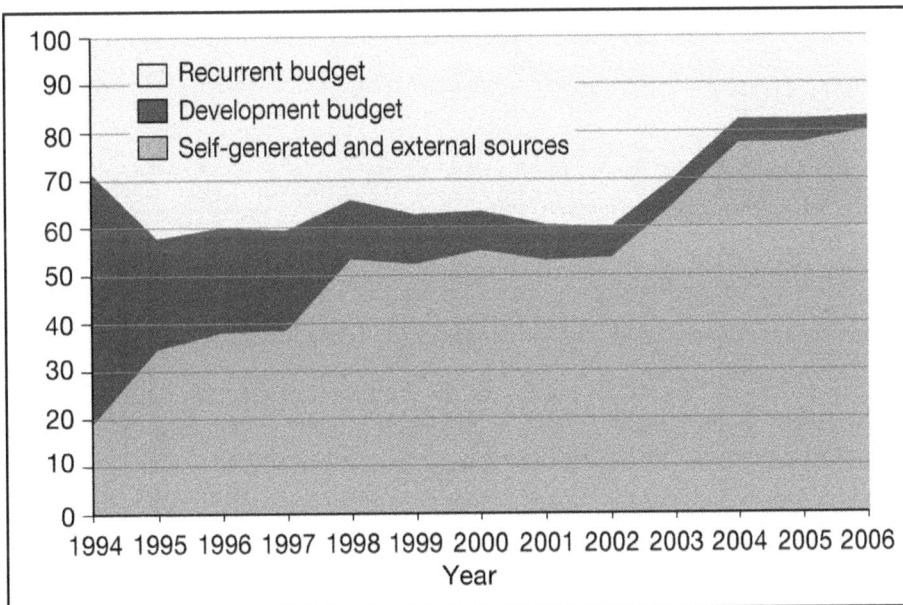

Figure 8.12 Composition of University of Indonesia's income sources

Source: Universitas Indonesia 2003, *UI dalam Angka.*

Conclusion

Indonesia's universities have a short history. During the past few decades, we have seen a rapid expansion of the higher education sector. This development has not, however, been followed by proper long-term planning, vision or good funding mechanisms. The universities have suffered internal inefficiency, poor initiatives (particularly in research) and lack of public accountability. Undoubtedly, these problems have had negative impacts on quality, efficiency and the relevance of higher education in Indonesia.

Facing these issues, the government, through the Directorate-General for Higher Education (DGHE), has undertaken major reform in order to improve the quality, efficiency and relevance of higher education in Indonesia. Some key points of the reform are the autonomy of university governance, its funding mechanism, the relationship between private and public HEIs, and the curriculum content that is set in line with the national development context. The reform has brought about considerable challenges for HEIs, particularly regarding financial matters, though it also offers opportunities in the context of independence and autonomy. After a decade, Indonesia's universities still seek the best format and practices so that they are best equipped to face the challenges of the future.

References

Bray, M. and Thomas, R. M. (eds) 1998, *Financing of Education in Indonesia*, Asian Development Bank, Manila.

Buchori, M. and Malik, A. 2004, 'Higher education in Indonesia', in P. Altbach and T. Umakoshi (eds), *Asian Universities. Historical perspectives and contemporary challenges*, The Johns Hopkins Press, Baltimore, pp. 249–78.

Davies, J. 2002, Empirical evidence on human capital externalities, RBC Financial Group Economic Policy Research Institute Working Papers No. 20035, University of Western Ontario, London, Ontario.

Directorate-General of Higher Education (DGHE) 2003, *Basic framework for higher education development KPPTJP IV (2003–2010)*, Technical Report, Directorate-General of Higher Education, Ministry of National Education, Jakarta.

Fahmi, M. 2007, *Indonesian higher education: the chronicle, recent development and the new legal entity universities*, Working Paper in Economics and Development Studies No. 200710, October, Department of Economics, Padjadjaran University, Bandung, Indonesia.

International Finance Corporation (IFC) 2006, *Sampoerna Student Financing Facility: Summary of proposed investment*, International Finance Corporation, Washington, DC, viewed 9 June 2008, <http://www.ifc.org/ifcext/spiwebsite1.nsf/2bc34f011b50ff6e85256a550073ff1c/bfa7100ccf2cdb6f8525719c0055cfeb?opendocument>

Moeliodihardjo, et al. 2000, Higher education strategy: implementation of the new paradigm, Background paper for university autonomy.

Moretti, E. 1998, *Social return to education and human capital externalities: evidence from cities*, Institute for Research on Labor and Employment Working Papers, University of California, Berkeley.

Nizam 2006, 'Indonesia: the need for higher education reform', in *Higher Education in South-East Asia*, UNESCO Asia and Pacific Regional Bureau for Education, Bangkok, pp. 35–68.

Purwadi, A. 2001, 'Impact of economic crisis on higher education in Indonesia', in N. V. Varghese (ed.), *Impact of the Economic Crisis on Higher Education in East Asia: Countries' experiences*, IIEP/UNESCO, Paris, pp. 61–75.

Triaswati, N. and Roeslan, F. 2003, *Senior Secondary Education and Access to Higher Education*, Higher Education Sector Study, Japan Bank for International Cooperation/Directorate-General of Higher Education, Jakarta.

Universitas Indonesia 2003, *UI dalam Angka*.

Welch, A. R. 2006, 'Blurred vision?: public and private higher education in Indonesia', *Springler Science + Business Media B.V.*, July.

9. Strategies for Financing Higher Education: The case of Thailand

Somkiat Tangkitvanich and Areeya Manasboonphempool
Thailand Development Research Institute

Introduction

Ninety years ago, the first university was established in Thailand. It was an elite approach to higher education with the main purpose being to train government officials to run the country (Krongkaew 2004). Since then, the Thai higher education sector has experienced remarkable development. Most notably, the number of higher educational institutions (HEIs) has increased to nearly 800, with the total number of students enrolled reaching 2.5 million. Thus, the Thai higher education sector has changed from elitist to a mass economic and social institution.

The purpose of this chapter is to discuss the main characteristics of the higher education sector in Thailand and review major policy developments with a special focus on how the country's higher education financing system has changed during the past decade. In particular, the chapter will discuss the role of student loan arrangements in funding higher education and assess its effectiveness.

We discuss the major developments of the Thai higher education sector during the past decade before exploring the role of the government in financing higher education and its effects on the efficiency and equity of the system. We then describe the Student Loans Fund (SLF)—the most important student loan scheme in Thailand—and provide an empirical assessment of its impacts. Finally, we summarise the main findings of the chapter and provide some policy recommendations.

Overview of the Thai higher education sector

Some key features of the Thai higher education system should be noted at the outset. First, even among East Asian countries that are well known for their emphasis on education, Thailand has a relatively high rate of participation in higher education. With 41 per cent of the gross enrolment ratio, the country ranks second only to Japan and higher than Malaysia and Hong Kong—both of which have higher income per capita (see Figure 9.1).

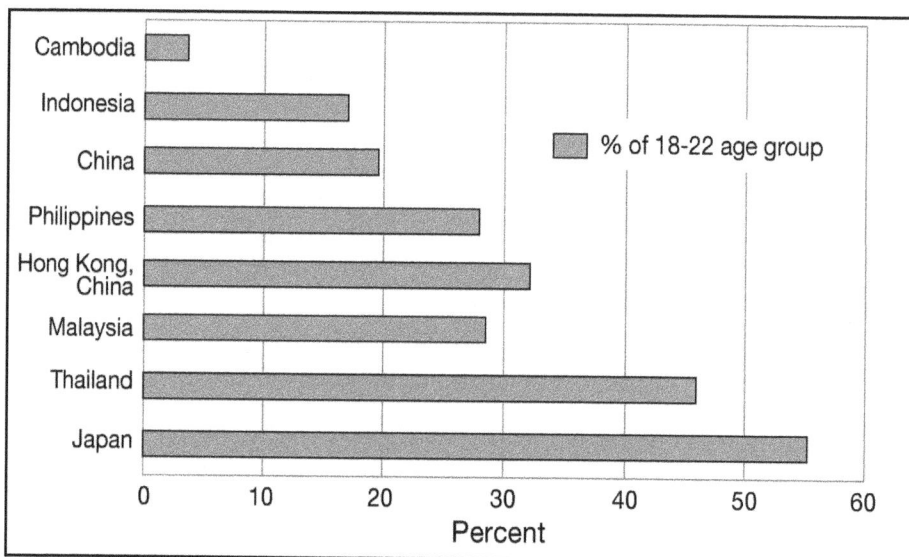

Figure 9.1 Gross enrolment ratios in higher education of selected East Asian countries, 2004

Source: *Edstats*, The World Bank.

This high level of enrolment is the result of rapid expansion of the sector in the past decade. As shown in Figure 9.2, the enrolment ratio has nearly doubled—from 22 per cent in 1996 to 43 per cent in 2005. As we will argue later, changes in the supply side are the main driving forces of the expansion.

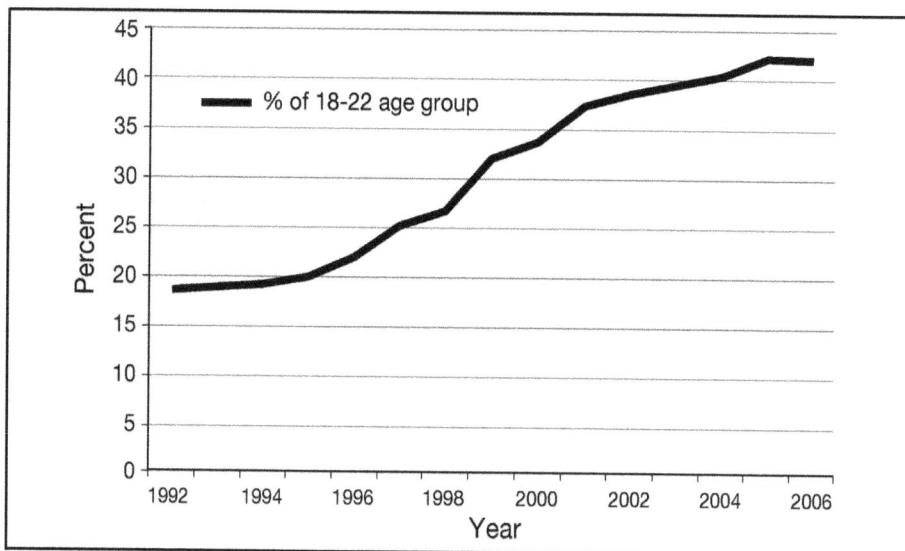

Figure 9.2 Changes in the gross enrolment ratio of higher education in Thailand, 1992–2006

Source: *Edstats*, The World Bank.

Another key feature of the Thai higher education system is that the public sector plays a very dominant role in education provision—with more than four-fifths of the total number of students enrolling in public institutions (see Figure 9.3). Institutions in the public sector are classified administratively into: 1) universities with limited admission; 2) open universities; 3) autonomous universities; 4) Rajabhat universities (former teachers' colleges); 5) Rajamangala universities of technology (former vocational colleges); and 6) public vocational colleges. These public higher educational institutions receive most of their funding from the government and a much smaller portion from tuition fees and other sources.

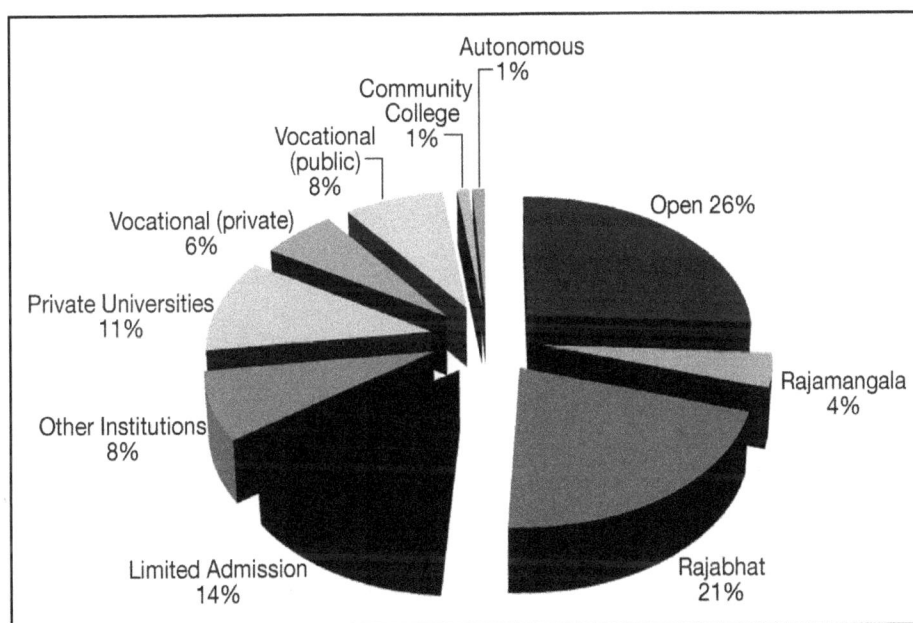

Figure 9.3 Student shares by types of education institution, academic year 2006

Source: Education statistics, Ministry of Education.

During the past three decades, continued efforts have been made to transform major limited-admission public universities into autonomous ones. The purpose of such attempts is to provide administrative flexibility to these universities, aiming to enhance their quality to an international level (Kirtikara 2004). So far, however, only seven public universities have been successfully transformed and a few more are in the pipeline.

Due to the domination of the public sector, private educational institutions play a relatively minor role in education provision. These institutions consist of private Thai universities, vocational colleges and international institutions.

International institutions are still marginal players, with a share of only 0.05 per cent of the total students due to a number of reasons, including the legal restrictions on foreign ownership of educational institutions.

The increase in enrolment during the past decade was driven mainly by the rapid expansion in the production capacities of many limited-admission and Rajabhat universities through the opening of 'special programs'. As these programs may charge high tuition fees, they are easy solutions to lecturers' calls for higher compensation[1] and the universities' needs to diversify their income sources away from the government budget to prepare for the transformation towards autonomous universities. In addition, two new limited-admission universities were also established. The expansion of the Rajabhat universities and limited-admission public universities has come at the cost of the open universities, while the number of students enrolling in private institutions in absolute term remains virtually unchanged (see Figure 9.4). In relative terms, however, the student share of private institutions has decreased from 24 per cent in 1996 to 17 per cent in 2006 (Figure 9.5).

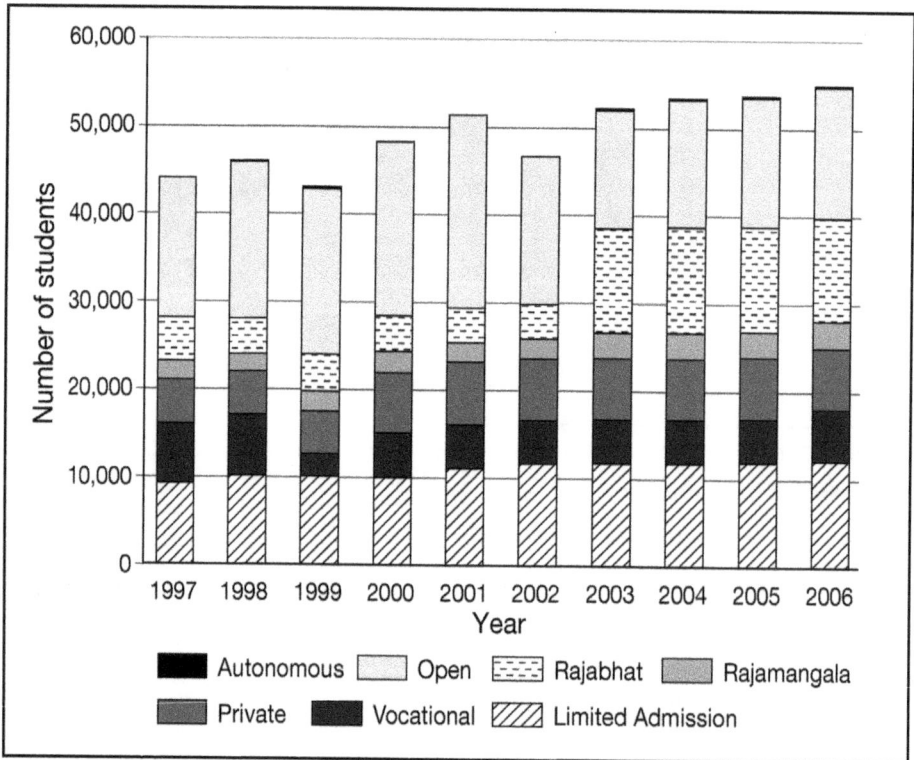

Figure 9.4 New students classified by type of institution, 1997–2006

Source: Education statistics, Ministry of Education.

---

1 According to our interviews with public university instructors, a lecturer who teaches a special program can earn 90 000 baht (US$2500) a month, which is more than four times his or her monthly salary.

To understand the sources of growth in enrolment from the demand side, we classify new higher education students into the group of new high-school graduates (that is, those just graduated from high school in the previous academic year) and the rest (that is, adult students and graduates from the non-formal education system). The analysis shows that while new high-school graduates remain the majority by a large margin, there has been a recent increase in the participation of adult students and those graduated from the non-formal system (Figure 9.6). Most of these students enrol in Rajabhat universities or special programs provided by limited-admission universities (Figure 9.7).

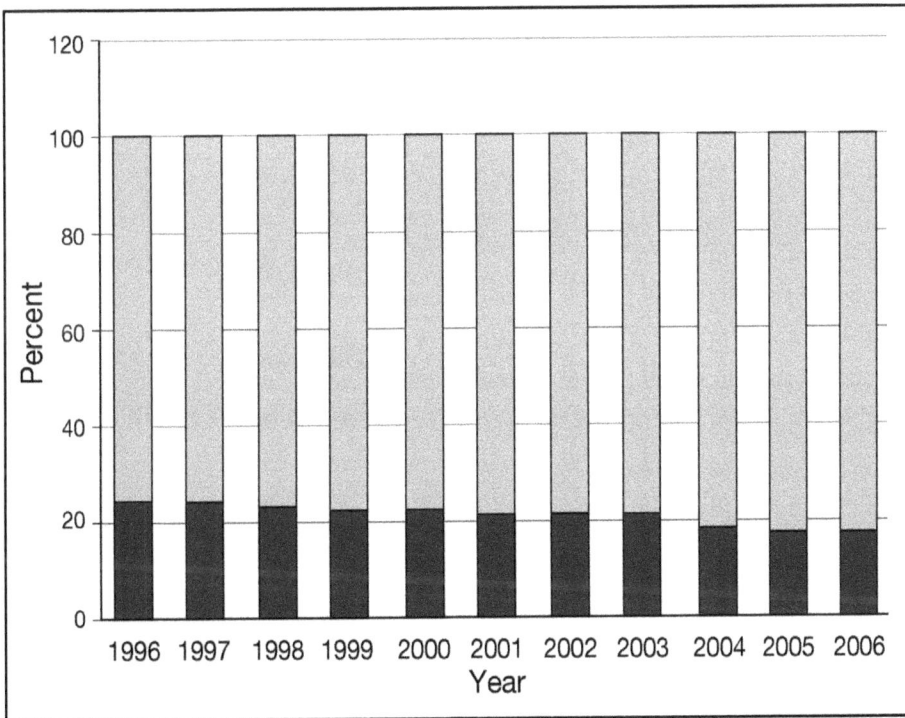

Figure 9.5 Changes in student shares of public and private institutions, 1996–2006

Source: Education statistics, Ministry of Education.

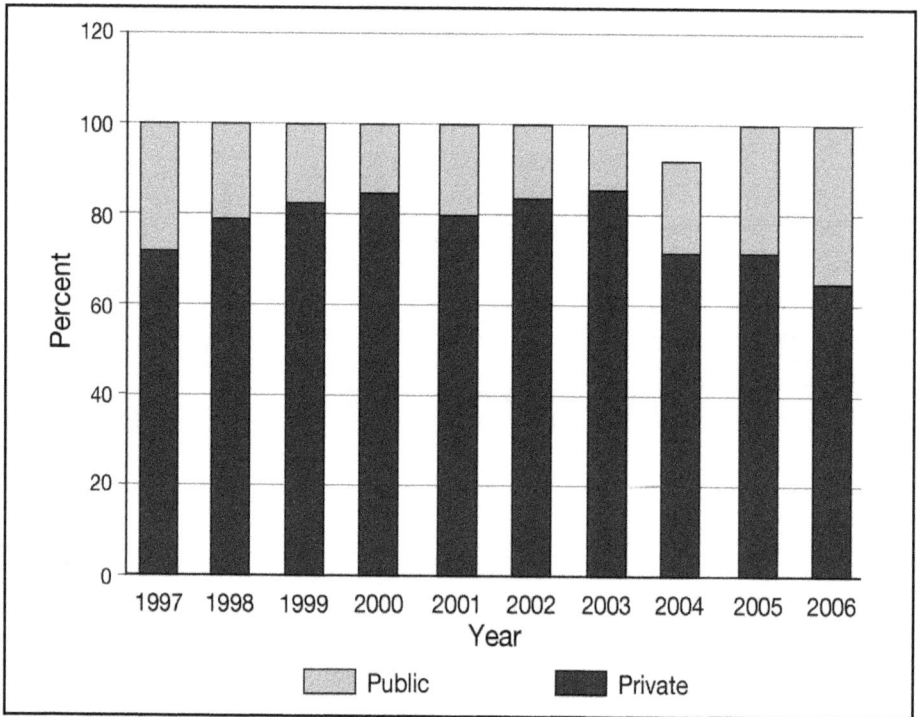

Figure 9.6 Composition of new enrolment in higher education, 1997–2006

Source: Education statistics, Ministry of Education.

There are at least two reasons for the dominant role of the public universities. First, many public universities were established decades before the private ones and thus are much better known. Second, due to their limited admission policy and the competitive entrance examinations, public universities can attract the best and brightest high-school graduates, which in turn reinforces their prestige. Finally, public universities have long been heavily subsidised by the government and thus can charge lower tuition fees—about half or even one-fourth of the fees charged by private institutions (see Table 9.1)—making them much more attractive from the students' perspective.

Another consequence of the rapid expansion of the Thai higher education sector is that the share of social science and humanity students has continued to increase from an already high level, reaching 73 per cent of the total number of students in 2007 (Figure 9.8). This is because the investment cost for training social science and humanity students is much less than that for physical and medical science students.[2]

---

2   To put this into perspective, the proportion of social science and humanity students in Thailand is slightly larger than that of the Organisation for Economic Cooperation and Development (OECD) average, which is about 68.5 and 53 per cent for female and male graduates, respectively.

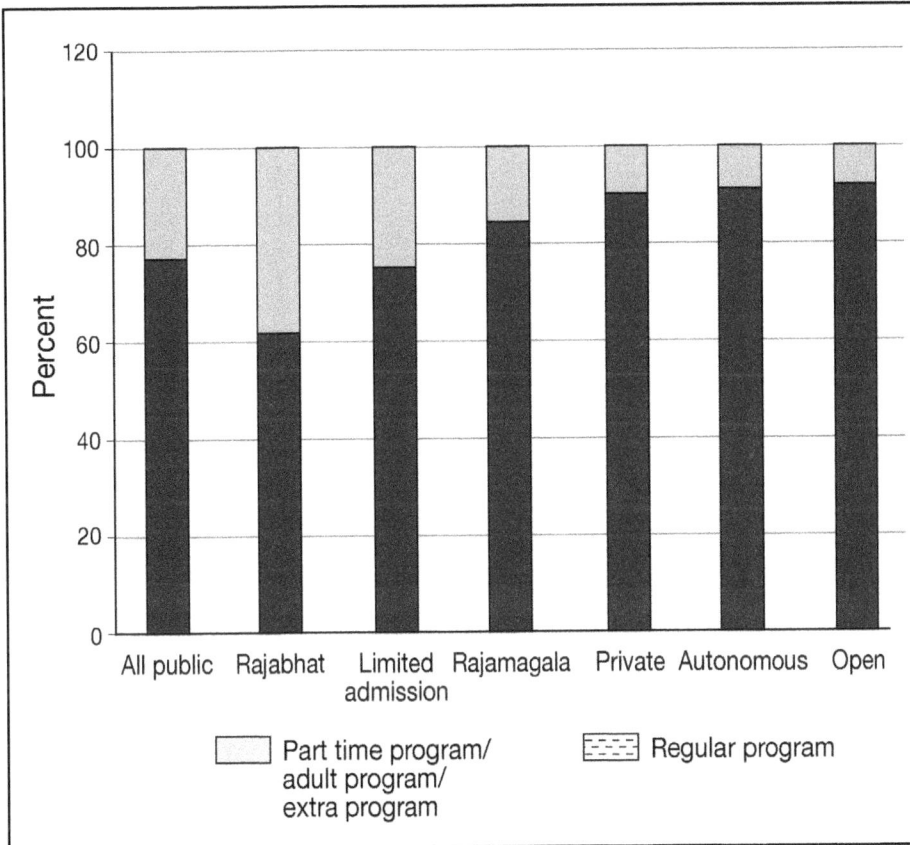

Figure 9.7 New enrolments by type of study program, 2007

Source: Education statistics, Ministry of Education.

Table 9.1 Tuition fees for bachelor degree (US$)

Types of institution	Courses	Tuition fee (per annum)		
		Minimum	Maximum	Median
Public institution				
Limited-admission university	Science and Technology	147	1224	387
	Health Sciences	144	723	395
	Social Sciences	152	578	291
Autonomous university	Science and Technology	546	1343	673
	Health Sciences	701	728	710
	Social Sciences	546	658	651
Open university	Science and Technology	47	994	99
	Health Sciences	93	106	99
	Social Sciences	46	96	82
Private institution				
Private university	Science and Technology	731	2571	1684
	Health Sciences	1302	4583	1766
	Social Science	568	1907	1072
Private college	Science and Technology	1079	2028	1376
	Health Sciences	1398	1979	1580
	Social Sciences	523	1547	972

Note: Tuition fees are converted from Thai baht to US dollars using the 2003 exchange rate (US$1 = B41.5).

Source: Weesakul et al. (2003).

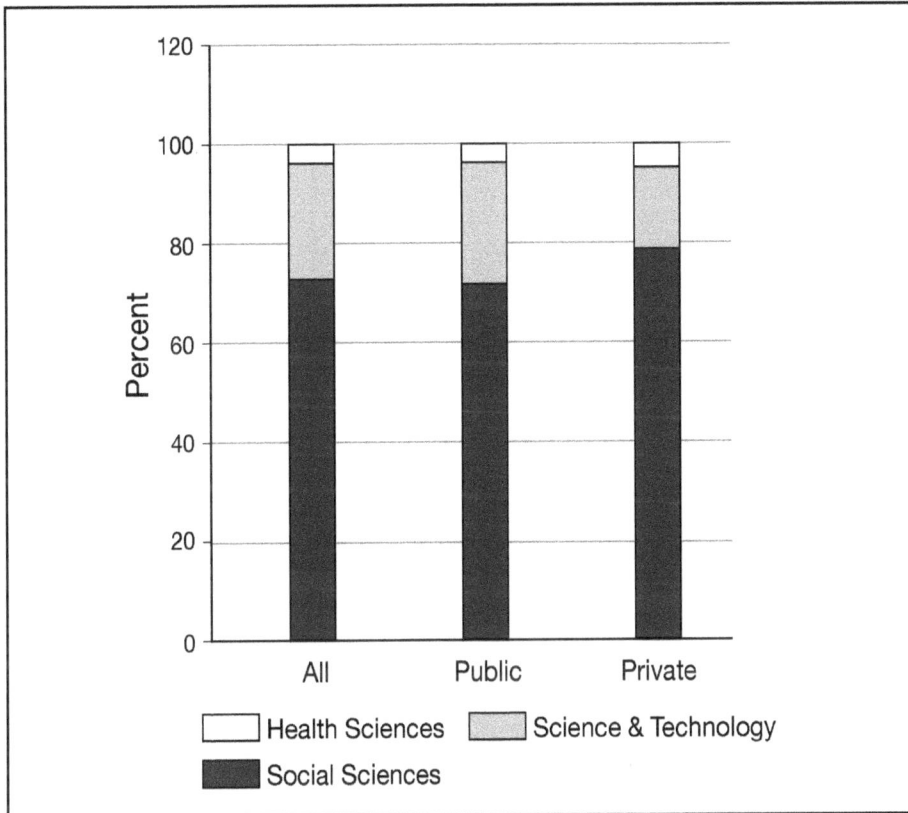

Figure 9.8 Total enrolments by field of education, 2007

Source: Education statistics, Ministry of Education.

Problems of the Current Education Financing System

Participating in higher education is a form of investment that can generate high returns. Using the Labor Force Survey data for 2001–03, Punyasavatsut et al. (2005) estimated that the rates of return on higher education were significantly higher than those for secondary education (Table 9.2).

Table 9.2 Estimates of rates of return on education (per cent)

Educational level	2001		2002		2003	
	Female	Male	Female	Male	Female	Male
Secondary school (academic)	14.74	20.80	14.22	19.14	15.81	18.72
Secondary school (vocational)	9.95	11.31	5.55	10.74	7.96	8.82
University, compared with secondary school level (academic)	16.34	20.40	17.77	20.25	17.51	19.94
University, compared with secondary school level (vocational)	13.51	15.67	13.21	16.05	13.58	15.06

Source: Punyasavatsut et al. (2005).

Due to imperfections in the capital market, however, not all high-school graduates can participate in higher education, especially those from low-income families. Using the 2002 Child and Youth Survey data, we found that high-school graduates who indicated that they would not enrol in higher education were mostly from low-income families. Two major reasons cited by them were the lack of financial resources and the need to earn a living (Table 9.3)—both of which reflect their financial constraints.

Table 9.3 Reasons cited for not enrolling in higher education

Reasons	Percentage
Lack of financial resources	71
Have to earn one's living/household's living	16
Have enough skill/knowledge for one's career	8
Sick/disability	1
Other	4

Source: Authors' calculations from the Child and Youth Survey, 2002.

The inability of low-income families to finance investment in higher education has implications for economic efficiency in that the investment in higher education is below an optimal level. It also has equity impacts in that low-income families are under-represented in higher education. As a result, government intervention is often required to correct this market failure. In the case of Thailand, the government intervenes in the higher education market by subsidisation of public educational institutions and student loans.[3]

---

3 There are also the grants in the form of scholarships to students, but their size has been marginal compared with the sizes of loans and subsidies.

Public funds account for nearly 80 per cent of the total funds for education in Thailand. In fact, education expenditures have been the largest component of the government's budget, ranging from 20 to 26 per cent of the total budget, or between 3.6 and 4.5 per cent of GDP (Punyasavatsut et al. 2005). Higher education expenditure ranges from 3.1 to 4.3 per cent of the total education budget, and 0.7 per cent of GDP, and has been relatively constant in the past decade (see Figure 9.9).

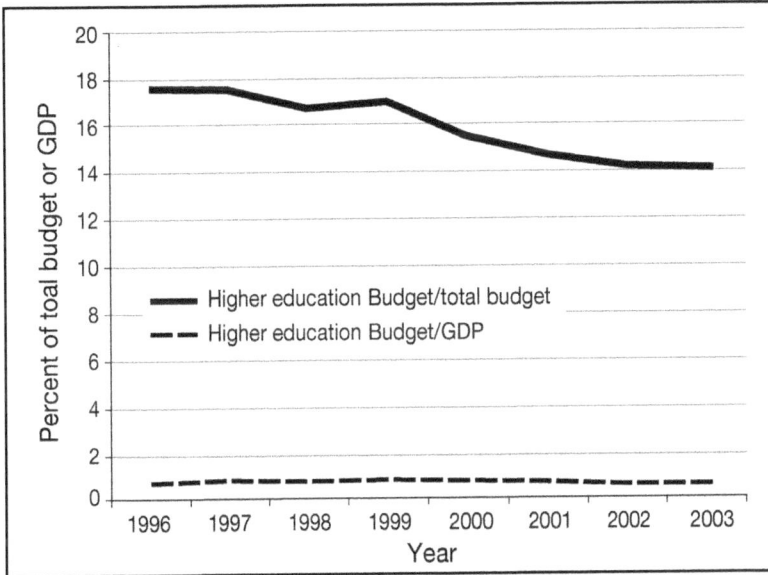

Figure 9.9 Public expenditure on higher education, 1996–2007

Source: *Budget in Brief* (calculated from nominal values).

Although a significant amount of public money has been allocated to the higher education sector, the sector's finances still suffer from a number of problems. First, it is mainly a supply-side financing system that cannot flexibly respond to the changes in students' needs. This is because most of the resources are channelled to producers of educational services—that is, universities and other higher educational institutions. A breakdown of government expenditure in Figure 9.10 shows that approximately 80 per cent of public expenditure goes to higher educational institutions, while the rest is used for student loans.

Second, the rapid growth in participation in higher education has exerted a lot of pressure on the current education financing system. In particular, the growth of budgets for education expenditure has not kept pace with the growth in the number of students enrolled (Figure 9.11). As a result, public expenditure on education per student has experienced a long-term downward trend (Figure 9.12). Since education investment has an impact on education quality, there is a risk of deterioration in quality unless there are other financial resources that grow sufficiently quickly.

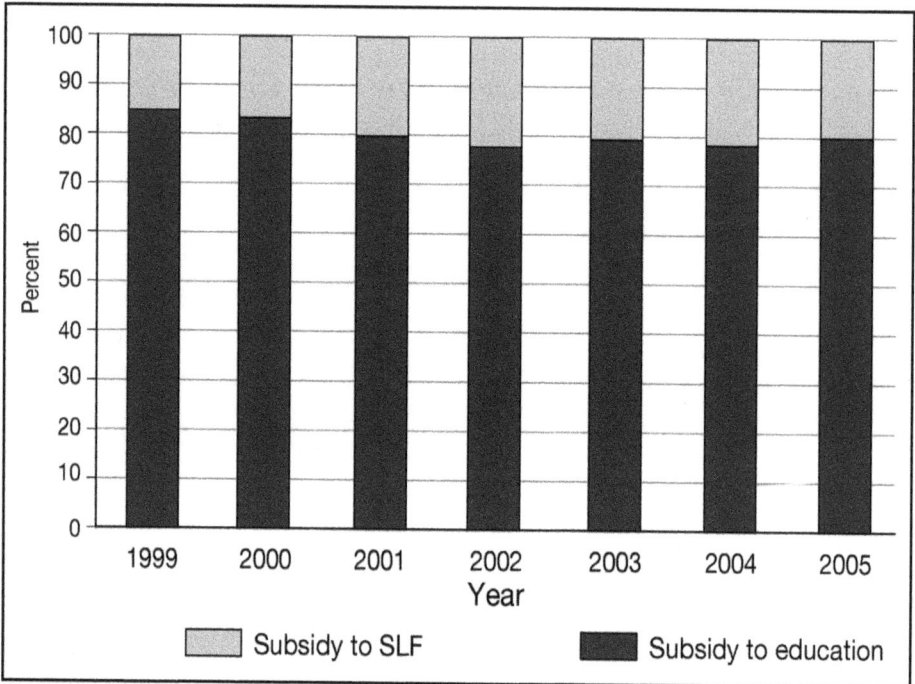

Figure 9.10 Composition of government support to higher education, 1999–2005

Source: Commission on Higher Education and Office of the Student Loans Fund.

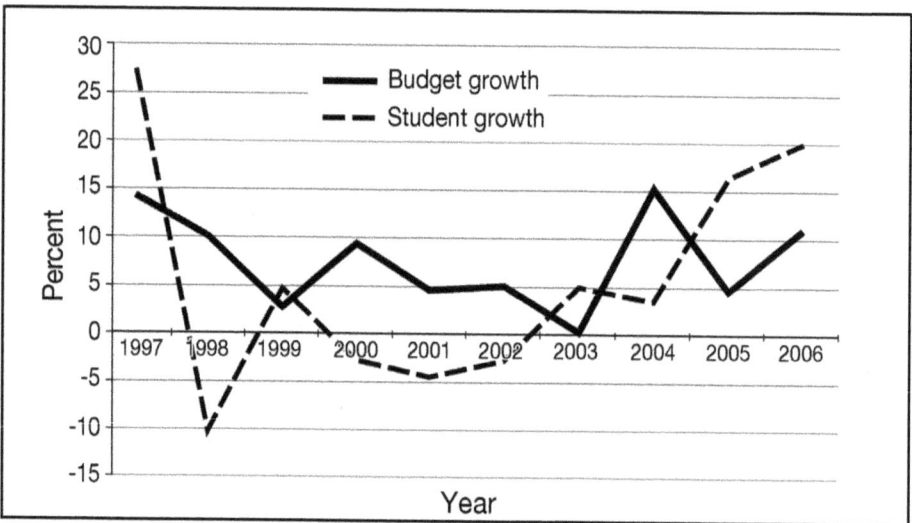

Figure 9.11 Growth rates of students and budget, 1997–2006

Source: *Budget in Brief* and Ministry of Education statistics (calculated from nominal values).

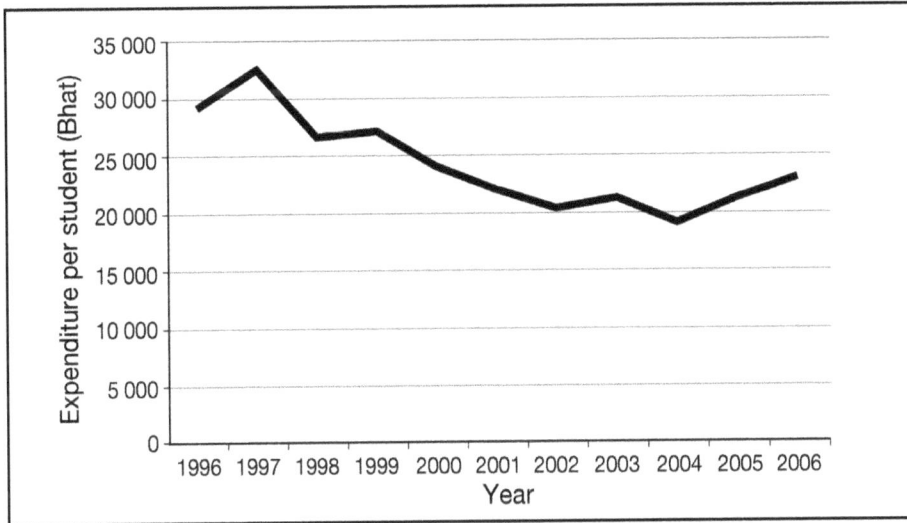

Figure 9.12 Public expenditure per student, 1996–2006 (baht p.a.)

Source: *Budget in Brief* and Ministry of Education statistics.

Third, enrolment in public HEIs is highly subsidised by the government—as a result of tuition fees that are set far below the actual costs. A study by King Mongkut's University of Technology Thonburi (KMITT 2005) found that, on average, a social science student is subsidised by 57 per cent of the operating cost while a public-health student is subsidised by 77 per cent (see Table 9.4). Since the poor are generally under-represented in higher education, subsidisation of higher education in this way is likely to be regressive. Based on a benefit-incidence analysis, we found that subsidy per capita actually grows with household income (Table 9.5).

Thus, there has been an urgent need to reform the Thai financing system for higher education. Experiences in other countries have shown that a properly designed student loan can provide a solution to the aforementioned problems.

Table 9.4 Public subsidy as a percentage of the total operating cost of educating a student

Field of education	Mean	Maximum	Minimum
Public health	77	93	29
Agriculture	76	94	56
Fine arts/architecture	69	94	24
Engineering/science	67	93	29
Medical sciences	63	91	28
Social sciences/arts	57	89	17

Source: KMUTT (2005).

Table 9.5 Benefit incidence of public education spending by income group, 2006

Decile	Per capita subsidy (baht)		
	All levels	Primary and secondary education	Higher education
1 (poorest)	11 188	11 148	40
2	14 860	14 687	173
3	15 751	15 428	323
4	17 744	17 277	467
5	18 891	18 128	763
6	20 725	19 541	1184
7	21 974	20 145	1829
8	23 173	20 436	2738
9	25 616	21 380	4237
10 (richest)	28 959	22 009	6950
Total	**19 889**	**18 018**	**1871**

Source: Authors' calculations from Socio-Economic Survey and the Bureau of the Budget.

Student loans Scheme in Thailand

In addition to the direct provision of higher education by public institutions, the Thai government has also provided loans to students since 1996. This section will discuss the Student Loans Fund (SLF)—so far the most important student loan scheme in Thailand—analyse its effectiveness and assess its financial sustainability.

Settings of the Student Loans Fund

The main objective of the SLF is to increase the opportunities for students from low-income families to continue their study. Other objectives are to promote a more equal income distribution in the long run and to develop a demand-side financing system by increasing the capacity of households to contribute more resources to education. The SLF loans cover tuition fees, educational-related expenses and other living expenses. Only high-school or tertiary-level students whose families' incomes are less than B150 000 per annum are eligible to apply for the loan. During the first 10 years of its operation, the SLF has lent to more than 2.6 million students, with the loan value totalling nearly B200 billion.

Organisational Structure of the SLF

Figure 9.13 shows the administrative structure of the SLF. At the top of the structure is the SLF Board, chaired by the Permanent Secretary of the Ministry of Finance. The board has the authority to set student loan policies and related regulations, and to decide the amount of budgets and administrative costs to allocate to related agencies. The SLF budget for loans is then divided into two portions: one for upper secondary level (high school and vocational school), which is supervised by the Sub-Committee on the First Expense Account; another for undergraduate level, which is supervised by the Sub-Committee on the Second Expense Account. The Krung Thai Bank, a major commercial bank owned by the government, has been hired to disburse the approved loans and collect repayments.

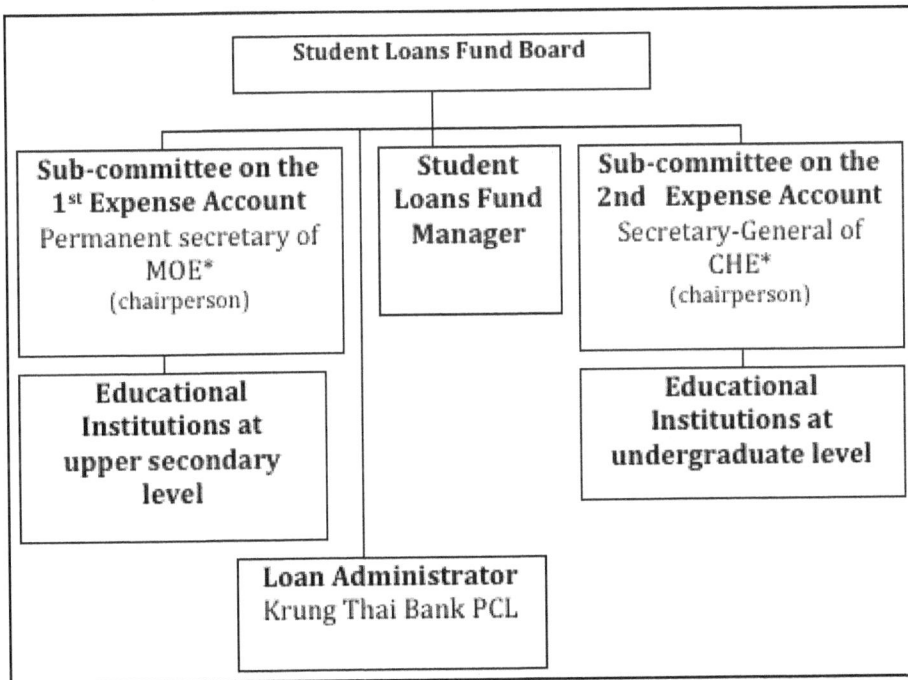

Figure 9.13 Organisational structure of the Student Loans Fund

* MOE = Ministry of Education
* CHE = Commission on Higher Education, under Ministry of Education
Source: Student Loans Fund officers' handbook, 2005.

Loan Application and Approval Procedures

The annual cycle of loan disbursement starts when the Sub-Committees on the First and the Second Expense Accounts allocate the approved budgets to educational institutions under their supervision. These institutions then call for loan applications from their students before the beginning of a new semester.

A committee in each institution then selects students to lend to by examining their applications and interviewing them. The time from loan application to the first loan disbursement is normally at least three months. As a result, selected students usually get their first tranche of loans near the end of the first semester.

Contrary to its objectives, the SLF still operates in a supply-side manner since all major decisions rest with the government committees and school administrators. Students will not be able to apply for loans before they are accepted by an educational institution. In addition, since the SLF loans are open to competition, applicants are not guaranteed selection for loans, but, in the case of being selected, will be able to borrow the full amount they requested. In fact, the amount of money a student may borrow depends on three factors: 1) the overall loans allocated to his or her educational institution, which is not directly linked to his or her financial needs; 2) the level of loan competition in his or her educational institution; and 3) the discretion of his or her school's authorised committee. This creates a high degree of uncertainty for applicants in need of financial support and is likely to be a barrier for them to enrol in higher education.

Loan Ceilings

The ceiling of loans for borrowing students is determined according to their educational levels, fields of education and types of expenses (Table 9.6). For example, the ceiling for a high-school student is currently set at B26 000 per annum, while that for a vocational-school student is B36 000 per annum. The maximum loan for an undergraduate student depends on the field of education, ranging from B84 000 per annum for social sciences, arts and humanities to B174 000 per annum for medical sciences.

Debt Repayment

Under the current scheme, borrowers have to begin to repay their debt two years after their graduation or after they stop borrowing, regardless of their income level. The rates of repayment are set progressively according to a pre-specified percentage of the total loan size, as shown in Table 9.7. The total repayment period is 15 years, with no interest charged in the first year. Borrowers are then charged an interest rate of 1 per cent of the outstanding loan in that year for the rest of the repayment period. It is important to note that interest is not charged before the repayment period and that even when it is charged, the rate is much lower than the commercial lending rates and the government's cost of capital, meaning that the government has to subsidise the interest rate. Borrowers would be penalised, however, at the rate of 12–18 per cent of the instalment loan for failure to repay their debts on time. Deferral of payment up to two years is allowed on a case-by-case basis if the borrowers can prove that they had incomes below B4700 a month or had been negatively affected by natural disasters, wars or riots. In addition, the outstanding debts would be forgiven if the debtors die or become handicapped.

Table 9.6 Loan ceiling by educational level and type of expense (baht per person p.a.)

Educational level/field of education	Tuition fee & education- related expenses	Living expenses	Total
1. High school	14 000	12 000	26 000
2. Vocational certificate	21 000	15 000	36 000
3. High vocational certificate/associate degree			
3.1 Business administration, arts, agriculture, domestic science, tourism	25 000	20 000	45 000
3.2 Manufacturing, information technology, communication	30 000	20 000	50 000
4.Undergraduate			
4.1 Social sciences, arts, humanities, education	60 000	24 000	84 000
4.2 Architecture	60 000	24 000	84 000
4.3 Engineering, sciences and technology	70 000	24 000	94 000
4.4 Agriculture	70 000	24 000	94 000
4.5 Public health, nursing, pharmacology	80 000	24 000	104 000
4.6 Medical science, veterinary science, dentistry	150 000	24 000	174 000

Source: Office of the Student Loans Fund, 2007.

Table 9.7 Repayment rate of the Student Loans Fund

Year	1	2	3	4	5	6	7	8	9	10	11	12	13	14	15	**Total**
Repayment (% of loan)	1.5	2	3	3.5	4	4.5	5	6	7	8	9	10	11	12	13	100

Source: Office of Student Loans Fund, 2007.

Impacts of Student Loans on Educational Opportunities

Although the SLF has been in operation for more than a decade, there has been no systematic evaluation of the scheme. In this section, we will present our empirical assessment of the impacts of the SLF by answering two questions.

1. To what extent did the loans reach the target group?

2. To what extent did the SLF increase educational opportunities for the borrowers?

Description of Data

The data used for evaluating the impacts of the SLF are derived from the Child and Youth Survey, which has been undertaken by the National Statistical Office every five years since 1974. These nationwide surveys cover information on education, employment status, leisure and social participation of children and youth, defined as those between three and twenty-four years of age. In our study, we use the latest round of the survey, 2002, which is the only round that was conducted after the full implementation of the SLF program.[4] We distinguish the SLF's borrower and non-borrower groups based on their answers to the question on their major sources of educational expenditure. There are 275 of 8290 students who answered that their major source of educational expenditure was the SLF loan.

Distribution of Loans to the Target Group

To begin with, it is natural to ask whether the SLF loans have actually reached the target group—that is, the students from families whose annual income is less than B150 000 a year. To answer this question, we rank the students by their average household income and divide them into five groups. Table 9.8 shows that, for upper secondary students, the SLF loans were targeted quite successfully to the intended group; only 7 per cent of total borrowers were not in the target group. For undergraduate students, however, nearly 19 per cent of the borrowers were not in the target group.

---

4   In fact, a previous survey was conducted, in 1997, right after the implementation of the SLF. Since the sample size of the students participating in the SLF was, however, very small in the 1997 survey, we consider it is more appropriate to use the 2002 survey for our study.

Table 9.8 Number of students borrowing from the SLF, classified by household income

Household income(baht p.a.)	Number of students(person)	Number of borrowers(person)	Share of total borrowers(%)
Upper secondary level			
0–50 000	1698	69	54.76
50 001–100 000	1857	35	27.78
100 001–150 000	1070	13	10.32
150 001–200 000	170	0	0.00
More than 200 000	1230	9	7.14
Total	**6025**	**126**	**100.00**
Undergraduate level			
0–50 000	348	43	28.86
50 001–100 000	647	53	35.57
100 001–150 000	466	25	16.78
150 001–200 000	89	5	3.36
More than 200 000	715	23	15.44
Total	**2265**	**149**	**100.00**

Source: Authors' estimations from the Child and Youth Survey data (2002).

These results indicate that the screening process of borrowers at the undergraduate institutions was much less effective than that of high schools. Our interviews with loan personnel of high schools and universities reveal that the former tend to have more information about the actual economic status of their students than the latter due to closer contact with the students' families. This could be the main reason for the differences in effectiveness of the screening.

Evaluation of Impacts on Educational Opportunity

As discussed in the previous section, there is some evidence that supports the view that financial barriers prevent many high-school graduates from low-income families from participating in higher education. Theoretically, the SLF should help reduce these financial barriers and thus promote greater participation in higher education.

To evaluate the impact of the SLF, we need to compare the actual outcome of having the SLF with the outcome of what would have happened in its absence, or the counterfactual. The key challenge is to construct a good counterfactual that permits us to compare participants (treatment group) and non-participants (comparison group) in the SLF. Ideally, we would like to compare the rate of higher education enrolment of high-school students who borrow from the SLF with that of the non-borrowers. This comparison requires panel data that track a given group of students over time, which are unavailable in Thailand. Fortunately, the Child and Youth Survey contains one question that asks whether a student borrows from the SLF and another that asks whether he or she intends to enrol in higher education after graduation. Combining the answers to both questions, we can assess the impacts of the SLF in influencing students' enrolment in higher education by a technique called matching.

Methodology

We adopt the Propensity Score Matching (PSM) technique to evaluate the impacts of the SLF program. The concept of PSM in our study is to find a comparison group that has the most similar profile to the borrower group except that they did not borrow from the SLF. This technique can help solve the selection-bias problems that are likely to occur in naive comparison of borrowers and non-borrowers. For example, it is likely that students who borrow from the SLF come from low-income families since the fund was designed to target poor families. Moreover, the poor generally have less educational opportunities than the rich. As a result, naively comparing the educational opportunity of borrowers and non-borrowers is likely to underestimate the impacts of the SLF in increasing educational opportunity for the poor.

The PSM technique solves these selection-bias problems by forming a comparison group by selecting an individual who has the probability—also known as the 'propensity score'—to borrow close to that of an individual in the borrowing group. In our case, the following steps were undertaken.

1. Final-year students of the upper secondary level (grade 12 students) are selected as the samples for the analysis.

2. The propensity-to-borrow score of each sample is estimated by a logit regression by using variables considered to affect the probability of borrowing. These explanatory variables are: 1) household income; 2) educational attainment of the head of the household; 3) the number of persons who are financially dependent in the household; 4) sex; 5) age; 6) type of educational institution (public or private); 7) field of education (academic or vocational); and 8) school location (rural or urban). See Appendix 9.1 for results of the logit regressions.

3. A comparison group is selected from the sample based on a number of matching methods (see Appendix 9.1). The treatment group and the comparison group are compared along a number of dimensions to ensure that the risks of selection bias are reduced by the matching process. As the five-nearest neighbours matching method resulted in the most similar comparison group, it is adopted as our matching technique.

4. The impact of SLF is estimated by comparing the intention to attend a higher education institution of the students in the treatment and the comparison groups. The difference derived from the comparison is called the Average Treatment effect for the Treated (ATT).

Results

Table 9.9 presents the estimated impacts of the SLF on the intention to attend higher education of the final-year high-school students. The result shows no significant differences between the two groups. Other matching methods also produced similar results, showing the robustness of our finding. Thus, it is found that the SLF has no significant impact on the intention of borrowing students to participate in higher education.

Table 9.9 Impact of the SLF on the intention of high-school students to enrol in higher education

Outcome	Five-nearest neighbours matching				Without matching			
	Treatment group	Comparison group	ATT	t-value	Treatment group	Non-borrower group	Difference	t-value
Intention to advance to higher education	95.65%	94.78%	0.87%	0.23	95.65%	96.35%	–0.7%	–0.23

Although it is found that the SLF has no significant impact on the overall borrower group, it could have some impact on some subsets of the borrowing group, especially low-income subsets. To test this hypothesis, we divide the sample into four subsets by household income into: 1) those with household income not more than B30 000 a year, which is close to the official poverty line of B28 650;[5] 2) those with household income between B30 000 and B60 000 a year; 3) those with household income more than B60 000 a year; and 4) those with household income not more than B150 000 a year, as set by the SLF's conditions. The results in Table 9.10 show that the intention to attend higher education for the treated subset with household income less than B30 000 a year is significantly higher than that of the comparison group by nearly 9 percentage points. No significant differences, however, for other subsets were found.

---

5   The official poverty line is B1190 per person per month (Jitsuchon et al. 2004). We assume that there are two income earners in a family: the head of the household and his or her spouse. Hence, the household income at the poverty line is B28 560 per annum.

Table 9.10 Impact of the SLF on intention to attend higher education institution, by household income

Sample group classified by household income (baht/month)	Intention to attend higher education institution			
	Treatment group	Comparison group	ATT	t-value
Income ≤ 30 000	100%	91.16%	8.84%**	3.39
Income 30 001–60 000	88.89%	94.44%	−5.56%	−0.26
Income > 60 000	100%	94.55%	5.45%	1.21
Income ≤150 000	95.76%	96.77%	−1.0%	−0.24

** significant at the 95 per cent confident level

Source: Authors' estimation from the Child and Youth Survey data (2002).

In summary, the SLF seems to have increased the educational opportunities of only the borrowers from families with income below the poverty line. Since this group constitutes only 13 per cent of the total borrowers, the income threshold set by the SLF appears to be far too high.

Financial Sustainability of the SLF

We now turn to the issue of the financial sustainability of the SLF. In this section, we will investigate the issue based on the approach used by Ziderman (2002).

Repayment Ratio

Based on the information about the repayment conditions described above, we estimate the SLF's repayment ratio, which assumes that all borrowers repay on time exactly according to the schedule set by the SLF (Table 9.7). Based on a discounted cash-flow calculation using various discount rates and assuming a constant inflation rate of 3 per cent per annum, repayment ratios are estimated (Table 9.11). It can be seen that the repayment ratios are lower than half in all cases—ranging from 24 to 42 per cent—depending on the period of borrowing and the discount rate used. The low level of repayment ratios reflects the generosity of the SLF's repayment conditions: the long grace period, the low interest rate and the long repayment period allowed.

Table 9.11 Ideal repayment ratios (per cent)

Borrowing period	Discount rate		
	4%	6%	8%
Upper secondary level (3 years)	41.81	33.22	26.65
Undergraduate (4 years)	40.48	31.82	25.27
Upper secondary plus undergraduate (7 years)	40.79	30.88	23.61

Recovery Ratio

The repayment ratio assumes that loans are repaid according to the set conditions. In addition to ignoring the administrative costs of the SLF, it also fails to take into account the fact that many borrowers will not repay on time and might even default on their loans. Table 9.12 shows the percentage of borrowers who did not repay on time. For instance, it shows that among the group of borrowers who were scheduled to repay in 2001, 54.8 per cent did not repay on time. This reflects a poor repayment-collection mechanism of the SLF. Since the SLF has not been operating long enough to reliably estimate the actual default rate, we assume the rate to be in the range of 10 per cent based on the SLF's estimation and 30 per cent based on our estimation using the 2005 repayment data. The administrative cost is estimated to be 1.6 per cent of the total outstanding debt.

Table 9.12 Percentage of borrowers who did not declare for obligatory repayment

| Year | Borrowers who did not declare for repayment by compulsory year | | | | | | |
	1999	2000	2001	2002	2003	2004	2005
2001	19.58	23.98	**54.80**				
2002	17.99	22.59	32.32	**56.85**			
2003	15.96	20.03	27.24	36.06	**57.44**		
2004	12.45	19.26	26.06	33.02	39.94	**55.61**	
2005	9.98	15.40	23.32	32.06	38.27	36.17	**56.87**

Source: Office of the Student Loans Fund.

Table 9.13 shows that the SLF has a very low recovery ratio—ranging from 25 to 35 per cent. Thus, the fiscal burden of the SLF could be very high in the long run unless the repayment conditions are changed or the repayment-collection system is strengthened.

Table 9.13 Estimated recovery ratios of the Student Loans Fund (per cent)

| Borrowing period | Discount rate | | | Default rate (for discount rate = 4%) | | |
	4%	6%	8%	10%	20%	30%
Three years (loans for upper secondary study)	24.9	19.6	15.6	33.3	29.2	24.9
Four years (loans for undergraduate study)	25.0	19.6	15.5	33.2	29.2	25.0
Seven years (loans for upper secondary and undergraduate studies)	26.4	19.9	15.2	34.7	30.6	26.4

Shifting to Income-Contingent Loans

The SLF was temporarily abolished and replaced with the Income Contingent Loan (ICL) scheme under the Thaksin government in 2006. The ICL, which was modelled after the loan with the same name in Australia, is different from the SLF in many important ways. First, it allows only undergraduates and not high-school students to borrow. In addition, it sets no condition on the household income of the borrowers. This means that all undergraduate students in any field may apply for the loan. Second, it covers only tuition fees, not other education-related expenses and living expenses. Third, it does not require the borrowers to start repaying until their incomes reach B16 000 a month (the minimum income level for the payment of income tax). The repayment rate is contingent upon the borrowers' incomes, and is progressively increased with higher income. Fourth, there is no interest charged under the ICL scheme, but the outstanding debt will be adjusted by inflation from the first year of borrowing. Finally, the revenue department is responsible for collecting the repayments.

Even though its supporters claim that the ICL is far superior to the SLF in many aspects, the ICL was short lived and the Surayud administration, which succeeded the Thaksin administration, decided to put the SLF back in place in 2007. Critics claim that, regardless of many improvements brought about by the ICL, the scheme is too fiscally expensive, especially when enrolments in higher education are expanding. The status of the ICL and of the SLF is again uncertain now that a new government, backed by Thaksin, gained power in early 2008.

Concluding Remarks

The Thai higher education sector has expanded quickly during the past decade, making a transition from an elitist to a mass institution. To cope with the enrolment expansion, the education financing system needs to be reformed. The current system of public subsidy to public educational institutions has proved to be inefficient, regressive and anti-competitive. The introduction of the SLF was supposed to be a step forward. Carefully designed, it has potential to be more efficient, fairer and more pro-competition. The current SLF scheme, however, contains too many flaws: its loan-screening system is far from perfect; it fails to disburse the loans on time; it has a very poor collection mechanism; and it is still based on the supply-side financing paradigm. Our analysis shows that it could not significantly influence the decisions of high-school students to continue their studies to a higher level, except for the poorest group, who were a minority among the recipients. In addition, the SLF is suffering from a serious financial sustainability problem due to its very low recovery rate.

The shift to the ICL brought about many important improvements, especially a potentially more effective repayment-collection system. Moreover, it was based on a demand-side financing paradigm that promoted more choices for students. The ICL is not, however, without its problems; it still unnecessarily subsidises the borrowers by charging a zero real interest rate. In addition, the ICL by itself cannot bring about the overall changes needed to the educational financing system unless other reforms are also undertaken.

More importantly, policy certainty is a prerequisite for long-term development of the system. Frequent policy reversals will not only bring about confusion to all stakeholders, they will also raise questions about the government's commitment to any loan programs. To prevent haphazard policy changes, policy makers should seek consensus from broad-based stakeholders before making any such major changes.

References

Jitsuchon, S., Plangprapan, J. and Kakwani, N. 2004, *Improvement of the official poverty line*, Final report, [in Thai], Office of National Economic and Development Board, Bangkok.

King Mongkut's University of Technology Thonburi (KMUTT) 2005, *The unit cost of higher education*, Final report, Commission on Higher Education, Ministry of Education, Bangkok.

Kirtikara, K. 2004, *Transition from a University Under the Bureaucratic System to an Autonomous University: Reflections on concepts and experience of King Mongkut's University of Technology Thonburi*, Office of the Education Council, Bangkok.

Krongkaew, M. 2004, The promise of the new university financing system in Thailand: the Income Contingent Loan (ICL) scheme, Paper presented at Monthly Workshop, the Monetary Policy Division, Bank of Thailand, Bangkok.

Lee, M.-J. 2005, *Micro-Econometrics for Policy, Program, and Treatment Effects*, Oxford University Press, New York.

Martins, J. O., Boarini, R., Strauss, H., de la Maisonneuve, C. and Saadi, C. 2007, *The policy determinants of investment in tertiary education*, Economics Department Working Paper No. 576, Organisation for Economic Cooperation and Development, Paris.

Punyasavatsut, C. et al. 2005, Efficiency of public expenditure in education, Component 1A, Technical Consultancy for the Country Development Partnership Program in Education—Component 1: school finance reform, The World Bank, Washington, DC.

Usher, A. 2005, Global Debt Patterns: An international comparison of student loan burdens and repayment conditions, Educational Policy Institute, Toronto.

Weesakul, B. et al. 2003, *Financing of Higher Education*, [in Thai], Office of the Education Council, Bangkok.

Ziderman, A. 2002, 'Financing student loans in Thailand: revolving fund or open-ended commitment?', *Economics of Education Review*, vol. 21, pp. 367–80.

Appendix 9.1

Table A9.1 Results of logistic regression

Variable	Coefficient	Standard error	P-value
Household income	−0.00001**	0.000	0.010
Education attainment of head of household	−0.47789	0.379	0.207
Number of members who are a burden on household	0.25866	0.268	0.334
Sex	−0.17533	0.433	0.685
Age	0.22761	0.146	0.119
Type of school	0.47168	0.732	0.519
Type of education	1.48395**	0.449	0.001
Location	−0.07549	0.421	0.858
Constant	−7.62449**	3.002	0.011

** significant at the 95 per cent confidence level

Table A9.2 Methods of matching

1. **One-to-one matching (1-nearest neighbour):** the method that chooses one comparison unit(non-participant) that has the closest propensity score with each treated unit.
2. **One-to-five matching (5-nearest neighbours):** the method that chooses five comparison units that have the closest propensity score with each treated observation.
3. **Radius matching:** each treated unit is matched only with the comparison units whose propensity score falls in a predefined neighbourhood of the propensity score of the treated unit.
4. **Kernel matching:** all treated are matched with a weighted average of all comparisons with weights that are inversely proportional to the distance between the propensity scores of the treated and comparisons.
5. **Mahalanobis matching:** this method does not use the propensity score for matching the comparison group. The similarity of a comparison to the treated is measured by a metric on variables.

Source: Lee (2005).

Table A9.3 Balancing property results for each matching method: all samples

Variable	One-to-one		5-nearest neighbours		Radius, kernel		Mahalanobis		No matching	
	Treatment group	Comparison group	Treatment group	Comparison group	Treatment group	Comparison group	Treatment group	Comparison group	Treatment group	Non-borrower
Household income (baht p.a.)	61 598	51 300	65 607	73 920	61 598	123 164	62 966	72 700	61 598	122 342
Education attainment of head of household*	2.2	1.6	2.3	2.4	2.2	3.4	2.2	2.4	2.2	3.4
Age	18.1	19.5	18.1	18.0	18.1	17.7	18.1	17.9	18.1	17.8
Sex (male)	34.8%	40.0%	35.7%	38.9%	34.8%	46.8%	36.4%	35.6%	34.8%	46.9%
Location (municipal area)	52.2%	60.0%	52.4%	51.4%	52.2%	62.3%	52.3%	51.1%	52.2%	62.0%
Type of school (public)	91.3%	90.0%	90.5%	89.7%	91.3%	91.1%	90.9%	91.1%	91.3%	91.2%
Type of education (vocational)	50.0%	100.0%	45.2%	41.1%	50.0%	21.1%	47.7%	48.9%	50.0%	21.8%
Members who are a burden on household (persons)	2.3	2.9	2.3	2.1	2.3	2.0	2.3	2.3	2.3	2.0

* education attainment of head of household ranges from '0 = no education' to '9 = doctoral degree'

Table A9.4 Sample with household income not exceeding B30 000 p.a.

Variable	One-to-one		5-nearest neighbours		Radius, kernel		Mahalanobis		No matching	
	Treatment group	Comparison group	Treatment group	Comparison group	Treatment group	Comparison group	Treatment group	Comparison group	Treatment group	Non-borrower group
Household income (baht p.a.)	19 500	17 250	19 500	20 770	19 500	19 044	19 636	20 250	18 965	20 684
Education attainment of head of household*	2.2	2.0	2.2	2.1	2.2	2.0	2.0	2.1	1.7	2.1
Age	18.0	20.0	18.0	17.8	18.0	18.1	18.0	17.9	18.1	17.8
Sex (male)	40.0%	50.0%	40.0%	43.7%	40.0%	32.6%	36.37%	33.4%	28.6%	43.05%
Location (municipal area)	50.0%	100.0%	50.0%	37.21%	50.0%	50.0%	45.46%	50.0%	57.14%	36.77%
Type of school (public)	100.0%	100.0%	100.0%	100.0%	100.0%	100.0%	100.0%	100.0%	100%	96.4%
Type of education (vocational)	50.0%	100.0%	50.0%	17.21%	50.0%	41.3%	54.55%	50.0%	64.29%	17.49%
Members who are a burden on household (persons)	2.1	2.0	2.1	1.9	2.1	2.0	2.1	1.9	2.3	2.0

* education attainment of head of household ranges from '0 = no education' to '9 = doctoral degree'

Table A9.5 Sample with household income in the range of B30 001–60 000 p.a.

Variable	One-to-one		5-nearest neighbours		Radius, kernel		Mahalanobis		No matching	
	Treatment group	Comparison group	Treatment group	Comparison group	Treatment group	Comparison group	Treatment group	Comparison group	Treatment group	Non-borrower group
Household income (baht p.a.)	45 079	41 400	45 079	42 682	45 079	44 720	45 250	44 167	45 079	44 680
Education attainment of head of household*	1.7	0	1.7	1.7	1.7	2.3	1.7	1.8	1.7	2.3
Age	17.9	18.2	17.9	18.1	17.9	18	17.9	18.1	17.9	17.9
Sex (male)	47.37%	40.0%	47.37%	48.05%	47.37%	44.0%	50.0%	50.0%	47.37%	43.9%
Location (municipal area)	36.84%	20.0%	36.84%	38.96%	36.84%	49.17%	33.34%	33.34%	36.84%	49.06%
Type of school (public)	94.74%	100.0%	94.74%	94.81%	94.74%	91.02%	94.5%	94.5%	94.74%	91.08%
Type of education (vocational)	42.11%	0%	42.11%	40.26%	42.11%	18.68%	38.9%	38.9%	42.11%	19.25%
Members who are a burden on household (persons)	2.1	2.0	2.1	2.0	2.1	1.9	2.0	2.1	2.1	1.9

* education attainment of head of household ranges from '0 = no education' to '9 = doctoral degree'

Table A9.6 Sample with household income more than B60 000 p.a.

Variable	One-to-one		5-nearest neighbours		Radius, kernel		Mahalanobis		No matching	
	Treatment group	Comparison group	Treatment group	Comparison group	Treatment group	Comparison group	Treatment group	Comparison group	Treatment group	Non-borrower group
Household income (baht p.a.)	130 773	95 455	130 773	133 966	130 773	163 353	129 964	146 786	129 964	162 818
Education attainment of head of household*	3.5	2.4	3.5	3.5	3.5	3.9	3.1	3.1	3.1	3.9
Age	18.0	20.0	17.5	17.5	17.5	15.9	18.1	17.6	18.1	17.8
Sex (male)	27.3%	36.4%	27.3%	35.7%	27.3%	50.1%	28.6%	41.3%	28.6%	49.7%
Location (municipal area)	63.6%	72.7%	63.6%	67.2%	63.6%	69.5%	64.3%	64.3%	64.3%	69.3%
Type of school (public)	91.0%	73.0%	90.9%	87.9%	90.9%	91.4%	78.6%	78.6%	78.6%	91.1%
Type of education (vocational)	45.5%	45.5%	45.5%	42.8%	45.5%	10.0%	42.9%	13.9%	42.9%	10.2%
Members who are a burden on household (persons)	2.1	3.3	2.4	2.4	2.1	2.0	2.8	2.5	2.8	2.1

* education attainment of head of household ranges from '0 = no education' to '9 = doctoral degree'

Table A9.7 Sample with household income not exceeding B150 000 p.a.

Variable	One-to-one		5-nearest neighbours		Radius, kernel		Mahalanobis		No matching	
	Treatment group	Comparison group	Treatment group	Comparison group	Treatment group	Comparison group	Treatment group	Comparison group	Treatment group	Non-borrower group
Household income (baht p.a.)	50 229	33 750	51 932	55 436	51 423	70 504	49 573	52 427	48 453	70 100
Education attainment of head of household*	2.9	2.1	2.9	3.0	2.9	3.3	2.8	2.8	2.7	3.3
Age	18.0	18.3	18.0	17.9	18.0	17.8	18.0	17.9	18.0	17.8
Sex (male)	40.00%	12.50%	40.54%	41.46%	38.46%	46.26%	39.02%	36.59%	37.21%	45.97%
Location (municipal area)	42.86%	62.50%	45.95%	54.27%	48.72%	55.37%	46.34%	51.22%	48.84%	55.28%
Type of school (public)	91.43%	100.00%	91.89%	94.51%	92.31%	92.23%	92.68%	92.68%	93.02%	92.23%
Type of education (vocational)	40.00%	62.50%	40.54%	35.37%	43.59%	22.35%	46.34%	43.90%	48.84%	22.95%
Members who are a burden on household (persons)	2.2	3.4	2.1	2.2	2.2	2.0	2.2	2.0	2.2	2.0

* education attainment of head of household ranges from '0 = no education' to '9 = doctoral degree'

10. Thailand's Student Loans Fund: An analysis of interest rate subsidies and repayment hardships

Piruna Polsiri, Rangsit Sarachitti and Thitima Sitthipongpanich
Dhurakij Pundit University

Introduction

Human capital is important for social and economic development. The most sensible way to enhance the quality of a country's human capital is to promote education. In developing countries, however, access to education, especially at high educational levels, is limited because large numbers of the population are poor. Therefore, the government has to play an important role in establishing a student loans scheme to reduce inequality in education, which will eventually increase the country's economic growth.

From the point of view of the government, as a loan provider, some key issues regarding a student loans scheme are: allocation and distribution, recovery, collection and administration, and repayment conditions.[1] The government also needs to be concerned about the efficiency of resource allocation to the student loan scheme. From the point of view of borrowers, although they receive the opportunity to access higher education and earn higher incomes, required loan repayments with strict conditions could increase the borrowers' repayment hardship. These issues lead to the trade-off between the government's subsidy and the borrowers' repayment difficulties.

Previous studies have investigated student loan schemes in many countries— for example, in Australia (Chapman 2006; Chapman and Ryan 2002), Europe and the United States (Johnstone 1986), Africa (Johnstone 2004; Johnstone and Amero 2001), and South-East Asia (Ziderman 2004).[2] Our goal is to fully analyse both the implicit subsidies related to the Student Loans Fund (SLF) and the repayment hardship of loan recipients in Thailand at an undergraduate level. An important and similarly motivated study by Ziderman (2003) comes to comparable conclusions with respect to both overall implicit subsidies and

---

1   Loan repayment conditions refer to interest charges and the repayment schedule.
2   Although Thailand's student loans cover upper secondary, vocational and undergraduate education, most student loan schemes around the world cover only higher education (Ziderman 2003). Therefore, in this chapter, our analysis will be based on higher education.

repayment hardships calculated at the mean of the data.[3] Most importantly, however, this study is the first to analyse the repayment hardship of SLF loans for graduates with very low incomes.

This chapter first describes the background of the SLF in Thailand, before discussing current issues of the SLF. We then analyse the implicit subsidy and repayment hardships.

Background of the Student Loans Fund

History of the Student Loans Fund

The history of student loans in Thailand began in 1996 when the government, led by the Chartthai Party, established the Student Loans Fund (SLF). The idea of student loans, nevertheless, originated in 1995 under the government led by the Democrat Party.[4] The main objective of the SLF is to enhance access to upper secondary and higher education for students from low-income families.[5] The ultimate goals are to reduce the inequality of education between the rich and the poor and to develop human resources in the country. This will at least help to achieve economic growth and enhance the competitive capacity of Thailand (*Student Loans Fund Act 1998*).

To serve its purposes, the SLF provides loans for upper secondary, vocational and undergraduate education to students whose family income does not exceed B150 000 per annum.[6] It has been allocated in the national budget, on average, B27 billion per annum. As reported by Krung Thai Bank in March 2008, the government had subsidised the SLF for the approximate total amount of B280 billion to about 2.9 million loan recipients from 1996 to 2007.

How the SLF Works

Loan Budget Allocation and Loan Distribution

In each fiscal year, the SLF will estimate the total amount of funds needed for loan distribution in that year, and submit a request to the Bureau of the

---

3   Examples of previous studies are Tangkitvanich and Manasboonphempool (2006) and Ziderman (2003).
4   Under the Thai Rak Thai Party government, the SLF scheme was changed to Thailand's Income Contingent and Allowance Loan (TICAL) scheme in 2006. When the government was ousted by the coup, the TICAL was switched back to the SLF. A detailed discussion of TICAL is provided in Chapman and Luonkaew (2008).
5   The average rate of continuing the upper secondary level, however, declined slightly during the period 1997–99, which was due mostly to the East Asian economic crisis in 1997 (Weesakul 2006).
6   The threshold family income of a loan recipient was originally set at B120 000 in 1996. It was then raised to B300 000 in 1997 and remained in place until 1999, when it was reduced to B150 000, which was the median household income in 2002 (Weesakul 2006; Ziderman 2003).

Budget in the Ministry of Finance. The annual allocated budget of the SLF will then be divided into: 1) the loan budget for upper secondary and vocational education; and 2) the loan budget for undergraduate education. For our focus, the loan budget for undergraduate education will be allocated directly to each university, through the Commission on Higher Education (formerly the Ministry of University Affairs). The loan budget allocated to a university is based on the number of loan recipients in previous years. At the institutional level, the university's loan committee authorises the distribution of the loan budget to eligible students and oversees the process of loan applications. Within the limitations set by the Commission on Higher Education, a university makes decisions on individual loans distributed to its students.

The SLF loans cover tuition fees and educational-related expenses, as well as living allowances during a study period. For the undergraduate level—which is the focus of our analysis—the loan ceiling for tuition fees and educational-related expenses is set differently, depending on the field of study, ranging from B60 000 to B150 000 per annum. The living allowance loan, including accommodation and personal expenses, is limited to B24 000 per annum (Office of Student Loans Fund web site: <www.studentloan.or.th>).

Loan Repayment

Since the SLF loans are provided to students from low-income families, the conditions for interest charges and principal repayments have been set to lessen the debtors' burden. First, there is a seven-year interest grace period between initial enrolment and the first debt repayment. Second, there is a two-year repayment grace period after a loan recipient graduates or stops borrowing. Following the two-year grace period, the loan recipient is required to repay his or her debt for 15 years.[7] Third, a flat interest rate of only 1 per cent per annum is charged throughout the repayment period. The annual loan repayment is calculated as the proportion of the total loan, ranging from 1.5 per cent in year one to 13 per cent in year 15.[8] It seems that the SLF loans have the potential to provide 'consumption smoothing', meaning that the proportion of the loan repayment grows with the borrower's expected earnings. Table 10.1 shows an example of a loan repayment schedule, assuming a loan amount of B200 000.

7 A loan recipient may choose to start repaying his or her debt during the two-year grace period. Also, a loan recipient may choose to pay off the debt in less than 15 years.
8 A loan recipient may, however, choose to repay the debt at a higher rate, or more quickly than what is specified in the repayment schedule.

Table 10.1 Loan repayment schedule of B200 000

Year of repayment	Loan repayment proportion (%)	Principal amount (baht)	Interest amount (baht)	Total amount (baht)	Outstanding principal (baht)
1	1.5	3000	-	3000	197 000
2	2.5	5000	1970	6970	192 000
3	3.0	6000	1920	7920	186 000
4	3.5	7000	1860	8860	179 000
5	4.0	8000	1790	9790	171 000
6	4.5	9000	1710	10 710	162 000
7	5.0	10 000	1620	11 620	152 000
8	6.0	12 000	1520	13 520	140 000
9	7.0	14 000	1400	15 400	126 000
10	8.0	16 000	1260	17 260	110 000
11	9.0	18 000	1100	19 100	92 000
12	10.0	20 000	920	20 920	72 000
13	11.0	22 000	720	22 720	50 000
14	12.0	24 000	500	24 500	26 000
15	13.0	26 000	260	26 260	-
Total	100.0	200 000			

Fourth, if a loan recipient is unemployed or encounters a natural disaster, riot or war, he or she may apply for a six-month suspension, but in total not more than two years. If a loan recipient's income falls below the threshold income of B4700 a month, he or she may request not to pay the total amount of the required payment. In this case, the borrower has to pay a minimum of B300 a month or B2400 per annum, and it has to be higher than the interest charged for that repayment period. If a loan recipient fails to repay his or her debt, he or she will face a penalty between 12 per cent and 18 per cent of the instalment principal. Finally, upon a loan recipient's death or disability preventing work, the loan will be automatically forgiven.

Loan Collection

Krung Thai Bank (KTB), a government-owned bank, is responsible for SLF loan collection. Once the two-year repayment grace period ends, due borrowers are required to contact KTB to arrange the loan repayment by 5 July in that year. The borrowers have two choices for paying back the debt. First, they may pay the total due amount for the particular period. Second, they may apply for an instalment of 12 monthly payments. During 15 years of the loan repayment period, the KTB will inform due borrowers of the amounts to be paid one month before the due date—that is, 5 July. Again, the borrowers have two choices to settle the repayment schedule for each particular year. If due borrowers fail to arrange the payment, follow-up by mail, telephone and a home visit will be made depending on the length of the delinquency period.

The Importance of Our Study

In this study, we focus on the analyses of the implicit subsidy by the government and the repayment hardship of SLF loan recipients. We realise that the implicit subsidy issues have already been discussed in Shen and Ziderman (2008), Tangkitvanich and Manasboonphempool (2006) and Ziderman (2003). There are similarities in many dimensions to the analysis of Ziderman and we consider this to be an important affirmation of policy concerns with respect to the SLF. As is the case with Ziderman (2003), we are able to show the extent to which the implicit subsidy can be traced to different policy components of the loan—that is, interest rates charged, interest grace periods, and repayment grace periods. We find that all components matter and that, roughly, the role of interest rate subsidies is about the same as the other factors combined.

As with Ziderman (2003), we calculate repayment hardships for loan repayments estimated with respect to average incomes; using more sophisticated earnings profiles, we come to quite similar conclusions. More importantly, our study contributes to the policy debate in two unusual respects concerning repayment hardships. First, we are able to calculate repayment burdens for graduates of different ages—and not just at the mean. Second, and most significantly, we are able to estimate the extent of repayment hardships for graduates with very low incomes—those in the bottom decile of the earnings distribution—by both sex and age. Our approach allows us to explore fairly specifically the potential policy trade-off between implicit interest rate subsidies and repayment burdens

Current Issues Concerning the SLF

Nominal Interest Rate of 1 Per Cent

The nominal interest rate charged to SLF loans is fixed at 1 per cent until the loans are fully paid. The 1 per cent interest rate assists loan recipients to bear a very low cost for their education because it is much lower than market interest rates. Currently, the term deposit interest rate of the Government Saving Bank is 3 per cent and the interest rate of long-term government bonds is 5 per cent (The Bank of Thailand, as of May 2008: <www.bot.or.th>). This means that the government has to subsidise the SLF at least 2–3 per cent over the 15-year repayment schedule.

Furthermore, the 1 per cent interest rate charged affects the present value of repayments in the future. Assuming that the average inflation rate is 4 per cent, the government subsidises loan recipients at about 3 per cent. The amount of repayment reduces through time at a real rate of 3 per cent. When the total loans—charged with a 1 per cent interest rate—are fully paid after 21 years (four-year course of study, two-year grace period and 15-year repayment period), the government will receive much less money in real terms.

Grace Period

The SLF allows loan recipients to start loan repayment two years after their graduation. The two-year grace period for repayment benefits loan recipients, but increases the government subsidy. Moreover, from the loan application date, the borrowers are not obliged to pay interest, or to make a repayment for seven years, meaning that the government has to bear a high cost of lending for the seven-year interest grace period. In addition to this, the SLF allows the borrowers to postpone their repayment for a total period of two years if they are unemployed or face a natural disaster, riot or war.

Administration/Collection Cost

It is arguable that the administration process under the SLF leads to high expenses because it involves several parties. The SLF hires KTB to be responsible for the loan-approval process and 'normal' loan collection. In the fiscal year 2008, KTB was allocated overall administration costs of about B227 million.[9] The bank is in charge of loan approval after receiving all relevant documents from borrowers' educational institutions. Through KTB, tuition-fee loans are paid directly to an educational institution, while monthly allowances and expenses are credited to borrowers' KTB accounts. During the loan-collection process, KTB will inform borrowers of the amount of payment, and, if the borrowers fail to repay the loan, KTB will follow-up by mail and phone.

After five years of the repayment schedule, the unpaid loans will be classified as 'delinquent' loans. For the delinquent loans, the Legal Affairs Division of the Office of the Student Loans Fund contracts out law firms to follow-up. From an interview with Professor Dr Boonserm Weesakul, an SLF honorary board member, we discovered that, at the steady state, approximately 34 000 cases are sent to law firms every year. The total cost for loan collection paid to law firms is about B521 million, and the SLF planned to spend B14.5 million to publicise the process of loan collection in the fiscal year 2008.[10]

---

9   B. Weesakul (Personal communication, 10 May 2008) referred to the figures from the SLF's 2008 budget.
10   The figures are from the SLF's 2008 budget.

Defaults

The high level of government subsidy to the SLF also stems from default losses. Several students might not meet their loan repayment obligation, meaning that when and if a borrower's income is low for a period, he or she will face difficulty in repaying the loan. Also, some students might still be unemployed after the two-year grace period finishes, or might continue a postgraduate course. In addition, the probability of default loss could be increased by contract breach or the death of loan recipients.

Table 10.2 shows the summary of loan repayments for 1999–2006 due for cohorts of borrowers. Official figures show that, for each due cohort, about 40 per cent of due borrowers commence their repayment in July of the first repayment year, while 60 per cent of due borrowers fail to make any repayment. The non-paying borrowers could include those who are not able to repay and who request a deferral of loan repayment, or those who do not commit to their loan repayment. After the first five years of the repayment schedule, the proportion of payers to due borrowers increases to about 80 per cent. This five-year period is a cut-off point for the Legal Affairs Division of the Office of the Student Loans Fund to handle delinquent loans. The legal procedure to some degree helps force due borrowers to repay loans. Therefore, the first two due cohorts—that is, due cohorts for 1999 and for 2000—show that about 15 per cent of the due borrowers do not pay after eight years, which should be considered as a steady state. This 15 per cent default loss will be used in implicit subsidy calculations.

Table 10.2 Proportion of payers to total number of due borrowers (per cent)

Due cohorts	Number of due borro-wers	Repayment year								
		July 1999	July 2000	July 2001	July 2002	July 2003	July 2004	July 2005	July 2006	April 2007
1999	18 672	15.93	68.18	76.84	81.00	82.85	85.56	88.58	89.77	88.51
2000	66 555		38.92	74.83	76.80	79.15	79.87	82.66	87.79	87.31
2001	135 314			41.21	66.60	72.00	73.22	73.85	80.05	82.65
2002	207 102				40.30	61.01	66.21	67.28	68.36	74.60
2003	226 105					39.19	58.78	61.06	62.63	62.78
2004	245 961						41.13	62.94	65.31	65.74
2005	281 070							39.34	60.38	63.50
2006	275 580								45.89	62.97

Source: Report on student loan payment and repayment, SLF (1999–2006) by KTB, as of May 2007.

Implicit Subsidies

In order to calculate the implicit subsidy, we first assume that an average loan per head of university students, including tuition fees and living expenses, is equivalent to B200 000 for a four-year course.

Table 10.3 shows an average tuition fee (four-year course) and the number of borrowers at each type of university in Thailand. The average tuition fee varies across the type of university. As expected, the average tuition fee per course at a private university is the highest: B180 000. A public university charges approximately B72 000 per course, while the average tuition fee at a Rajamangala university of technology is B48 000 per course. The lowest average tuition fee is B48 000 per course at a Rajabhat university. The proportion of borrowers is 37 per cent at a Rajabhat university, followed by 30 per cent at a private university, 22 per cent at a public university and 11 per cent at a Rajamangala university of technology.

Table 10.3 Average tuition fee per course and number of borrowers, 2003

Type of university	Average tuition fee (baht)	No. of borrowers
Private university	180 000	100 489
Public university	72 000	75 469
Rajamangala university of technology	48 000	39 069
Rajabhat university	36 000	125 546

Source: Office of Student Loans Fund.

Weighted average tuition fee =

$$\frac{\text{Average tuition fee per course} \times \text{Number of borrowers at each type of university}}{\text{Total number of borrowers}}$$

From these figures, we calculate the weighted average tuition fee per course in 2003, which is about B88 000 per person. To make a simple calculation, we assume that the weighted average tuition fee per course in 2008 is approximately B100 000 per borrower. In addition, university students can borrow monthly expenses, including accommodation and living expenses, from the SLF. According to the borrowing conditions of the SLF, each student may borrow a personal expense loan of B2000 a month (Office of Student Loans Fund 2007). Hence, the total personal-expense loan amount for a four-year course is B96 000 per person. We assume that, together with the tuition-fee loan, an approximate total loan for a four-year university course is B200 000 per person.

Furthermore, we assume an inflation rate of 4 per cent, which was the average inflation rate from 2004 to 2007.[11] The inflation rate is used to adjust the amount of loan repayment in each year over the 15-year repayment period to a real term of money. We also assume a discount rate of 3 per cent, which is quoted by a general agreement of Times Preference Experts. We use the discount rate to calculate the present values of total payment, loan amount, and collection costs.

The collection cost is assumed to be 3 per cent of the total payment over the 15-year repayment period and it is added to the total loan amount per borrower. Referring to the previous section, the total collection cost is B763 million per annum, including fees paid to KTB and law firms and expenses to promote loan repayment. The approximate collection cost of 3 per cent is the proportion of total collection costs (B763 million) to outstanding loans per annum (B27 billion).

The default loss of 15 per cent is used to adjust the total repayment over the 15-year repayment period. Default loss is assumed to mean that 15 per cent of the borrowers pay nothing over the repayment period, while 85 per cent of the borrowers pay the full amount. These figures are from Table 10.2, which shows that it is likely that 85 per cent of total due borrowers pay back the loan at the steady state (B. Weesakul, Personal communication, 10 May 2008).

The calculation of the implicit subsidy in this study turns out to be similar to Shen and Ziderman's (2008), which is shown in Table 10.4.

$$\text{Implicit subsidy} = 1 - \left[\frac{\text{PV of total payment adjusted by loan loss}}{\text{PV of total loan amount} + \text{PV of total collection cost}} \right]$$

The current SLF is examined under repayment conditions of a 1 per cent nominal interest rate charged to the total loan amount, a two-year grace period of repayment, interest charged three years after graduation, and a repayment schedule of 15 years. In addition to the analysis of the current SLF, we also analyse three comparison SLF schemes, which vary in terms of the number of grace periods of repayment and interest charged. Moreover, we propose to analyse the schemes with the adjustment of the interest rate—1 per cent versus 7 per cent. The nominal interest rate of 7 per cent is equivalent to a real rate of interest of 3 per cent, given that the inflation rate is 4 per cent. If the government's cost of borrowing is 3 per cent, this interest subsidy will be removed. Table 10.4 shows the results of implicit subsidy calculation of four different schemes with two interest rate regimes.

---

11   The Bank of Thailand reported inflation rates of 2.7 per cent in 2004, 4.5 per cent in 2005, 4.7 per cent in 2006, and 2.3 per cent in 2007 (<www.bot.or.th>).

Table 10.4 Implicit subsidies (per cent)

Nominal interest rate	1%	7%
Two-year repayment grace period and interest rate charged three years after graduation	65.68	44.62
No repayment grace period and interest rate charged three years after graduation	60.57	36.44
Two-year repayment grace period and interest rate charged on enrolment	50.55	20.29
No repayment grace period and interest rate charged on enrolment	46.60	19.92

Table 10.4 shows that the implicit subsidy of the current SLF is 65.68 per cent, which is similar to Shen and Ziderman (2008) and Tangkitvanich and Manasboonphempool (2006). Specifically, Shen and Ziderman (2008) report 28.21 per cent of the loan recovery ratio, incorporating default loss, which is equivalent to 71.79 per cent of the implicit subsidy. Using the same approach as Shen and Ziderman (2008), Tangkitvanich and Manasboonphempool (2006) show that the loan recovery ratio is 33.2 per cent (that is, the implicit subsidy is 66.8 per cent), assuming a discount rate of 4 per cent and the default rate of 10 per cent. The differences in the implicit subsidy calculations derive from different estimation formulas and assumptions of inflation rate, discount rate, default loss, and collection costs.

As with Ziderman (2003), our results indicate that the implicit subsidy is affected significantly by the interest rate charged, the grace period of repayment, and the grace period in which interest is not charged. Interest rate subsidies are an important aspect of the government subsidy and these arise because interest rates charged on debt are typically lower than the government's borrowing cost. If we adjust the nominal interest rate from 1 per cent to 7 per cent—meaning that the real interest rate is 3 per cent (equivalent to the discount rate we use)—the implicit subsidy decreases to 45 per cent. This could be roughly summarised as: 1 per cent of the interest rate charged to the loan reduces the implicit subsidy by about 3.5 per cent.

We estimate also the effect of changes in the repayment grace period on the subsidy. Based on other conditions of the current SLF system, the implicit subsidy declines from 65.68 per cent to 60.57 per cent if borrowers are required to make a repayment after graduation (zero repayment grace period). The interest grace period also has an impact on the implicit subsidy. If the interest is imposed on enrolment, the implicit subsidy reduces to 50.55 per cent. Even assuming no grace period of repayment and interest charged on enrolment, the implicit subsidy roughly declines from 65.68 per cent to 46.6 per cent. These results indicate that the impact of the interest rate charged on the implicit subsidy is much stronger than that of the repayment grace period and that of the interest grace period.

Under the schemes of a 7 per cent interest rate charged on the SLF, the implicit subsidy decreases to 36.44 per cent when there is no grace period of repayment. If we drastically alter the current SLF, assuming a 7 per cent interest rate charged, zero repayment grace period and interest rate charged on enrolment, the implicit subsidy substantially reduces—to 19.92 per cent,[12] or to less than one-third of the estimate for the current SLF of about 65 per cent. The findings of Table 10.4 suggest that the impact of grace period parameters on the implicit subsidy is greatest at the high interest rate.

We also calculate the implicit subsidy assuming that the default loss is 20 per cent and everything else remains constant. This 20 per cent default loss refers to the proportion of unpaid due borrowers after the five-year cut-off point for the Legal Affairs Division of the Office of the Student Loans Fund to handle delinquent loans. Results available from the authors show that at the interest rate of 1 per cent, the implicit subsidy increases by about 2 per cent, while at the interest rate of 7 per cent, it increases by about 4 per cent, compared with the current SLF with an assumed 15 per cent default loss. As expected, at a higher interest rate charged, the impact of default loss on the implicit subsidy is greater. Adjusting the default loss does not, however, significantly change our analysis of the implicit subsidy.

Repayment Hardships

Data and Methodology

To investigate the repayment hardship of loan recipients, we use the age–earnings profile of average Thais with an undergraduate degree provided by Chapman and Lounkaew (2008).[13] They construct age–earnings profiles of Thai graduates using data from the 2006 Labour Force Survey conducted by the National Statistical Office. The sample is classified into female and male graduates. Their income is measured as wages from their main jobs with a minimum of 20 working hours a week, and the estimated income of average graduates is constructed based on the ordinary least squares (OLS), which is estimated using potential experience (in a quadratic form) and educational background.[14]

---

12   The fact that some subsidies remain can be traced to overall defaults and administration costs built into the analysis.
13   Ziderman (2003) calculates repayment burdens using average earnings only.
14   There is a possible unemployment issue; however, it is probably not very serious because the average unemployment rate of female and male graduates during the 15-year repayment period is only about 8 per cent and 4 per cent, respectively.

Table 10.5 shows the descriptive statistics of the sample's earnings. The number of observations is 6899 and 9871 for male and female graduates, respectively. On average, female graduates earn approximately B172 000 per annum, which is lower than the male graduates' earnings of about B190 000 per annum. The minimum wage of female graduates is B13 200 per annum, while male graduates earn at least B18 200 per annum.

Moreover, to examine how the repayment hardship of loan recipients under the SLF scheme will be different when the loan recipients earn much less than the average, we use the age–earnings profile of graduates whose income is in the bottom 10 per cent—that is, unlucky graduates. To calculate the estimated future income of unlucky graduates, we also use the same regression model as that for average graduates. The descriptive statistics of unlucky graduates in Table 10.5 show that the number of observations for unlucky graduates is 1038 and 668 for female and male graduates, respectively. The minimum earnings of unlucky female graduates is B12 500, but on average they earn B75 994.96. As for unlucky male graduates, their average income is B78 972.62, which is higher than that for females.

Table 10.5 Descriptive statistics of age–earnings profile data

Sub-sample	No. of observations	Min.	Max.	Mean	Median	Std dev.
Female graduates	9871	13 200	480 003	172 116.10	148 800	85 172.42
Male graduates	6899	18 200	521 440	190 350.20	180 000	88 589.68
Unlucky female graduates	1038	12 500	130 600	75 994.96	71 400	25 485.52
Unlucky male graduates	668	6250	149 400	78 972.62	74 600	22 092.78

The age–earnings profiles over the working life of average female and male graduates and that of unlucky female and male graduates are shown in Figures 10.1 and 10.2, respectively.

To calculate the repayment hardship, there are four sub-samples in our analysis—that is, average female graduates, average male graduates, unlucky female graduates and unlucky male graduates. The repayment hardship is calculated as below:

The total loan repayment of each period is adjusted to a real term, using the inflation rate of 4 per cent and total income, estimated by the regression model, in a real term.

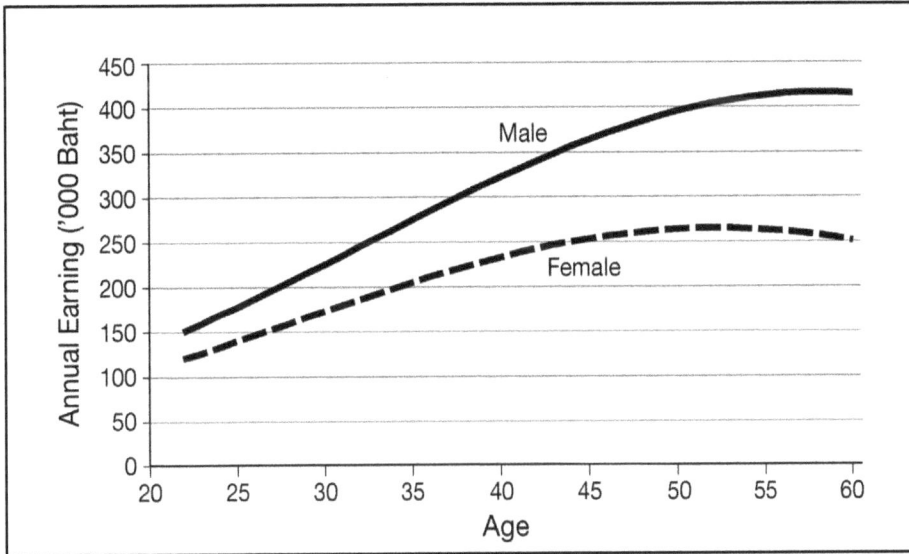

Figure 10.1 Age–earnings profile of average graduates

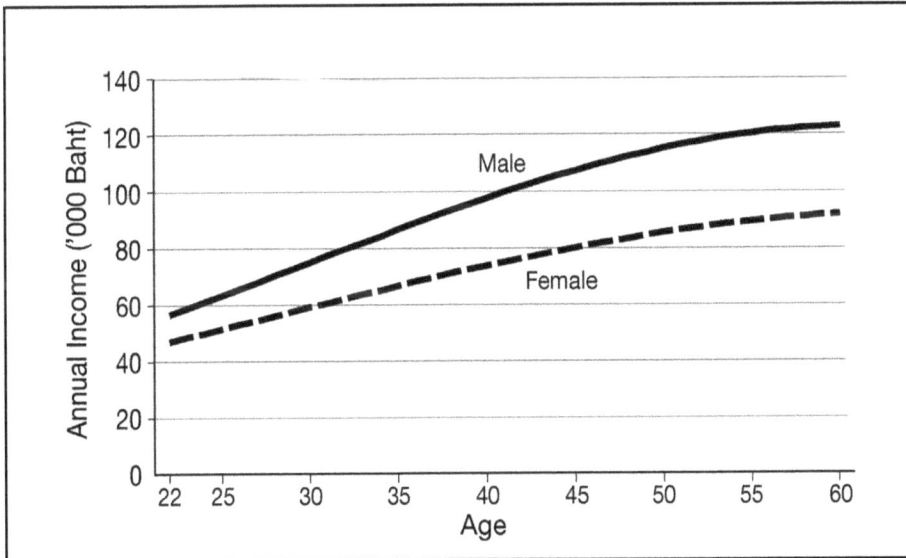

Figure 10.2 Age–earnings profile of unlucky graduates

Analysis

Consistent with the implicit subsidy analysis, we calculate the average repayment hardship over the 15-year repayment period of average female and male graduates as well as unlucky female and male graduates under the four different SLF schemes. The results are presented in Table 10.6.

Table 10.6 Average repayment hardships (per cent)

Schemes	Interest rate 1%				Interest rate 7%			
	Average		Unlucky		Average		Unlucky	
	Female	Male	Female	Male	Female	Male	Female	Male
2 Rep, 3 Int[a]	4.19	3.47	12.44	9.72	6.87	5.74	20.13	15.81
0 Rep, 3 Int[b]	4.55	3.76	14.20	11.21	7.45	6.22	23.01	18.28
2 Rep, 0 Int[c]	4.46	3.70	13.21	10.33	9.72	8.17	28.32	22.30
0 Rep, 0 Int[d]	5.12	4.33	14.79	11.69	10.22	8.78	28.95	23.06

a *2 Rep, 3 Int* = 'Two-year repayment grace period and interest charged three years after graduation'

b *0 Rep, 3 Int* = 'No repayment grace period and interest charged three years after graduation'

c *2 Rep, 0 Int* = 'Two-year repayment grace period and interest charged on enrolment'

d *0 Rep, 0 Int* = 'No repayment grace period and interest charged on enrolment'

As expected, under the current SLF scheme (*2 Rep, 3 Int* with the interest rate of 1 per cent), the average repayment hardship of the borrowers is the lowest among all schemes. For females and males, we find repayment burdens of 4.2 and 3.5 per cent, respectively. Ziderman (2003) has similar findings—of 3.5 and 2.2 per cent, respectively. The findings of most interest from our exercises relate to repayment hardships for our unlucky graduates.

We find that for unlucky female and male graduates, the average repayment hardship is about 12 and 10 per cent, respectively. Given that Ziderman (2003) argues that repayment burdens of about these levels are acceptable in terms of loan design when calculated at the average, it follows that the current SLF can be considered quite generous.

When we design a comparison SLF by changing the interest rate from 1 per cent to 7 per cent (*2 Rep, 3 Int* with the interest rate of 7 per cent), the average repayment hardship of average graduates increases by roughly 2–3 per cent. The average repayment hardship of unlucky graduates, however, increases about 6–8 per cent.[15]

As previously discussed, the implicit subsidy is very high under the current SLF scheme, but it can be lowered considerably if we remove all forms of subsidisation. The question here is what will happen to the repayment hardship of loan recipients? In other words, how much will the repayment hardship change when: 1) the interest rate increases from 1 per cent to 7 per cent; 2) there is no grace period for loan repayment; and 3) the interest is charged on enrolment? Table 10.6 shows that the average repayment hardship under this radically modified SLF scheme (*0 Rep, 0 Int* with the interest rate of 7 per cent) is twice as much for all sub-samples, compared with the current SLF scheme.

---

15   Again, these findings, based on average incomes, are not very different to those of Ziderman (2003).

More precisely, the average repayment hardship increases from 4.19 per cent and 3.47 per cent, to 10.22 per cent and 8.78 per cent for average female and male graduates, respectively. As for unlucky female and male graduates, the average repayment hardship increases from 12.44 per cent and 9.72 per cent, to 28.95 per cent and 23.06 per cent, respectively. These findings show that for unlucky graduates, if the government decides to reduce the subsidy for student loans, they might have to pay as much as one-fourth of their income for the loan, on average.

We then compare the repayment hardship over the 15-year repayment period of the current SLF with the radically modified SLF scheme (*0 Rep, 0 Int* with the interest rate of 7 per cent) for all sub-samples. Figure 10.3 shows that under the current SLF scheme, an average female graduate pays somewhat less than 4 per cent of her income at the beginning of the repayment period, reaching about 5 per cent at the end of the repayment period. Similarly, for an average male borrower, the proportion of loan repayment to income increases from about 3 per cent in the first year to about 4 per cent in the final repayment year.

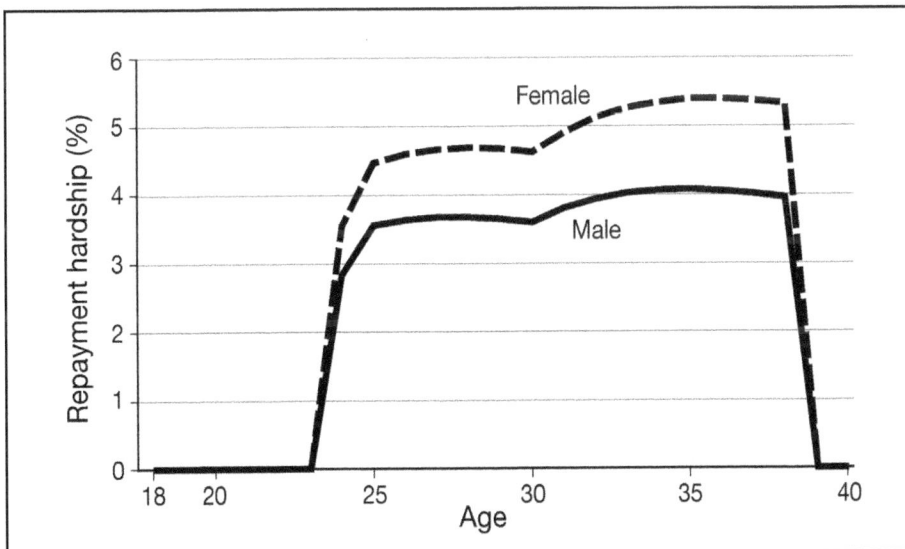

Figure 10.3 Proportion of total payment to total income of average graduates: current SLF

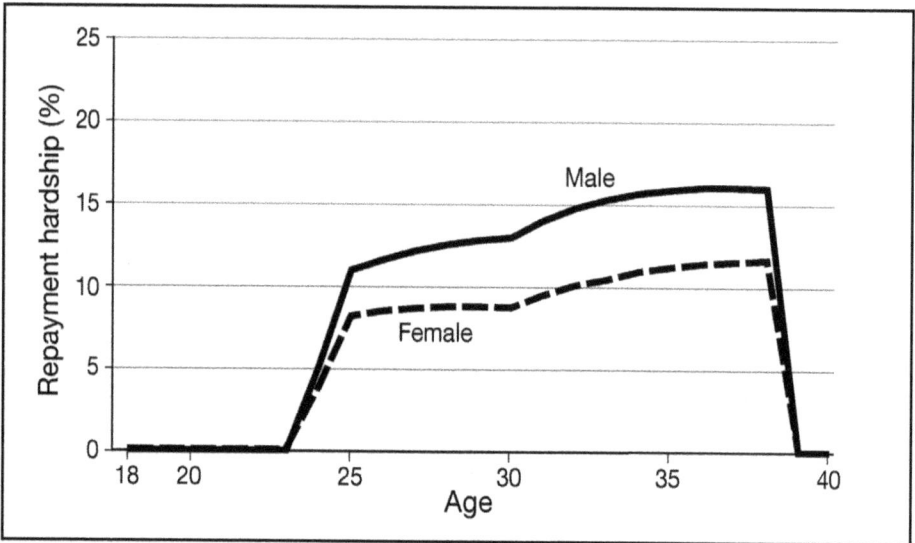

Figure 10.4 Proportion of total payment to total income of unlucky graduates: current SLF

Figure 10.4 shows the repayment hardship of unlucky graduates over the repayment period.

Compared with that of average graduates, the ratio of repayment to income for unlucky graduates is much higher. More precisely, the proportion of loan repayment to income is the lowest at about 8–11 per cent in the first year of repayment, rising to about 12 per cent and 16 per cent for females and males, respectively, in the final repayment years.

The proposed SLF scheme that charges 7 per cent interest on enrolment and requires borrowers to pay immediately after graduation demonstrates a different pattern of repayment hardship than that of the current SLF. This is shown in Figure 10.5 for borrowers (male/female) earning average incomes.

With the subsidies considerably reduced, the data from Figure 10.5 show that an average female borrower repays about 9 per cent of her annual income at the start of the repayment period. This proportion increases consistently, to reach nearly 14 per cent of annual income in the final year of the repayment period. The results are similar for an average male borrower. Nevertheless, the repayment hardship of a male borrower is about 1–3 per cent lower than that for a female borrower at any given age during the repayment period.

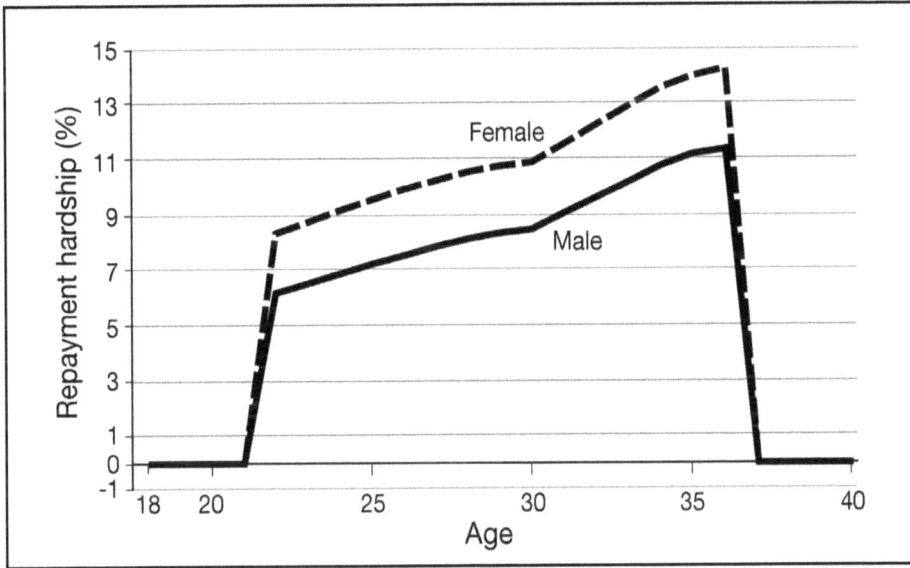

Figure 10.5 Proportion of total payment to total income of average graduates, 7 per cent interest rate, and no repayment and interest grace periods

The repayment hardship of unlucky borrowers is shown in Figure 10.6.

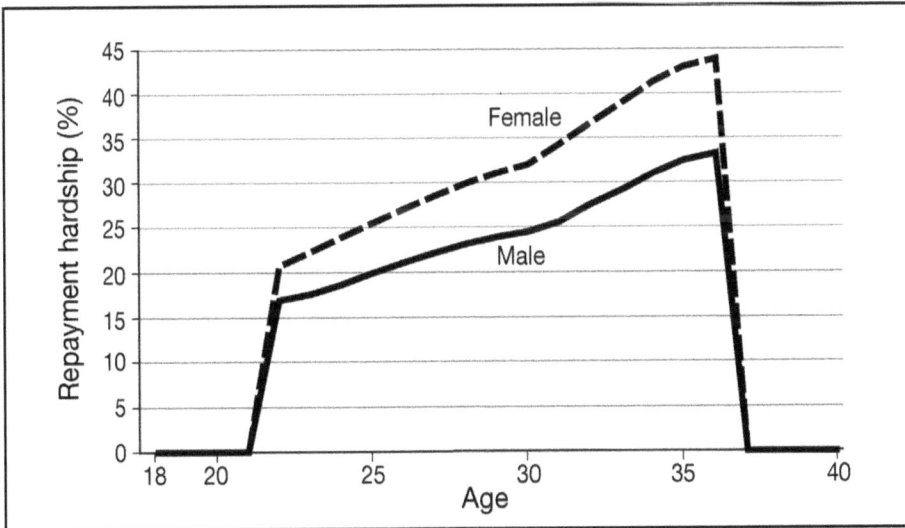

Figure 10.6 Proportion of total payment to total income of unlucky graduates, 7 per cent interest rate, and no repayment and interest grace periods

The clearest point from Figure 10.6 is that the proportion of repayment to income for unlucky borrowers is substantially greater than that for graduates earning average incomes. Specifically, the proportion peaks about 43 per cent and 32 per cent for unlucky female and male graduates, respectively, in the final year of the repayment period, after being about 20 per cent and 18 per cent, respectively, of annual income in the first repayment period.[16]

The analyses of the implicit subsidy and the repayment hardship suggest that if the government modifies the current SLF by increasing the interest rate to 7 per cent with no grace periods on repayment and interest, a very significant portion of the subsidy is reduced. More precisely, from Table 10.4, the implicit subsidy is reduced by more than two-thirds, while borrowers face greater difficulties in repaying the loan, especially in the first several years. This, then, is the dilemma facing the Thai government with respect to the SLF: the implicit interest rate subsidies are so high as to render the scheme close to a grant, but removing these subsidies results in what could be seen as highly undesirable repayment hardships for the members of some groups. This will undoubtedly lead to higher defaults.

Conclusion

We have analysed for Thailand the implicit subsidy of the current SLF and the repayment hardships of borrowers. We compare the current SLF with alternative SLF schemes, assuming different grace periods on interest charged and loan repayments. In addition, we assume a 7 per cent nominal interest rate—instead of 1 per cent—for all schemes. This 7 per cent rate is to make the real interest rate of the SLF loan equivalent to the discount rate we have used in the analysis.

Our analysis shows that the implicit subsidy drastically reduces—by approximately 46 percentage points (to less than one-third)—when the nominal interest rate is increased from 1 per cent to 7 per cent and there is no grace period for both the interest charge and the loan repayment. With no changes to grace periods, but using an interest rate of 7 per cent, the implicit subsidy declines by about 21 percentage points. In the case that the interest rate remains 1 per cent, and if the grace periods on interest charges and loan repayments are removed, the implicit subsidy drops by about 20 percentage points. These findings are similar to those reported by Ziderman (2003), implying a strong consensus in this area of analysis with respect to the SLF.

---

16   We allow direct comparisons of the repayment hardships between average and unlucky graduates under the current SLF and the three proposed SLF schemes in Appendix 10.1.

We considered also repayment hardship under the current SLF, and, as with Ziderman (2003), we did the calculations using average earnings data. We found the repayment hardships of average female and male graduates to be about 4 per cent and 3 per cent, respectively. But the story becomes much more interesting when we consider repayment burdens for graduates earning in the bottom deciles by age and sex. Specifically, for the SLF, repayment hardships for unlucky female and male graduates are about 12 per cent and 10 per cent, respectively. Given that Ziderman argues that burdens of these levels are acceptable (if estimated at the mean of the data), and we are considering the outcomes for very poor graduates indeed, the SLF is clearly a very generous student loan scheme.

Assuming that the interest rate increases to 7 per cent and the grace periods on interest charged and loan repayments are eliminated, the average repayment hardship of female graduates increases to about 10 per cent, and is about 9 per cent for males (Ziderman 2003 makes very similar findings). A critical finding, however, is that under the same conditions, the average repayment hardship of unlucky female graduates rises to about 29 per cent and for males the figure is 23 per cent. But it is important to note that there are differences between age groups in estimations of repayment hardships, with the figures reaching 43 per cent and 32 per cent for females and males respectively in the last year of repayment. These burdens should be considered excessive and unacceptable in policy terms.

To sum up, the current SLF is very generous in terms of repayment hardship for the borrowers. The scheme appears, however, to be unsatisfactory in terms of the extent of the implicit subsidies. In other words, the repayment hardship of loan recipients is relatively low, while the implicit subsidy is relatively high. Nevertheless, if all forms of subsidy are taken away (that is, the nominal interest rate increases and there are no grace periods on repayment and interest charges) that proportion of graduates earning very low incomes will likely experience great difficulties in repaying the loan.

References

Chapman, B. 2006, *Government Managing Risk: Income contingent loans for social and economic progress*, Routledge, London.

Chapman, B. and Lounkaew, K. 2008, Income contingent student loans for Thailand: comparative analysis, Paper presented to Student Loans in South and East Asia Conference, The Australian National University and Dhurakij Pundit University, Bangkok, 15–16 July.

Chapman, B. and Ryan, C. 2002, 'Income-contingent financing of student charges for higher education: assessing the Australian innovation', *The Welsh Journal of Education*, vol. 11, no. 1, pp. 64–81.

Johnstone, D. B. 1986, *Sharing the Costs of Higher Education: Student financial assistance in the United Kingdom, the Federal Republic of Germany, France, Sweden, and the United States*, The College Board, New York.

Johnstone, D. B. 2004, 'Higher educational finance and accessibility and student loan in sub-Saharan Africa', *Journal of Higher Education in Africa*, vol. 2, no. 2, pp. 11–36.

Johnstone, D. B. and Amero, A. 2001, *The applicability for developing countries of income-contingent loans or graduate taxes, with special consideration of an Australian HECS-type income-contingent loan program for Ethiopia*, Working Paper, University of Buffalo Center for Comparative and Global Studies in Education, NY.

Office of Student Loans Fund 2007, *SLF's Handbook*, (in Thai), Office of Student Loans Fund, Bangkok.

Shen, H. and Ziderman, A. 2008, *Student loans repayment and recovery: international comparisons*, Working Paper, Department of Economics, Bar Ilan University, Tel Aviv.

Tangkitvanich, S. and Manasboonphempool, A. 2006, *Policy evaluation of Student Loans Fund*, Working Paper, Thailand Development Research Institute, Bangkok.

Weesakul, B. 2006, Student loans in Thailand: past, present and future, Mimeo., Dhurakij Pundit University, Bangkok.

Ziderman, A. 2003, *Student Loans in Thailand: Are they effective, equitable, sustainable?*, United Nations Educational, Scientific and Cultural Organisation, Bangkok.

Ziderman, A. 2004, *Policy Options for Student Loan Schemes: Lessons for five Asian case studies*, International Institute for Educational Planning, United Nations Educational, Scientific and Cultural Organisation, Paris.

Appendix 10.1 Repayment Hardships of Average Graduates Versus Unlucky Graduates under Four Different SLF Schemes

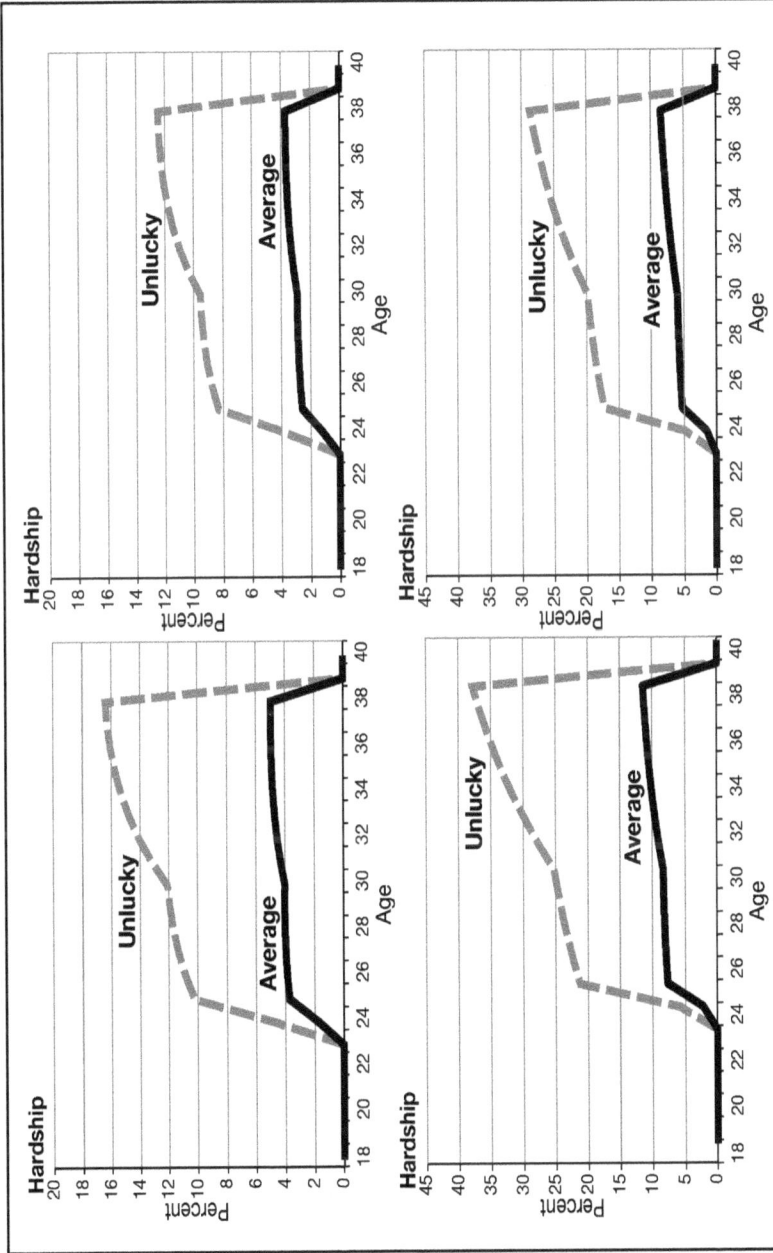

Figure A10.1 Proportion of total payment to total income for average and unlucky graduates (two-year repayment grace period and interest charged three years after graduation)

Top left: 1% interest rate, female. Top right: 1% interest rate, male. Bottom left: 7% interest rate, female. Bottom right: 7% interest rate, male

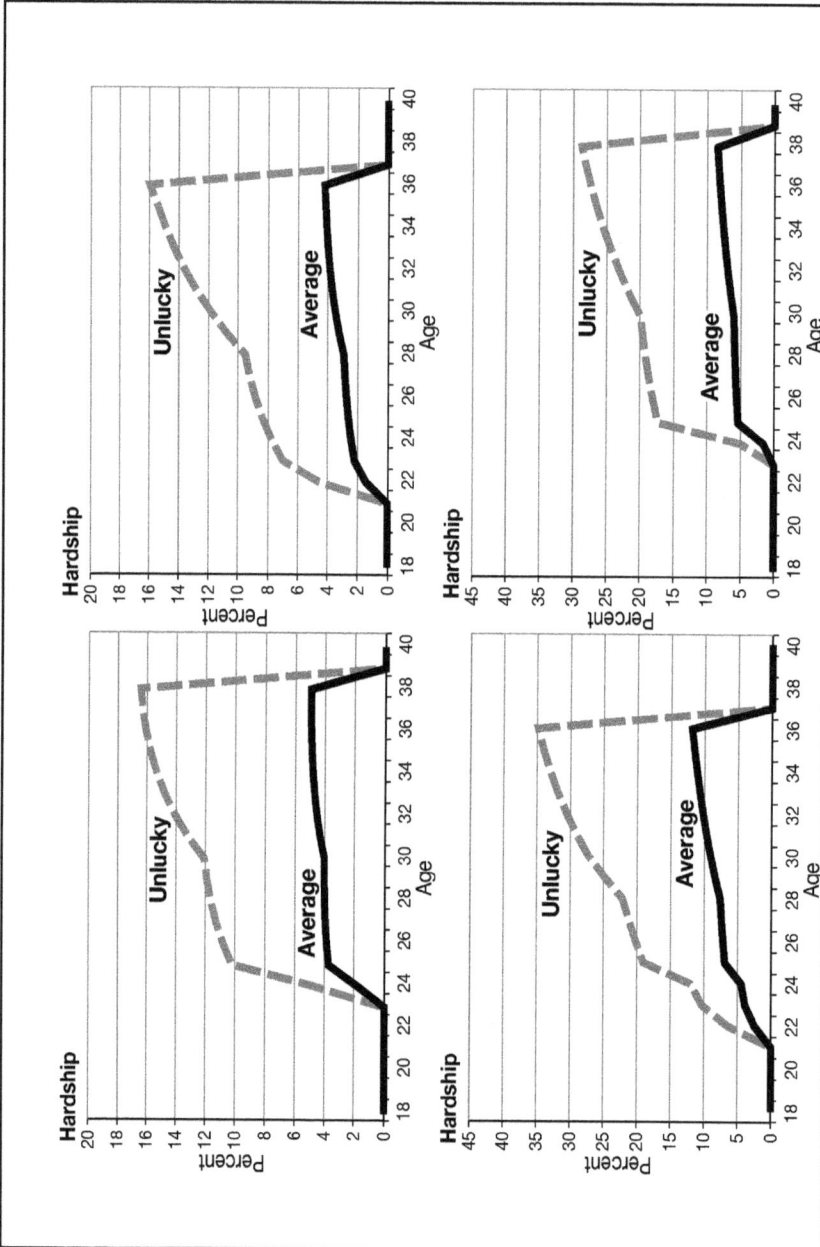

Figure A10.2 Proportion of total payment to total income for average and unlucky graduates (no repayment grace period and interest charged three years after graduation)

Top left: 1% interest rate, female. Top right: 1% interest rate, male. Bottom left: 7% interest rate, female. Bottom right: 7% interest rate, male

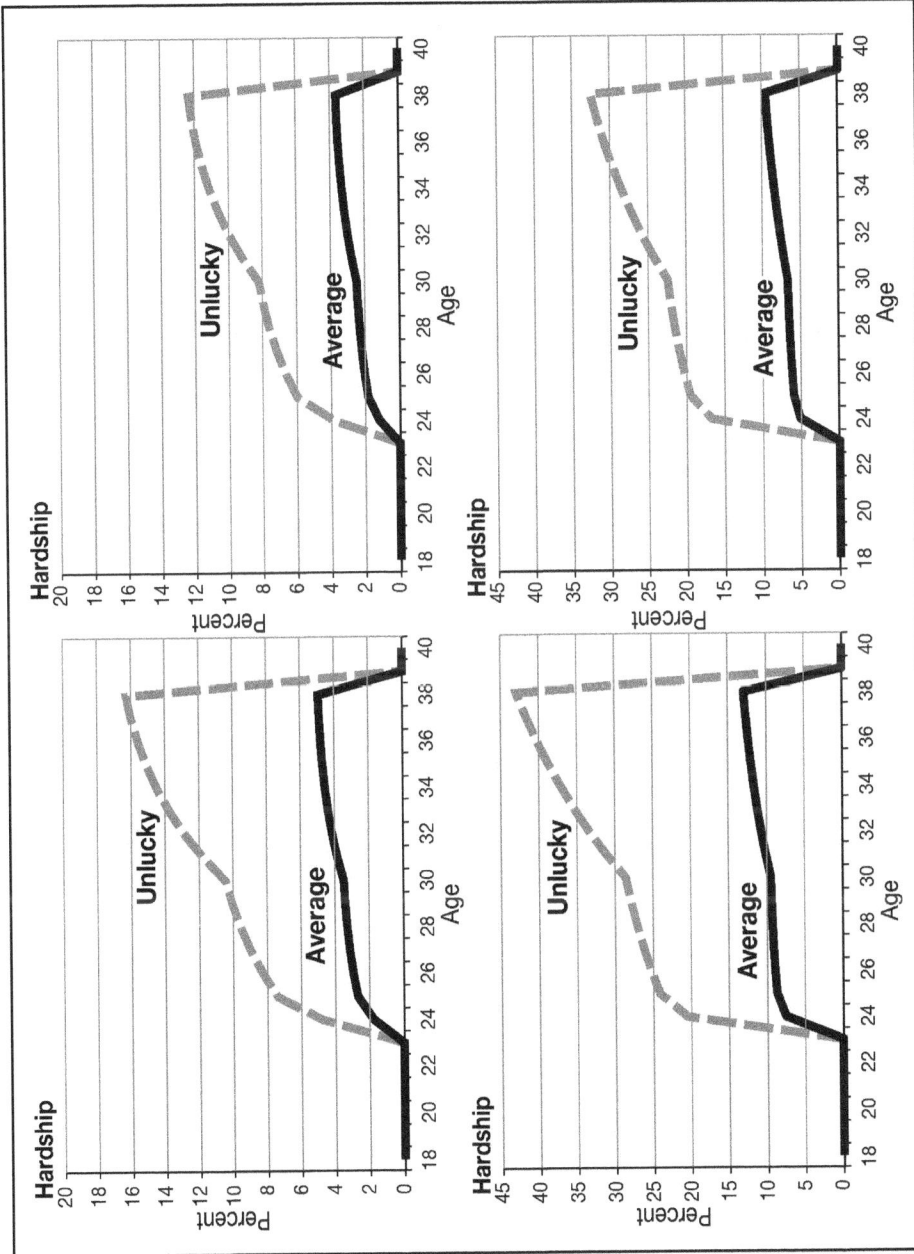

Figure A10.3 Proportion of total payment to total income for average and unlucky graduates (two-year repayment grace period and interest charged on enrolment)

Top left: 1% interest rate, female.Top right: 1% interest rate, male. Bottom left: 7% interest rate, female. Bottom right: 7% interest rate, male

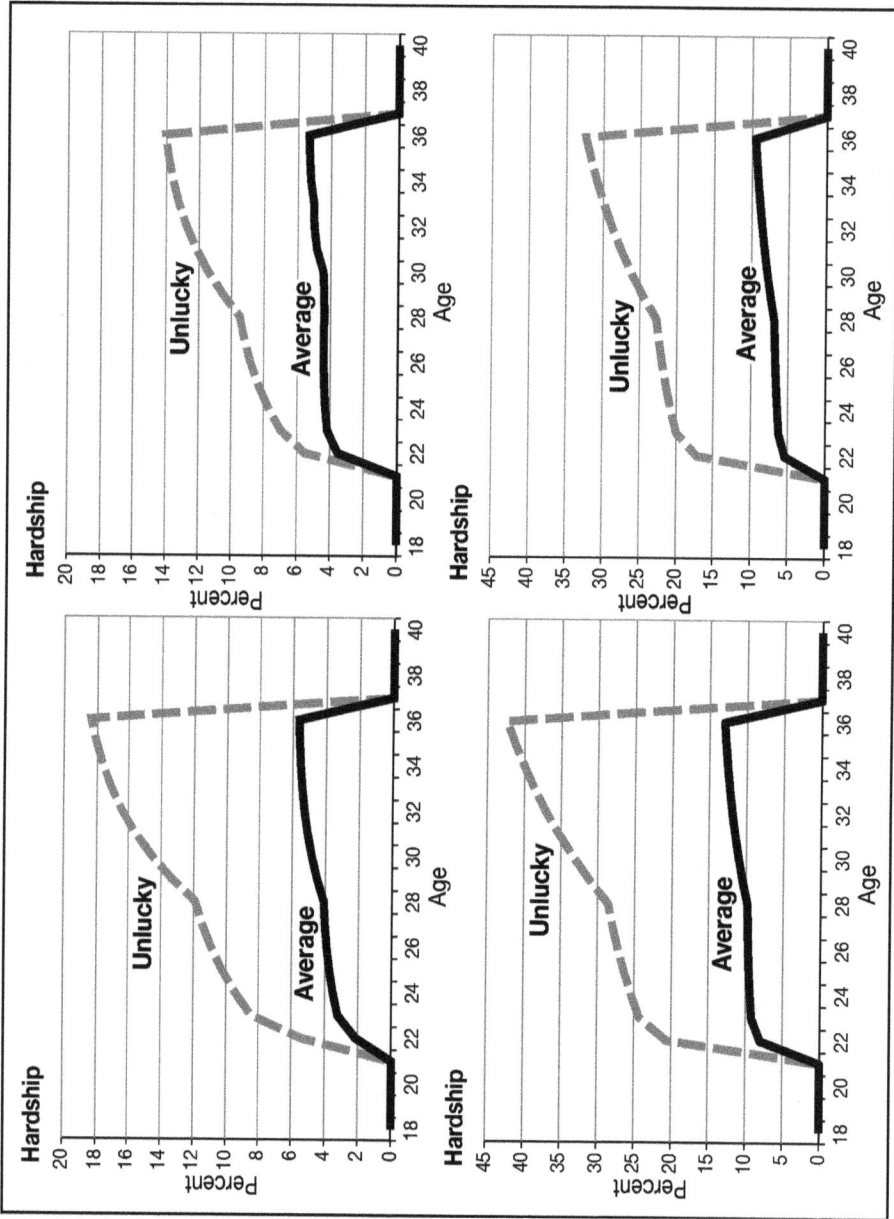

Figure A10.4 Proportion of total payment to total income for average and unlucky graduates (no repayment grace period and interest charged on enrolment)

Top left: 1% interest rate, female. Top right: 1% interest rate, male. Bottom left: 7% interest rate, female. Bottom right: 7% interest rate, male

11. Income-Contingent Student Loans for Thailand: Alternatives compared

Bruce Chapman and Kiatanantha Lounkaew
Crawford School of Economics and Government,
The Australian National University

Summary

In Thailand there is an ongoing debate concerning the most desirable form of higher education financing, with the critical concern being the form such a loan scheme should take. Conceptually, there are two generic possibilities: a mortgage-type loan, in which repayments are made on a consistent basis over a set period; and an income-contingent loan, in which the level and timing of repayments depend on a borrower's future income stream.

From 1996 to 2006, Thailand's preferred approach to higher education financing took the form of a mortgage-type loan known as the Student Loans Fund (SLF). The SLF involved targeted funds being allocated for both income support and tuition, with a time-limited repayment period of 17 years after graduation. Piruna et al. (2008) analysed the SLF with respect to two important dimensions: taxpayer-financed interest rate subsidies; and measures of so-called 'repayment hardships'—calculations of the proportion of borrowers' future incomes that would need to be allocated to SLF repayments.

Very similarly to the findings of Adrian Ziderman and others, Piruna et al. (2008) conclude that the SLF is associated with very substantial subsidies—perhaps of the order of 65 per cent. The source of the subsidy can be traced overwhelmingly to the interest rate regime. Consistent with these high subsidies, and in a unique contribution, they find also that the SLF has low rates of repayment hardship of about 4 per cent on average and only about 10 per cent for graduates whose future earnings are very low. In short, the SLF is a very generous scheme for students.

In this chapter, we seek to replicate some significant aspects of Piruna et al. (2008) with respect to various suggested forms of income-contingent loan schemes for Thailand. By definition, this type of loan has 'repayment hardship' set as a collection parameter—for example, in the Thai Income Contingent Allowance and Loan (TICAL) system explained below and in place in Thailand for 2007 only, the highest rate of repayment was set at 12 per cent of a borrower's income, and with the current Australian system the figure is 8 per cent. For these schemes, repayment hardships are not an issue.

There can be, however, considerable implicit interest rate subsidies with income-contingent loan schemes. The major contribution of this chapter lies in the illustration of the extent of these subsidies for four different possible income-contingent loan policies for Thailand. We show that the size of the subsidies is of the order of 25–40 per cent for a TICAL-type arrangement calculated for graduates with average earnings, and for this group these subsides can be almost eliminated with alternative loan schemes with a form of real rate of interest. But a more disaggregated, and preferred, approach to computing loan subsidies reveals that TICAL-type schemes have subsidies of 30–55 per cent, and even improved loan systems with respect to interest rate regimes have the potential to result in subsidies of 3–18 per cent, even for low levels of debt.

A major benefit of our approach is that we have used the same data, econometric techniques and present-value methods as employed by Piruna et al. (2008), providing a consistent basis from which to assess alternative loan schemes. We find that in design terms, and with respect to taxpayer subsidies, there seem to be viable possibilities for an income-contingent loan scheme for Thailand. But this conclusion is more credible for relatively low levels of debt than for the sizes of tuition fees that are more likely to be associated with higher-price private institutions. In this latter case, the subsidies of even well-designed schemes can be as high as 50 per cent. Whether or not Thai institutional and administrative arrangements are well suited to the collection of an income-contingent loan is a critical policy issue not addressed in what follows.

Introduction

In 2007, for one year only, Thailand introduced an income-contingent loan system for higher education, known as the Thai Income Contingent Allowance and Loan (TICAL) system. TICAL was based on Australia's Higher Education Contribution Scheme (HECS)—an income-contingent loan system in which tuition charges are collected through the income tax system depending on a student's future income. HECS was instituted in 1989, and similar student loan policies commenced throughout the 1990s and beyond in, among other countries, New Zealand, Chile, South Africa, Ethiopia, Hungary and the United Kingdom. Other countries—notably, Colombia and Israel—are involved currently in research-based debate on the usefulness of income-contingent loan approaches to higher education financing.

This chapter examines the conceptual bases of alternative student loan systems, and it is argued that income-contingent approaches are generally seen as desirable arrangements compared with alternatives. Such an assessment is, however, associated with two extremely important qualifications: one is that the administrative institutions of a country are such as to allow efficacious collection of a former student's debt; and two, that an income-contingent scheme needs to be properly designed with respect to some key parameters.

We are unable to ascertain with complete certainty if potential Thai collection arrangements are such as to enable efficient and fair collection of an income-contingent loan, and we leave the answer to that critical question to administrative, tax and/or social security specialists.[1] Our aim is instead to throw significant light on the second concern—the importance of design parameters with respect to the likely outcomes of such a system—with our focus on the critical issue of implicit taxpayer interest rate subsidies. Internationally, this is now perhaps the most important non-administrative design issue for an assessment of the efficacy of income-contingent loan schemes.

Interest rate subsidies, along with loan repayment hardships, have been explored by Piruna et al. (2008), who are concerned with analysis of the previous Thai student loan scheme, the Student Loans Fund (SLF). Piruna et al.'s (2008) and our analyses use exactly the same data set and empirical methods, so we can compare and contrast confidently the effects of disparate past and prospective Thai student loan arrangements.

While interest rate subsidies are a major aspect of our chapter, it is useful to make a comment on the other major component of Piruna et al.'s (2008) analysis: so-called repayment hardships associated with the SLF. The results of their research are summarised below, and it is important to recognise that one of the principal benefits of an income-contingent loan system is that, unless the loan is designed poorly, it is not possible to incur important repayment hardships, as measured by the proportion of a graduate's income that needs to be allocated to the repayment of a student loan. That is, because such a loan is repaid up to a maximum percentage of income, there will not be repayment hardships. In the Australian system, this maximum is 8 per cent, and for TICAL it is 12 per cent; for mortgage-type loans, these figures could be very different.

There are, however, important reasons to explore the findings of Piruna et al. (2008) with respect to implicit interest subsidies for the SLF, and, in this chapter, various forms of income-contingent loans for Thailand. As implied above, all the

---

1 The analysis below of requirements suggests the importance of being able to collect the debt on the basis of observed lifetime incomes, and this might imply for Thailand the use of the social security system instead of the income tax system. With the former, there are already income-contingent collections of funds for pensions.

authors collaborated closely in the two exercises in order to be in a position to make similarly based assessments of the effects of the different schemes in terms of subsidies.

Piruna et al.'s (2008) results can be compared with our findings for two different interpretations of how TICAL might have worked in practice had it not been discontinued, as well as with an alternative proposed income-contingent loan scheme for Thailand. Two versions of the latter are explained and explored, with these variants having been motivated by our curiosity with respect to the possible role played by different forms of the requirement that former students cover, at least in part, the opportunity cost to the government of borrowing to finance the income-contingent loan. As with Piruna et al. (2008), we use not only average predicted lifetime graduate incomes for our empirical exercises, but also low, median and high estimates of incomes, and for both sexes.

Our estimates and calculations illustrate the empirical significance of different levels of income thresholds for repayment, and for disparate approaches to the imposition of real rates of interest for a wide spectrum of graduate incomes, and take into account the possible roles of graduate unemployment rates and potential loan losses associated with collection inefficiencies. The findings suggest that in design terms an income-contingent loan scheme is a viable option for Thailand, but this conclusion seems to be more credible for relatively low levels of debt than for the sizes of tuition fees that are more likely to be associated with higher-price private institutions.

Traditional Student and Income-Contingent Loan Schemes: Conceptual issues

The Need for Government Intervention in Higher Education Financing

A significant financing issue for higher education is that there is generally seen to be a case for both a contribution from students and a taxpayer subsidy (Barr 2001; Chapman 2006). An important question is: is there a role for government beyond the provision of the subsidy?

An understanding of the issue is facilitated through consideration of what would happen if there was no higher education financing assistance involving the public sector. That is, a government, convinced that there should be a subsidy, could simply provide the appropriate level of taxpayer support to higher education institutions, and then leave market mechanisms to take their course. Presumably, this would result in institutions charging students up-front on enrolment for the service.

There are, however, major problems with this arrangement, traceable in most instances to the potent presence of risk and uncertainty. This critical point was first raised by Friedman (1955). The argument can be best understood with reference to the nexus between labour markets and human-capital investments. The essential point is that educational investments are risky, with the main areas of uncertainty as follows.[2]

Enrolling students do not know fully their capacities for (and perhaps even true interest in) the higher education discipline of their choice. This means, in an extreme, they cannot be sure that they will graduate, with, in Australia, for example, about 25 per cent of students ending up without a qualification.

Even given that university completion is expected, students will not be aware of their likely relative success in the area of study. This will depend not just on their own abilities, but also on the skills of others competing for jobs in the area.

There is uncertainty concerning the future value of the investment. For example, the labour market—including the labour market for graduates in specific skill areas—is undergoing constant change. What looked like a good investment at the time it began might turn out to be a poor choice when the process is finished.

Many prospective students, particularly those from disadvantaged backgrounds, might not have much information concerning graduate incomes, due in part to a lack of contact with graduates.

These uncertainties are associated with important risks for both borrowers and lenders. The important point is that if the future incomes of students turn out to be lower than expected, the individual is unable to sell part of the investment to refinance a different educational path, for example. For a prospective lender—a bank—the risk is compounded by the reality that in the event of a student borrower defaulting on the loan obligation, there is no available collateral to be sold—a fact traceable in part to the illegality of slavery. And even if it was possible for a third party to own and sell human capital, its future value might turn out to be quite low, taking into account the above-noted uncertainties associated with higher education investments.

It follows that, left to itself—and even with subsidies from the government to cover the value of externalities—the market will not deliver propitious higher education outcomes. Prospective students judged to be relatively risky,

---

2   As discussed by Barr (2001), Chapman (2006) and Palacios (2004).

and/or those without loan-repayment guarantors, will not be able to access the financial resources required for both the payment of tuition and to cover income support. There would be efficiency losses (talented but poor prospective students would be excluded) and distributional inequities (the non-attainment of equality of educational opportunity). Government intervention of some form is thus required.

The governments of most countries apparently understand the capital-market failure with respect to higher education financing, given that public-sector loan interventions are commonplace internationally. Until recently, government intervention often took the form of public-sector guarantees for commercial bank provision of education loans, but over the past decade or so this has increasingly involved income-contingent loans. While quite different in practice, both approaches are motivated in part by the recognition that, left alone, higher education markets will function poorly.

The Costs and Benefits of Mortgage-Type Loans

A possible solution to the capital-market problem described above used in many countries is the provision of student loans—either directly by the government or indirectly through guarantees of repayments to banks by the government in the event of default. Typically, and most simply, these loans involve fixed repayments, as, for example, with a house mortgage. While this seems to address the capital-market failure, it raises other problems.

Students face an important default issue. This is that some might be reluctant to borrow for fear of not being able to meet future repayment obligations. Not being able to meet repayment obligations has the potential to inflict significant damage to a person's credit reputation (and thus access to future borrowing— for example, for the purchase of a house). These concerns imply that there will be less borrowing than there would be in the absence of this default concern.

A reluctance to borrow due to the uncertainty of repayment constitutes what might be labelled an *ex ante* default problem for prospective students. There is also an *ex post* problem, which is that a proportion of those students who took the credit risk of borrowing for a human-capital investment will end up not being able to repay because of low incomes. In these circumstances, default imposes a potentially large cost on those unlucky borrowers who do poorly in the labour market. Significantly, research suggests that members of the default group are predominantly those who ultimately experienced relatively high unemployment rates and relatively low earnings.[3]

---

3 Dynarski (1994) used the National Post-Secondary Student Aid Study and found strong evidence that experiencing low earnings after leaving formal education is a strong determinant of default. Importantly,

The prospect and consequences of a student defaulting on a loan obligation are potentially critical issues for borrowing to finance human-capital investments, due to the uncertainties noted above. A consequence is that some eligible prospective students will not be prepared to take bank loans. This problem can be traced, in part, to the fact that bank-loan repayments are insensitive to the borrower's financial circumstances.

A final possible practical problem of government-guaranteed bank loans relates to the fact that in many countries loans of this type are not universally available, or available loan levels are limited.[4] This is because loan provision and/or amounts available are usually means tested on the basis of family income. This raises the important issue explained by Carneiro and Heckman (2002) concerning the role of the sharing of financial resources within families. Some students will be unable to access necessary levels of borrowing and will face the same credit-market failure as they would in the absence of a government guarantee of a bank loan. Making loans available on a means-tested basis (as is the case in the United States and Canada) suggests that some prospective students will have difficulties accessing the system.

The bottom line is that, even though government-assisted conventional loans are a common form internationally of public-sector involvement in higher education financing, such an approach has several apparently very significant weaknesses.

The Costs and Benefits of Income-Contingent Loans

A different approach to student financing involves income-contingent loans, such as Australia's HECS. The attraction of these schemes is that they can be designed to avoid many of the problems associated with alternative financing policies.

First, there is no concern with intra-family sharing so long as the scheme is universal. That is, no students would be denied access through the imposition of means-testing arrangements that could exclude some whose parents or partners are unwilling to help.

Second, given an efficient collection mechanism, there is no default issue as such for the government. That is, if the tax system works well and is used to collect the debt (at least for Australia, this is essential because the Australian Taxation Office is the only institution with reasonably good information on a former student's income), it is extremely difficult for the majority of graduates to avoid

---

borrowers from low-income households and minorities were more likely to default, as were those who did not complete their studies.

4   Eligibility for Canadian student loans is limited to less than half of all students (Finnie and Swartz 1996).

repayment. There is a form of a default issue in that some students will not pay back in full, because income-contingent systems are designed to excuse some former students' payments because their lifetime incomes are too low. Harding (1995) calculates that the total repayments remaining uncollected because of the nature of HECS would be of the order of 20 per cent for the original scheme (when the repayment conditions were particularly generous for the student). Other reasons loans might not be repaid include death and emigration.

Third, because repayments depend on income, there should be no concerns by students with respect to incapacity to repay the debt, or hardships associated with repayments. That is, once an individual's income determines repayment, and so long as the repayment parameters are sufficiently generous, it is not possible to default for hardship because of a lack of capacity to pay. This is the critical practical advantage of income-contingent collection schemes: unlike any other form of assistance, there is insurance against default and repayment difficulties.

Income-contingent schemes have significant advantages over alternative financing arrangements, in that they can be designed to avoid the major problems of their alternatives. This does not make such approaches a panacea generally, however; for an income-contingent scheme to be made operational, it is essential that there is an efficient administrative collection mechanism.

The matter of collection is of great importance for the introduction of income-contingent loans in countries without the necessary institutional apparatus. Chapman (2006) argues that the minimum conditions for a successful income-contingent loan seem to be

1. accurate record keeping of the accruing liabilities of students

2. an effective collection mechanism with a sound and, if possible, computerised record-keeping system

3. an efficient way of determining with accuracy, over time, the actual incomes of former students.

While most Organisation for Economic Cooperation and Development (OECD) countries will have income tax or social security systems that enable efficient collection of income-contingent debts, it is very unlikely that developing countries have the capacity to meet requirement (3) above. This issue requires critical attention in the Thai policy context.

The Student Loans Fund, TICAL and the Need for Alternatives

The Recent History of Student Loans in Thailand

A loan scheme for Thailand's higher education students, the SLF was introduced in 1996, and has been analysed extensively by Piruna et al. (2008) and Ziderman (2003). The main features of the loan scheme are documented in Piruna et al. (2008), with the most important design issues for our purposes being as follows.

The SLF is in essence a traditional student loan scheme, with a fixed repayment period of 15 years after a grace period of two years, but with the novel feature that the proportion of the total debt-repayment obligation increases with time, starting at 1.5 per cent in the first year and reaching 13 per cent of the total debt in the final year. This aspect of the SLF can be seen as a part-concession to the benefits of income-contingent loans, since the repayment obligations will be correlated with increases in average earnings with age, as is clear from the analysis presented in this chapter. What these arrangements mean for repayment hardship is summarised below.

An important feature of the SLF relates to the nature of the interest rate subsidies. As pointed out in Piruna et al. (2008) and Ziderman (2003), these arise principally from: the zero nominal interest rate in the period before repayment begins; and the fact that the nominal interest rate of 1 per cent per annum, when imposed, is significantly below the true cost of borrowing for the government of perhaps 2–3 per cent in real terms per annum. The importance of these arrangements in an understanding of the overall interest rate subsidies is summarised below.

In 2007, the SLF was suspended and was replaced with the (short-lived) TICAL. The main design features of TICAL, and its financial implications, are explained and examined in detail below. In 2008, TICAL was replaced with what is essentially a new form of the SLF, but with the same fixed repayment period of 17 years. This new scheme has not been analysed by Piruna et al. (2008) and it will not be explored here, but it is very likely that the new loan system's implications for both repayment hardship and interest rate subsidies are very similar to those of the SLF.

The Effects of the SLF in Summary: Repayment hardship and interest rate subsidies

Piruna et al. (2008) analysed two critical aspects of the former Thai SLF: repayment hardships and interest rate subsidies. The former is defined as the proportion of a graduate's income that is used to repay the loan, and is calculated both for graduates earning average incomes in the periods of repayment and so-called 'unlucky graduates' who earn in the bottom 10 per cent of the graduate income distribution by age and sex.

For the same sample of graduates used in this chapter, and using the same methods to project graduate incomes by age and sex, Piruna et al. (2008) find that the measures of repayment hardship on average are about 4 and 3.5 per cent for females and males, respectively. For the 'unlucky graduates', the results are about 12.4 and 9.7 per cent for females and males, respectively. It is reasonable to describe these outcomes as fairly low—certainly compared with the situation in other countries with similarly motivated and designed student loan schemes.[5]

Related to the above finding is that the SLF delivers very considerable interest rate subsidies, of the order of 67 per cent overall—a finding very similar to that found also for the SLF by Ziderman (2003). These very high subsidies are explained by a combination of policy parameters, but by far the most important empirically can be traced to the fact that SLF debt is adjusted annually by a nominal rate of interest of only 1 per cent—implying a real rate of interest of about −3 per cent per annum. Interest rate subsidies are a very important aspect of the Thai student loan debate, and they are now considered further with respect to the design of alternative possible income-contingent loan schemes for the country.

TICAL and an Alternative Form of an Income-Contingent Loan Described

TICAL was motivated by the perceived benefits of income-contingent loans considered in section two, although it is reasonable to suggest that there are some controversial design aspects of the scheme. There are several important and arguably contentious design issues associated with the scheme that are addressed in our empirical exercises.

The first relates to the first income threshold of repayment, set at B192 000 per annum, which seems to be very high given the age–earnings profiles of

---

5   Recent calculations by Bruce Chapman and Colombian education officials illustrate that for the ICETEX loan scheme in that country, the repayment hardship results for unlucky graduates are of the order of 35–45 per cent.

graduates presented below.[6] This matters particularly if the debt has no real rate of interest, since it is necessarily the case that the longer it takes to repay a government loan that does not have a real rate of interest, the greater is the size of the associated subsidy from taxpayers. A major goal in what follows is to illustrate the empirical significance of this feature of TICAL.

Because the first income threshold of repayment of TICAL seems to be very high, we suggest a different income-contingent loan model for Thailand for illustrative purposes, and we label this 'ILLUSTRATIVE'. It has two repayment features different to TICAL: 1) the first income threshold of repayment is very much lower, at B100 000 per annum; and 2) the rates of repayment we have chosen are much closer to those of HECS, meaning that they are considerably lower than is the case for TICAL, particularly at high levels of income. Table 11.1 presents the repayment thresholds and rates of income for the two broad schemes.

Table 11.1 Repayment thresholds and collection parameters (percentage of taxable income)[7] of different income-contingent loan schemes for Thailand

TICAL		ILLUSTRATIVE	
Annual income (baht)	Collection parameters	Annual income (baht)	Collection parameters
Less than 192 000	0.00	Less than 100 000	0.00
192 000–360 000	0.05	100 000–110 000	0.03
360 001–840 000	0.08	110 001–120 000	0.04
Higher than 840 000	0.12	120 001–130 000	0.05
		Higher than 130 000	0.06

A second design issue concerns the indexation arrangements with respect to the income thresholds of repayments, and this is a critical point in trying to understand what the effects of TICAL might have been. The concern is that it is not clear if the income threshold for repayment of the loan was to be indexed, and to what, as is the case for all relevant parameters of Australia's HECS, for example. To address this, we raise two possibilities.

The first possibility is that the income thresholds are eventually indexed to average nominal wage increases, but we are unsure what this means in a Thai context in which regular indexing is typically not part of the economic policy

---

6   For example, from the data presented in this chapter, it would seem to take an average female graduate about 12 years before any TICAL repayments are made.

7   This form of collection is the same as that used in the Australian loan scheme, HECS, in which once a given threshold of income is reached, a given proportion of total income is owed. While this seems to imply an extremely high effective marginal tax rate at the first income threshold, work by Chapman and Leigh (2006) suggests this has only small behavioural effects.

fabric. To illustrate the significance of this possibility, however, it is necessary that an indexation arrangement of some form is imposed and the one we have chosen is full (assumed to be 5 per cent per annum) wage indexation being imposed 10 years after the initiation of the policy, and continuing annually after that. This scenario of eventual indexation of the repayment thresholds is referred to as 'TICAL1'.

The second possibility is that the TICAL thresholds are not to be indexed, meaning that over time as nominal wages increase the threshold becomes effectively lower and graduates would increasingly be repaying their debts earlier; in the event of real interest rate subsidies, this would mean lower taxpayer subsidies over time. This unindexed scenario is referred to as 'TICAL2'.

A third, related and controversial aspect of TICAL is that there is no real rate of interest on the debt, with an adjustment being made annually to a student's or graduate's debt for changes in the consumer price index (CPI) only. This aspect of the scheme looks to be identical to Australia's HECS arrangement, but there is a critical difference. This is that for HECS there is a 20 per cent discount for an up-front payment of the tuition obligation, which in effect means that students choosing to take the debt are subject to a 25 per cent surcharge[8] (meaning that effectively there is a blunt form of real interest rate for HECS). The motivation for analysing in depth the conceptual issues associated with interest rate regimes, and for providing an empirical approach to explore this further, is now considered.

Understanding the Role of the Form of Real Interest Rates

The issue of interest rate subsidies in student loan schemes is extremely important. Moreover, there are major differences between countries even with apparently similar approaches to income-contingent loan policies. As examples: given the write-off of the interest rate of loans in nominal terms in New Zealand, the effective interest rate for that country is negative in real terms; for both the United Kingdom and TICAL, the real rate of interest is zero; and for HECS, there is a surcharge on the debt once it is incurred, but the ongoing adjustment of the debt is equal only to the rate of price inflation.

There are important disagreements between researchers on the appropriate level and form of a rate of interest on the debt associated with income-contingent loans. Barr (2007) makes a compelling case that the Australian form, which uses a surcharge, introduces distortions in both efficiency and equity terms,

8 This can be explained as follows. If there is a charge of $1000, a student may avoid the debt by paying $800; this means that students paying later take on an additional 25 per cent—that is, $200/800.

although on average it still means that there is some attempt to require students to contribute to the government's opportunity costs of borrowing. Chapman (2006) argues that the issue is quite complex in the case of an income-contingent loan, since such schemes are designed to offer insurance against the costs of poor future outcomes; and, in the case of a former student experiencing low future incomes, they might find themselves in an *ex post* situation of accumulating high real debts due simply to unpredictable poor luck.

Three broad points can be highlighted.

1. There is a strong case for an income-contingent loan scheme to require borrowers to contribute to diminishing the costs of borrowing for the loan for the government (which must mean that the UK scheme and TICAL, and now the New Zealand system, have important design weaknesses).

2. In the circumstances in which loans are offered in part for income support (as they are in New Zealand, but not in Australia), the case for having an ongoing real rate of interest such as suggested by Barr is strong, since otherwise some borrowers will be able to use their loans to make profits in the commercial money market—at taxpayers' expense.

3. There might be a case for a surcharge instead of an ongoing real rate of interest for tuition charges if borrowers are averse to having rapidly increasing debts in times of ongoing low incomes—a possibility that seems to be recognised through most loan schemes having a so-called 'forgiveness' clause, after which all the outstanding loan is written off.

We are unable to determine with confidence what the correct form of a real rate of interest should be for income-contingent tuition charges in the Thai context, so in what follows we have designed two alternative forms of the suggested TICAL1 and TICAL2, and this is known as ILLUSTRATIVE. The first form is called 'ILLUSTRATIVE1', and this variant imposes the same rule as HECS by adding a surcharge of 25 per cent to the debt, after which the real rate of interest is zero (that is, with an ongoing CPI adjustment only).

The second is called 'ILLUSTRATIVE2', which has a conventional real rate of interest imposed on the debt of 3 per cent real per annum, with adjustments beginning immediately after the debt is incurred.[9] It is a significant goal of our research to determine the extent to which these different approaches matter with respect to the extent of taxpayer subsidies, and whether the size of the debt matters to an assessment of the relative appeal of these different approaches. This last point might become very important if the income-contingent loan system is allowed to move to the private sector where tuition charges are much higher.

---

9   Very roughly, this is about the long-term government bond rate, at least for Australia.

The Data and Earnings Function Results

Motivation

We are interested in estimating earnings functions in order to provide structure and understanding of the lifetime earnings streams of male and female graduates, on average. This will assist in an overall understanding of the Thai graduate labour market, allowing insight into increments to wages from additional education, and the internal rate of return to investing in a university education. In this sense, our single cross-section provides restricted but complementary information for the exercises reported in Lathapipat (2008).

More significantly, for the policy aspect of our exercise, the ordinary least squares (OLS) results will allow us to determine the extent of interest rate subsidies on average from our four different variants of income-contingent loans for Thailand. This is done by using predicted smoothed average earnings to ascertain the timing and structure of loan repayments under different debt obligation parameters.

It is also interesting and important for subsidy calculations to examine the extent to which interest rate subsidies vary between debtor groups with quite different *ex post* income levels. This is approached in a separate exercise explained and reported below by truncating the earnings data—our preferred method to the use of quantile regressions, for reasons to be explained. Our method reveals that the use of OLS to determine interest rate subsidies from different forms of income-contingent loans has the potential to overstate aggregate loan repayments and thus to understate loan subsidies. The differences are not trivial, and this matters for the policy debate.

The Data

We use cross-sectional individual survey data from the Labour Force Survey (LFS), collected in the third quarter of 2006. The LFS is administered by the National Statistical Office, and it contains information on individuals' characteristics such as age, marital status, household size, educational attainment, and geographical location, as well as job-related information such as employment status, occupation, earnings, and hours of work. The LFS covers every province in Thailand and has a total sample size of more than 200 000; thus, it is the most comprehensive data set for the labour market available in Thailand to be used for analysing returns to education at the aggregate level. Summary statistics are presented in Table 11.2.

Our analysis is restricted to individuals aged from fifteen to sixty.[10] We have omitted: a very small number of individuals whose earnings are significantly different from the population at large; the self-employed; part-time workers;[11] and those who work in the agricultural sector.

The major points are as follows. There are 19 856 males and 17 491 females in the sample. Earnings per hour are calculated as weekly earnings received from the main job divided by total hours worked in the main job per week, and gross hourly wages in 2006 for males and females are B52.47 and B54.68, respectively, and we have adjusted these to derive average annual earnings for men and women, of B106 769 and B108 385, respectively.

Binary variables (0, 1) are used to represent the highest educational qualification of each individual in the sample, and in the econometric work we use individuals who did not complete primary school as the reference point for comparisons. About 18 per cent and 13 per cent of males and females, respectively, have the highest qualification recorded as being primary-school level or lower, and about 32 per cent of males and 29 per cent of females have attained lower secondary or upper secondary education. The receipt of an undergraduate qualification differs markedly between males and females, with the proportions being 17 per cent for males and 33 per cent for females.[12] Average hours of work a week are 45.7 for men and 44.9 for women.

One drawback of the LFS is that respondents are not asked how long an individual has been employed in paid work—an important variable in the estimation of the earnings functions. To deal with this issue, we have constructed the usual proxy, known as 'potential experience', which is the difference between age and the sum of total years of schooling and the minimum age required to begin school. Based on this calculation, average potential experience is 19.4 years for males and 17.3 years for females.

---

10   Sixty is the official retirement age in Thailand.
11   A part-time worker is defined as a person who works less than 20 hours a week.
12   These sex differences in university participation are commonly found in Thailand. It is an area of future research by one of the authors of this chapter.

Table 11.2 Variable definitions and summary statistics

Variable	Definition	Male		Female	
		Mean	Std dev.	Mean	Std dev.
Dependent variables					
Earnings per hour	Gross hourly wages from main job in 2006 (baht)	52.47	42.67	54.68	45.83
Annual earnings	Gross annual earnings in 2006 (baht)	106 769	77 680	108 385	812 491
Educational variables					
Incomplete school	Dummy = 1 if did not complete school	0.178	0.383	0.154	0.361
Primary school	Dummy = 1 if highest qualification is primary	0.184	0.387	0.133	0.339
Lower secondary	Dummy = 1 if highest qualification is lower secondary	0.178	0.383	0.123	0.329
Upper secondary	Dummy = 1 if highest qualification is upper secondary	0.148	0.355	0.148	0.355
Diploma	Dummy = 1 if highest qualification is diploma	0.082	0.275	0.080	0.271
Undergraduate	Dummy = 1 if highest qualification is undergraduate	0.172	0.376	0.337	0.473
Postgraduate	Dummy = 1 if highest qualification is postgraduate	0.020	0.140	0.025	0.025
Other variables					
Hours per week	Hours of work per week in main job	45.72	8.10	44.87	7.86
Potential experience	(Maximum) time in paid work in years	19.38	10.89	17.32	10.14
Number of observations		19 856		17 491	

OLS Earnings Functions

The standard earnings equation is used in this study and is of the following form:

$$\ln w_i = \mathbf{X}_i'\hat{\mathbf{a}} + \mathring{a}_i$$

in which $i = 1, 2, 3, \ldots, n$ represent individuals, w_i is the gross hourly earnings of individual i, and $\mathbf{X}_i'$ is a vector of characteristics that determine earnings.

We employ three variations of the model: the first uses years of schooling as a proxy for educational attainment; the second variant uses the education dummies described earlier; and the third extends the second model to include interaction terms between education dummies and potential experience. The last of these is essentially a relaxation of the restriction imposed in the second model, which constrains returns to experience to be identical between education levels. The estimations for these models are carried out separately for males and females.

Based on the years-of-schooling coefficient model, on average, the earnings increases for one additional year of education are about 11.2 per cent for males and 12.9 per cent for females. Our estimates are reasonably close to the results from previous studies. The results from this study and selected previous studies are now shown in Table 11.3 (see Appendix 11.1 for the regression result).

Table 11.3 Selected comparisons of returns-to-schooling estimates for Thailand

Author	Year of data	Method	Return to one additional year of schooling (%)	
Psacharopoulos (1994)	1971	The coefficient on years of schooling	Overall 10.4	
Patrinos (1995)	1986	The coefficient on years of schooling	Overall 12.4	
Patrinos (1995)	1989	The coefficient on years of schooling	Overall 11.5	
Psacharopoulos (1994)	1972	Returns to education by level of education and gender	Male 9.1	Female 10.0
This study	2006	The coefficient on years of schooling	Male 11.2	Female 12.9

Source: Psacharopoulos and Patrinos (2002) and authors' (2008) estimate.

Results from the dummies-and-interaction terms are reported in Appendix 11.1. The findings from this model are consistent with economic theory—that is, earnings increase with education and experience, with the rate of increase with experience falling over time. The earnings–experience slopes are relatively steep for graduates, although not by much; this is as expected—a prediction that follows from the general view that university graduates are more likely to be in higher-training jobs with concomitant steeper earnings–experience slopes.

The percentage differences in earnings associated with educational qualifications are shown in Table 11.4. The reference group is made up of individuals who did not complete school.

The data from Table 11.4 show that, on average, without any prior market experience, a male primary-school graduate earns 15 per cent higher than a male without any formal qualifications, and this commensurate figure for females is 14 per cent. A male and female with lower secondary education experience higher earnings by 25 per cent and 22 per cent, respectively. Upper secondary qualification increases earnings by 32 per cent for males and 35 per cent for females. Average male and female diploma-holders earn 58 per cent and 55 per cent, respectively, more than the 'incomplete school' individual, with the earnings advantage for university graduates 78 per cent for males and 86 per cent for females. These earnings advantages for postgraduate males and females are 102 per cent and 110 per cent, respectively.

Table 11.4 Percentage differences in earnings

Educational attainment	Male	Female
Primary	15	14
Lower secondary	25	22
Upper secondary	32	35
Diploma	58	55
Undergraduate	78	86
Postgraduate	102	110

Age–Earnings Profiles and Internal Rates of Return

We use the estimation results in Appendix 11.1 to construct age–earnings profiles.[13] These profiles are used to derive the earnings path for males and females with upper secondary qualifications and undergraduate qualifications.[14]

---

13 The predicted value of earnings has been adjusted by the formula; $\hat{y} = \exp^{\left(\frac{s^2}{2}\right)} \cdot \exp^{\left(\ln \hat{y}\right)}$. See Wooldridge (2006) for details.

14 Observations with age greater than fifty-five years were dropped due the presence of several large outliers.

The profiles for average males and females are shown in Figures 11.1 and 11.2, respectively. These profiles assume that the full working life of an average upper secondary high-school graduate is 42 years—from age eighteen to sixty. For those who decide to undertake undergraduate study for four years, the full working life is reduced to 38 years—from age twenty-two to sixty. As well, we adjusted the age–earnings profiles by 1.5 per cent to capture productivity growth, with the choice of this adjustment factor based on the average real wage growth in Thailand for 2003–06.

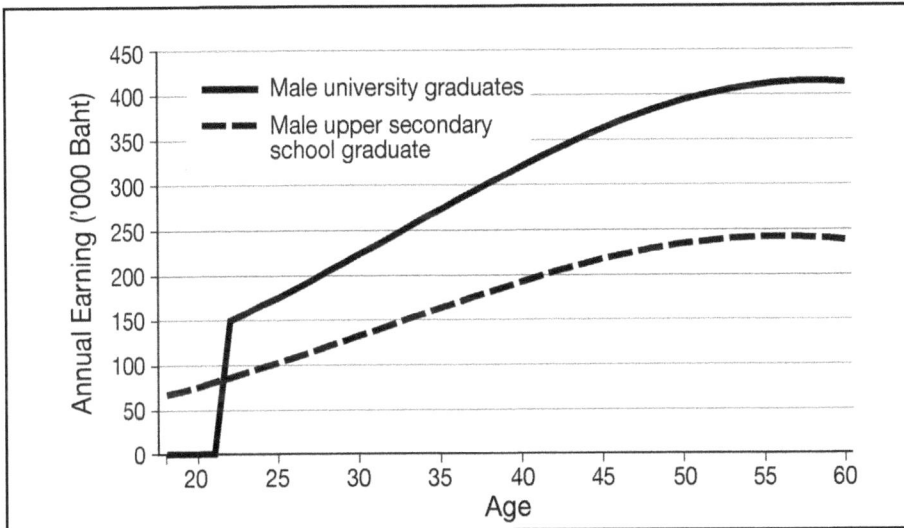

Figure 11.1 Average male age–earnings profiles: Thailand, 2006

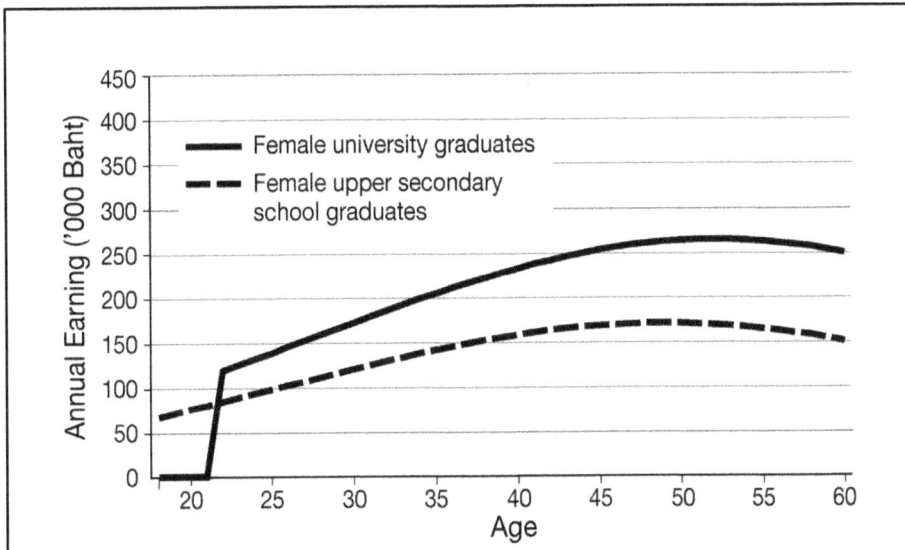

Figure 11.2 Average female age–earnings profiles: Thailand, 2006

As can be seen from the figures, earnings increase at a decreasing rate with age (experience) for both upper secondary graduates and university graduates. The age–earning profiles for both male and female university graduates are (slightly) steeper than they are for secondary school graduates. It is of comfort to note that these relationships are familiar with respect to the findings for a large number of countries at different points of time.

We can use these results to calculate the so-called internal rate of return (IRR) to investment in university education—a measure of the value in earnings terms of process. Formally, the IRR is defined as the discount rate that equates the present value of additional benefits from the investment to the present value of the cost of obtaining the additional education. The benefits are additional earnings from higher education, and the costs are tuition fees plus the opportunity cost of not working in paid employment after the completion of upper secondary school. It should be noted that the result from the IRR estimate is contingent upon both the cost of investment and the earnings streams.

In our estimates, we assume that university graduates undertake study on a full-time basis for four years and receive zero income at that time. The calculations have been carried out for a diversity of tuition fees—from B36 000 to B350 000 per program—which reflects very broadly the current range of Thai higher education annual tuition charges for different institutions. Table 11.5 shows the results with the IRR, and these range from 8 to 12.8 per cent per annum for males, and 4.5 to 7.9 per cent per annum for females—estimates that are roughly in line with international experience (see Psacharopoulos and Patrinos 2002). This familiarity should leave us with some confidence that the data and the methods employed are useful for describing the Thai graduate experience.

Table 11.5 IRR estimates (per cent per annum)

Tuition prices by type of institution*		Total tuition fee (baht)*	Male	Female
Public university	Low price	36 000	12.79	7.93
	High price	144 000	10.41	7.13
Private university	Low price	192 000	9.23	5.55
	High price	350 000	8.04	4.48

* average estimates from various universities

To this point the analysis has been based on average age–earnings profiles derived from OLS estimations. In order to better capture the heterogeneity of outcomes across different age–earnings groups, a truncated approach to estimation has been employed and this is now explained and the results are shown. A main reason that this more disaggregated approach is likely to be of considerable importance for the policy debate is that income-contingent loan schemes typically have a first income threshold of repayment; this can mean that a small proportion of the graduate population does not repay (even the nominal debt) in full and this could have marked effects on estimations of interest rate subsidies that will not show up with the use of OLS.

Deriving Truncated Age–Earnings Profiles

While it is of considerable interest to understand the earnings relationships at the mean of the data—which is what is happening with the use of OLS—a fuller understanding of the implications of different income-contingent loan schemes requires a more disaggregated method. We have approached this by doing the analysis separately for three parts of the lifetime graduate earnings distributions, and have thus divided the earnings data into three groups by year of age and sex: the bottom third, the middle, and the top third of earnings.[15]

There is an important reason for considering the earnings and loan experiences for different parts of the earnings distribution, which is that for TICAL1, TICAL2 and ILLUSTRATIVE1 (but not ILLUSTRATIVE2)[16] there will be different subsidies depending on the lifetime earnings streams of hypothetical graduates; it is of interest to determine how big these are, and how much they differ between those earning low, medium and high lifetime incomes.

The truncation exercise provides an indication of the distributional effects of policy regimes and, related to this, the possible future contributions of taxpayers given marked movements in graduate income distributions. More significantly, and as noted above, when loan schemes have the potential to have less than full collection from some parts of the graduate earnings distribution, this needs to be explicitly modelled in order that we estimate implicit interest rate subsidies properly.

There is, however, a major limitation of this approach. It is the implicit assumption that graduates remain in the low, middle or top third of the earnings distribution throughout their lives, and this is clearly not going to be the case.

---

15 An alternative but similar way to have addressed this issue would be through the use of quantile regression techniques, which effectively divide the distributions into earnings categories. This approach, however, assigns weights to all the data points in the sample, with the weights being lower the further the data point is from the group under consideration. Because of this weighting procedure, we are unconvinced that such an approach usefully helps us understand the impact on subsidies of graduates in different thirds of the earnings distribution. Our approach using truncations implicitly assigns a weight in the regression of zero to all data points outside the group.

16 This is because ILLUSTRATIVE2 imposes the same real rate of interest on the borrowings as the real discount rate, and this must mean that there are no subsidies involved for any income groups, so long as all members of the group eventually pay off their debts in full.

Even so, the approach employed allows us to determine upper boundaries of implicit interest rate subsidies (for the lowest third of earnings) and lower boundaries of implicit interest rate subsidies (for the highest third of earnings).

The estimated parameters from the truncated OLS estimations are shown in Appendix 11.1 and these have been used to construct age–earnings profiles for the three different graduate earnings groupings.[17] These are shown for males and females in Figures 11.3 and 11.4, respectively.

The results illustrated in the figures show quite different earnings outcomes for graduates by age and sex. For both sexes, it is apparently the case that those in the highest third of the earnings distribution start out with earnings that are about 2.5 times higher than is the case for those in the bottom third of the distribution, and that this advantage increases considerably as age increases; at age fifty, for example, the earnings advantage of the top third compared with the bottom third has grown to about five times for females and to about 3.5 times for males. The size of these differences suggests strongly that estimated variations in implicit interest rate subsidies as a result of the parameters of the income-contingent loan schemes are likely to be very important.

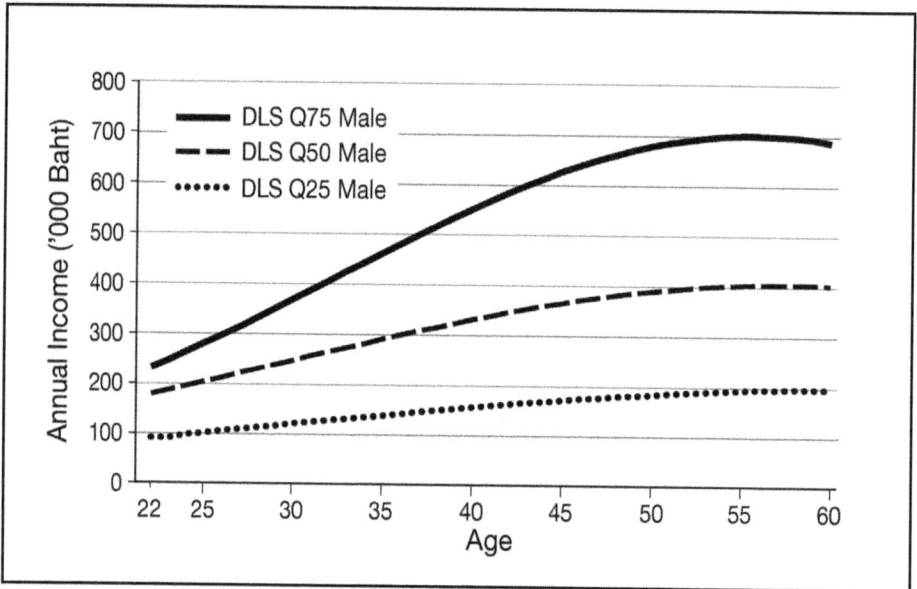

Figure 11.3 Male graduate age–earnings profiles for low, median and high earnings groups

17   The profiles are adjusted for productivity change by the same method used for adjusting the OLS predictions.

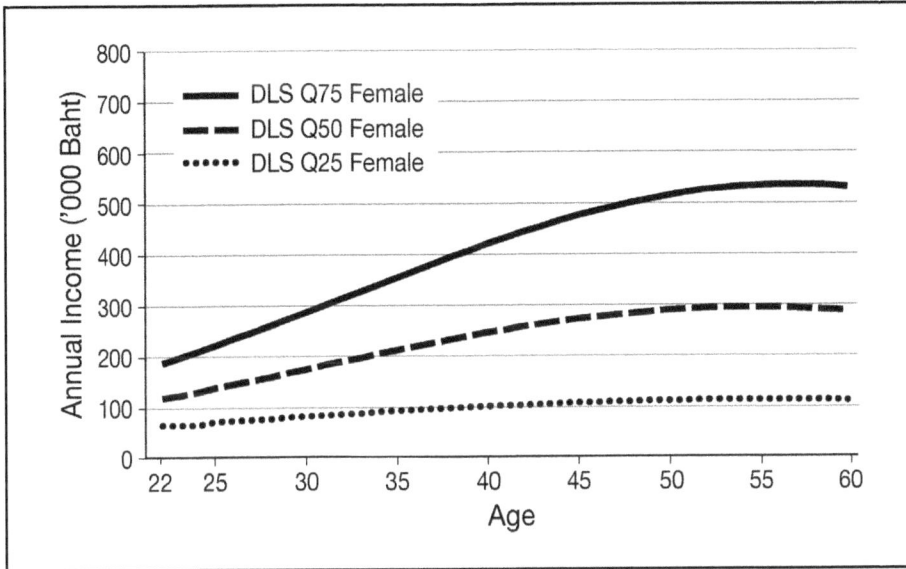

Figure 11.4 Female graduate age–earnings profiles for low, median and high earnings groups

Loan Repayments and Interest Subsidies for Four Income-Contingent Loan Schemes

The Implicit Subsidy Calculation: Concepts and assumptions

From a financial point of view, the efficiency and sustainability of loan programs depend significantly upon the level of loan recoverability. In turn, this is linked to the repayment conditions—the most important being: 1) the level and form of the real rate of interest on the debt; 2) the first income threshold of repayment; and 3) the rates of repayment as a proportion of income.

The difference between the present value of the sum of the repayment stream and the present value of the tuition fee paid through the loan scheme is called an 'implicit subsidy', and it is likely to be an unintended consequence as a result of the design of the financing scheme. The word 'implicit' is used to distinguish this form of subsidy from the intended tuition fee subsidy usually provided to public universities.

For our exercises, and those reported in Piruna et al. (2008), we used the following formula for calculations of implicit subsidies.[18]

$$\% \text{ of Implicit Subsidy} = \left[\frac{\sum_{t=1}^{n} \frac{T_t}{(1+r)^{t-1}} - \sum_{l=1}^{N} \frac{P_l}{(1+r)^{1+l-1}}}{\sum_{t=1}^{n} \frac{T_t}{(1+r)^{t-1}}} \right] \times 100$$

Where

T_t = tuition fee paid in year t

t = year of tuition fee payment

P_l = loan repayment in year l

l = length of time to repay the loan

r = discount rate

An implication of the above formula is that a loan package that takes longer to pay will result in a lower present value of repayment, and thus a higher subsidy, for all schemes except ILLUSTRATIVE2.[19] This is an important issue for loan design and, as is shown below, it is a critical point with respect to whether or not it is possible to develop a workable income-contingent loan scheme for Thailand in circumstances in which debts are much higher than the low levels modelled here initially.

In what now follows, we present calculations of the implicit subsidy with respect to the collection of tuition fees for four possible income-contingent loan schemes for Thailand—described above and known as TICAL1, TICAL2, ILLUSTRATIVE1 and ILLUSTRATIVE2. The assumptions used in estimating the subsidies are as follows.

1. Real interest rates: zero for TICAL1 and TICAL2, as proposed for the original TICAL. A 25 per cent tuition surcharge with a zero real interest rate afterwards for ILLUSTRATIVE1, which is the same as is the case for HECS. A 3 per cent real rate of interest calculated from the beginning of the debt for ILLUSTRATIVE2, to represent a conventional method of covering the government's cost of borrowing.

2. Discount rate for the present value calculations: 3 per cent per annum in real terms.[20]

---

18 Subsequently and fortunately, we ascertained that it is the same formula derived by Adrian Ziderman (2003).

19 As long as the nominal debts are paid in full using a real rate of interest equal to the discount rate (both are set at 3 per cent per annum for ILLUSTRATIVE2), this must result in implicit interest rate subsidies of zero.

20 The choice of discount rate is somewhat subjective, but can be justified with reference to some data. For example, in Australia from December 2001 to 2004, accountants used a 5.6 per cent nominal discount rate,

3. Full employment: the hypothetical graduates are assumed to be engaged in full-time year-round paid work.

4. Tuition fee (initially): the tuition fee is set at B100 000 for a four-year undergraduate degree. This is approximately equal to the weighted average tuition fee of public and private universities in Thailand, and is equivalent to the tuition fee imposed in Piruna et al.'s (2008) exercises. This assumption is relaxed later.

As noted above, we approach the interest rate subsidy calculations with both OLS and truncated estimations, beginning with the former.

The Streams of Repayments and Interest Rate Subsidies: OLS

Using these assumptions and average earnings profiles predicted from the OLS coefficients, we are able to construct repayment streams under all four schemes. The annual payments are shown in Figures 11.5 and 11.6.

A critical reason that the repayment streams differ is that the first income repayment threshold for the two versions of TICAL is almost twice as high as is the case for the two versions of ILLUSTRATIVE. The very high first threshold means that under TICAL1 an average male does not start to repay the debt until he is twenty-six years old, and the non-payment period of an average female is even longer, with repayment not beginning until she is thirty-two years old. It is also worth noting that the presumed indexation arrangement for the former TICAL is very important to the timing of repayment streams, with the non-indexed version resulting in repayments beginning three and six years earlier for males and females, respectively. A final obvious point is that the different forms of the real interest rate for ILLUSTRATIVE1 and ILLUSTRATIVE2 appear to deliver almost identical repayment streams.

All the above points are broadly true for both males and females, with the main differences in the results lying in the timing of repayments. Because they earn lower incomes, females start to repay later with TICAL1 and TICAL2, and repay for longer and at lower rates with ILLUSTRATIVE1 and ILLUSTRATIVE2.

Table 11.6 reports the implicit subsidies associated with these streams of repayment in combination with the interest rate parameters of each of the schemes.

---

and the average inflation rate was 2.3 per cent during that period, giving a real interest rate of 3.3 per cent per annum. Further, the real long-term bond rate is about the same as this. Piruna et al. (2008) also used a real rate of discount of 3 per cent.

Table 11.6 Implicit interest rate subsidies for average graduates (per cent)

	TICAL1 (indexed)	TICAL2 (not indexed)	ILLUSTRATIVE1 (25% surcharge)	ILLUSTRATIVE2 (3% real interest)
Male	31.54	26.20	2.03	0.01
Female	42.23	33.72	2.90	0.02

The major points with respect to the implicit subsidies from the four income-contingent loan policies are

1. having a zero real rate of interest, in combination with very high first income repayment thresholds, results in the high implicit interest rate subsides for both TICAL1 and TICAL2—of about 30–40 per cent for the former, and 25–34 per cent for the latter

2. while the TICAL subsidies can be considered high and reflective of less-than-perfect design, it is worth recording that these subsidies are much less than those reported in Piruna et al. (2008) for the SLF—of about 60 per cent

3. it is clear that having a form of real rates of interest for ILLUSTRATIVE1 and ILLUSTRATIVE2 has a marked effect on calculations of subsidies compared with the two versions of TICAL

4. it is apparent that a 25 per cent surcharge with no further real interest rate adjustment (ILLUSTRATIVE1) delivers much the same implicit subsidies of about zero[21] as having an ongoing real rate of interest of 3 per cent per annum[22] (ILLUSTRATIVE2).

These findings are an important part of our contribution. The results from the use of basic econometric techniques promote for discussion the advantages of an income-contingent loan with a relatively low first income threshold of repayment, and with some form of a real rate of interest. The approach adopted thus far, however, reveals only subsidies for the schemes at the means of the data by age and sex, since our method uses OLS earnings function results. We now move to consider the subsidies associated with the schemes for quite different lifetime earnings distributions.

---

21 The slight difference between the subsidies found for ILLUSTRATIVE2 and zero is the result only of a rounding error.

22 This is very close to the results found for the HECS system for public-sector undergraduates (Chapman and Lounkaew 2008).

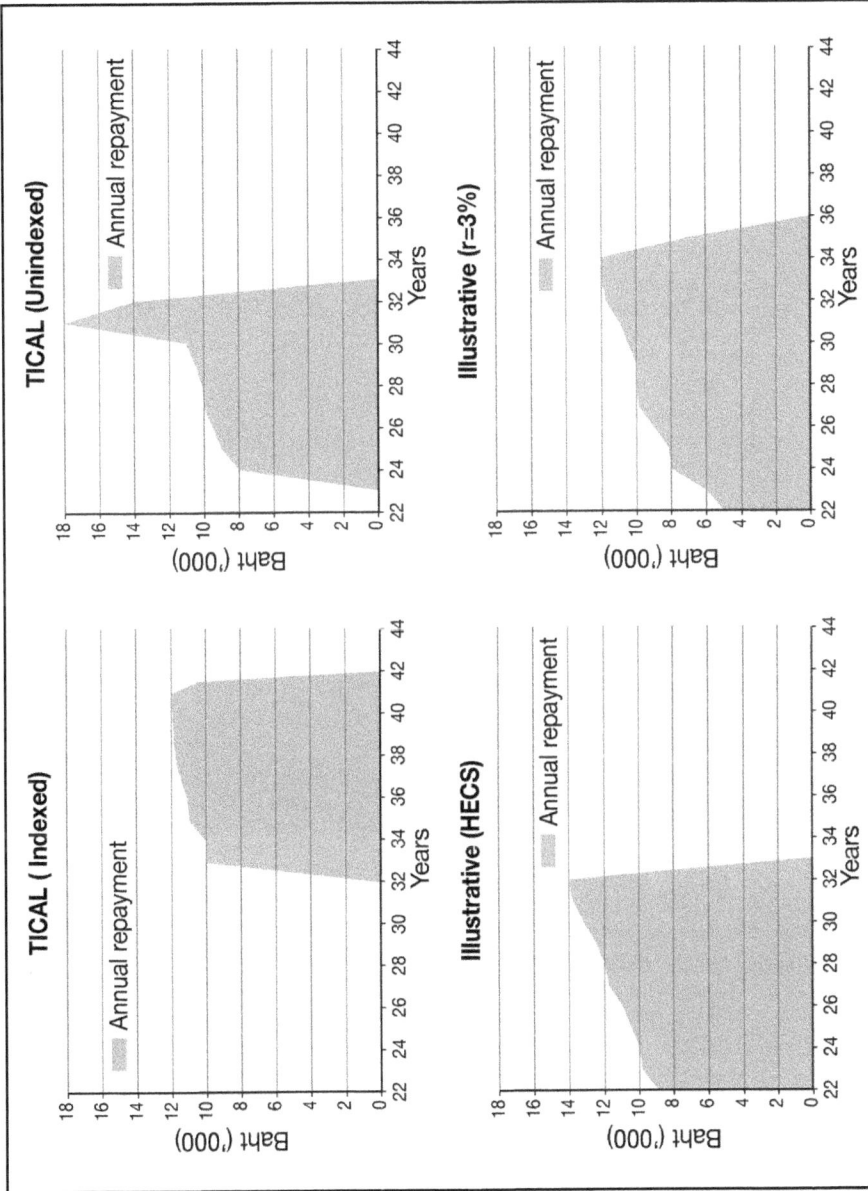

Figure 11.5 Male graduate average repayment streams under alternative schemes.

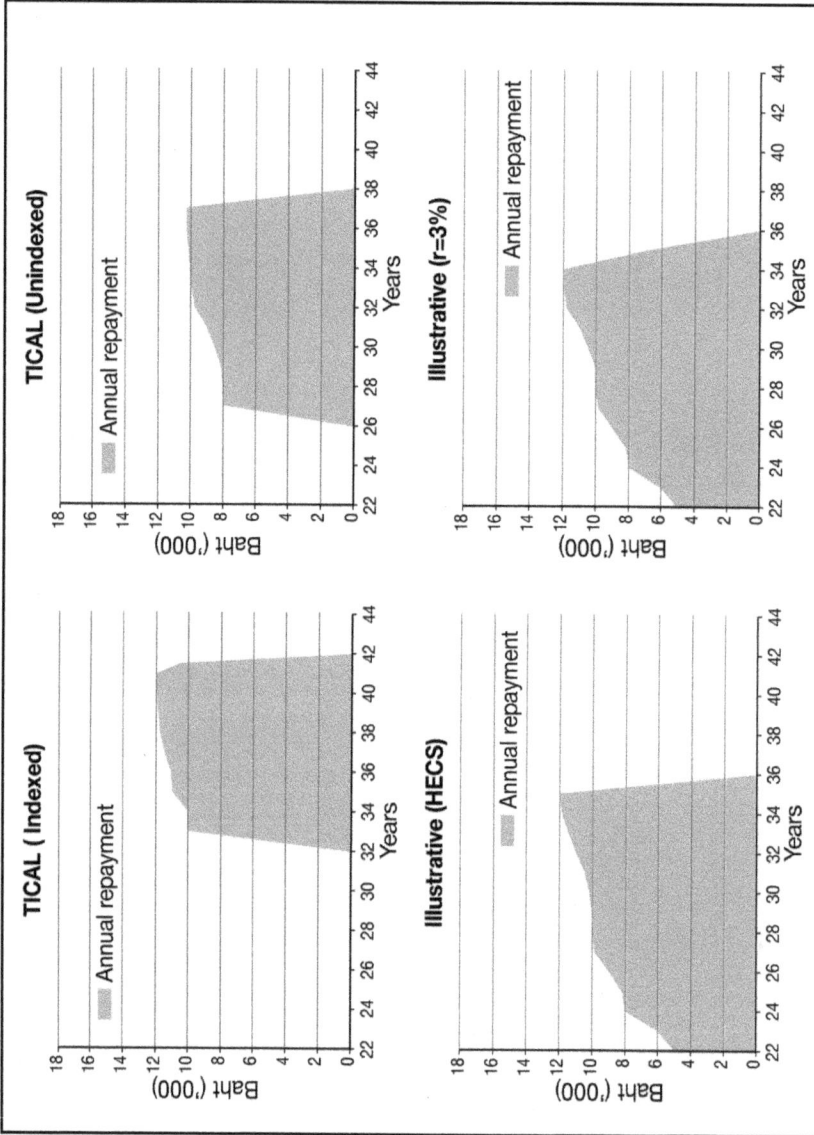

Figure 11.6 Female graduate average repayment streams under alternative schemes The Streams of Repayments and Interest Rate Subsidies: Truncations.

What now follows illustrates the streams of repayments and implicit subsidies of the three different lifetime earnings groups for both sexes illustrated in Figures 11.3 and 11.4: high earners (Q75), median earners (Q50), and low earners (Q25).[23] Table 11.7 shows the implicit subsidies for males and females for each of the three lifetime earnings distributions for the four loan schemes.

Table 11.7 Implicit interest rate subsidies for low, median and high earnings groups (per cent)

Group		TICAL1 (indexed)	TICAL2 (not indexed)	ILLUSTRATIVE1 (25% surcharge)	ILLUSTRATIVE2 (3% real interest)
Male	Q25	77.42	43.20	17.40	0.05
	Q50	25.23	23.18	−0.85	0.00
	Q75	18.91	18.38	−9.01	0.00
	Average	**40.52**	**28.25**	**2.51**	**0.01**
Female	Q25	100.00*	100.00*	58.90*	53.04*
	Q50	42.71	33.42	1.42	0.02
	Q75	20.62	20.62	−6.92	0.00
	Average	**54.44**	**51.35**	**17.80**	**17.69**

An important aspect of the data from Table 11.7 needs to be explained, and this relates to the measure of the so-called 'average'. The calculation is the average of the three cohort-specific implicit taxpayer-subsidy calculations and can be interpreted with the use of the following example with respect to the findings for males under the TICAL1 scheme.

The results suggest that if there are 100 men taking TICAL1 loans, about 33 of them will earn in the bottom third of graduate earnings for the period in which the loan is collected, and for this group the estimated subsidy is about 77 per cent; an important part of this subsidy can be attributed to the fact that when the retirement age is reached, the loan is not paid off in full (in nominal terms). There will also be 33 men in the top third of graduate earnings in the period in which the loan is collected and for this group the estimated subsidy is about 19 per cent. Combined with the subsidy of about 25 per cent for the middle third of the male graduate earnings distribution, we can then calculate the (weighted) average for males as a whole under TICAL1. In this case, the answer is about 40 per cent ([77 + 25 + 19]/3).

The strength of this calculation compared with the use of earnings data at the mean only is that it broadly takes into account the importance of subsidy differences across the earnings distribution. This must matter because income-contingent loans require no repayments from debtors at the time that they experience low earnings, meaning that there are important asymmetries with

---

23 The repayment streams data are available from the authors.

respect to collection above and below the first (and later) income threshold at which repayments exist. Our method is necessarily more accurate than the estimates using OLS only.

The major points with respect to the implicit subsidies from the four income-contingent loan policies taking into account the earnings distributions are

1. in all cases—except for males in ILLUSTRATIVE1 and ILLUSTRATIVE2—estimates of implicit interest rate subsidies are higher than is the case for the calculations done at the mean only

2. with TICAL1, the subsidies are now calculated to be about 40–55 per cent for males and females, which is not very different to the estimates from Piruna et al. (2008) for the SLF, of about 65 per cent

3. with TICAL2, the subsidy for males remains relatively low—about 28 per cent—but increases to more than 50 per cent for females

4. with both ILLUSTRATIVE schemes, the subsidies remain about zero for males—an interesting component of this result being that for males in the top third of the earnings distribution under ILLUSTRATIVE1, there is a negative subsidy of 9 per cent; this is because the 25 per cent surcharge on the debt represents an effective real rate of interest in excess of 3 per cent per annum

5. with both ILLUSTRATIVE schemes, the average subsidy for females increases to about 18 per cent, and this is due almost entirely to the fact that the subsidies for females in the bottom third of the earnings distribution are very large (59 and 53 per cent for ILLUSTRATIVE1 and ILLUSTRATIVE2, respectively). This important finding can be traced to the fact that a large proportion of women experiencing low earnings have unpaid debt at the end of their working lives and thus the end of their debt repayments—of about 45 per cent.

The final point above is critical to our understanding of the potential for having an efficacious income-contingent loan scheme for Thailand. It means that, with reasonable repayment parameters and a real rate of interest, there remain important subsidies associated with income-contingent loan schemes for some groups. This is because the lifetime earnings of some graduates are not sufficient to repay the debt in full, and this is traceable to the fact that Thailand's per capita real incomes are relatively low when considered in an international context. This is unlike the situation in many countries with income-contingent loans such as Australia, New Zealand and the United Kingdom.

The results of Table 11.7 imply that schemes with design arrangements similar to TICAL are associated with very considerable subsidies and their level might be such as to suggest that alternative income-contingent loan policies are more appropriate. While the subsidies for schemes with forms of a real rate of interest and a much lower first income threshold of repayment are not insignificant, for the policy debate, it could be concluded that arrangements of this kind are acceptable with respect to taxpayer contributions.

It needs to be recognised, however, that our subsidy calculations have been undertaken for a total tuition debt of B100 000, and it will certainly be the case that with higher charges—and thus higher debt—these subsidies will increase. This issue matters with respect to the coverage of an income-contingent loan for Thailand because outside the public sector, university tuition charges are generally and significantly higher.

Interest Rate Subsidies for Higher Debts

The exercises reported above involve estimations of implicit subsidies from income-contingent loans of various forms for a total tuition charge of B100 000. While it can be argued that this is appropriate and typical for public-sector universities in Thailand, the story is different in the case of the private sector, where charges are much higher than this.

Our best estimate of a typical tuition charge for the private sector is a total of about B350 000.[24] Assuming an income-contingent loan facility is offered by the government to cover this charge, we are able to estimate the implicit subsidies associated with the four schemes. The calculations are presented in Table 11.8.

The main points from Table 11.8 are

1. with a much higher charge of B350 000, the implicit subsidies are higher for all four schemes, although the increases for TICAL1 and TICAL2—to between 44 and 63 per cent—are not as high as the increases for ILLUSTRATIVE1 and ILLUSTRATIVE2; this is due to the fact that both TICAL arrangements involve quite high collection rates (of up to 12 per cent of income) at higher levels of earnings

2. with the higher charge, there is now very little difference between the subsidies associated with TICAL1 and TICAL2 and those found for the SLF and reported in Piruna et al. (2008)

3. having a surcharge of 25 per cent on the loan and no real rate of interest after the debt is incurred (ILLUSTRATIVE1) is associated with quite high subsidies—of about 38 for males and 51 per cent for females

---

24 This is about the same as tuition fees for the undergraduate business program at Assumption University.

4. even with an income-contingent loan with an ongoing real rate of interest of 3 per cent per annum (ILLUSTRATIVE2), high charges are associated with important levels of subsidies—of about 17 per cent for males and 34 per cent for females.

Table 11.8 Implicit interest rate subsidies for low, median and high earnings groups with high debts (per cent)

Group		TICAL1 (indexed)	TICAL2 (not indexed)	ILLUSTRATIVE1 (25% surcharge)	ILLUSTRATIVE2 (3% real interest)
Male	Q25	93.55*	66.38*	49.29	50.41*
	Q50	40.55	35.72	35.18	0.00
	Q75	30.30	28.47	30.04	0.00
Average		**54.80**	**43.52**	**38.17**	**16.80**
Female	Q25	100.00*	100.00*	84.33*	86.58*
	Q50	54.28	45.15	38.08	16.07*
	Q75	36.10	30.62	31.42	0.00
Average		**63.46**	**58.59**	**51.28**	**34.23**

These findings are very important for Thailand's higher education financing debate, since they imply that widespread reform of student loans, including their provision for relatively high-cost courses, is likely to involve sizeable taxpayer subsidies. We have not determined the possible overall costs for the government of broadly based coverage, and these might not be such as to undermine the basis for a universal income-contingent loan facility since we note that private universities apparently enrol about 15 per cent of all undergraduates (National Statistical Office 2006b).

On the other hand, the income-contingent loan schemes under consideration for our exercises have involved debts for tuition only. Since additional loans for income support would also seem to be a propitious aspect of higher education financing reform, the level of debts modelled, of B350 000, could well be required for the public sector as well.

Conclusion

There is an ongoing and very important debate in Thailand concerning higher education financing policy. For the 10 years prior to 2007, a traditional mortgage-type loan—known as the Student Loans Fund (SLF)—was in operation, and, after this was suspended, a system very similar to the SLF was reintroduced in 2007. Piruna et al. (2008) analyse the SLF with respect to both taxpayer interest rate subsidies and graduate loan repayment hardships. As found also by Ziderman (2003), it is clear that the SLF has very high interest rate subsidies and, consistent with this, it is associated with low repayment difficulties for former students.

The main contributions of this chapter are as follows. First, we present a comparison in conceptual terms of the costs and benefits of schemes such as the SLF with the other main alternative: income-contingent loans. Income-contingent loans have advantages over mortgage-type loans in terms of providing insurance against both default and repayment hardships. A critical issue for this approach for many countries, however, concerns the efficacy of collection on the basis of a student's future income stream—it being the case that quite sophisticated institutional mechanisms are required. It is unclear to us whether or not the Thai income tax and/or pension collection schemes are such as to make effective and operative the collection of an income-contingent loan.

Using the same data, econometric approaches and accounting methods as those employed by Piruna et al. (2008), we are able to estimate the implicit interest rate subsidies for four different income-contingent loan arrangements, differing importantly with respect to collection parameters and interest rate regimes. For the first time in analyses of the effects of income-contingent loans, we demonstrate that the use of averages provides misleadingly low estimates of the extent of interest rate subsidies. As well, it appears that schemes with high first income thresholds of collection, and without a real rate of interest, are associated with significant interest rate subsidies, and, for high debts, these subsidies are not very dissimilar to those estimated for the SLF.

Further, it is also apparent that, for relatively low levels of debt income, contingent-loan policies with relatively low first income thresholds of repayment and with real rates of interest can be designed to be workable for Thailand in an aggregate financial sense. As debt levels increase, however, so too do the interest rate subsidies, with an important part of this result being due to the fact that Thai graduate incomes per capita are just not high enough for many groups to be able to repay all the debt before they leave the labour force.

Some important caveats are warranted. One is that we have not taken into account loan losses through poor collection outcomes, and this has the clear potential to reduce repayments and thus increase subsidies. Related to this is that graduate unemployment rates are quite high for the first several years after the completion of a university degree, and, from our calculations, with the SLF remain as high as 5 per cent even five years after labour-force participation begins. Taking this into account would necessarily increase subsidy estimates, and preliminary work in this area suggests that the figures would be about 5 percentage points higher.

Finally, it has to be stressed that our conclusions are derived on the basis of particular design rules concerning different income-contingent loan approaches, and this should matter very significantly to the debate concerning the efficacy of income-contingent loan approaches in Thailand. The important point is that subsidy calculations are very sensitive to choices concerning: the first income threshold of repayment; the proportions of income required for loan repayment; and real interest rates. The next step is to ascertain the extent to which our broad conclusions are reinforced or compromised with alternative loan design parameters.

References

Barr, N. 2001, *The Welfare State as Piggy Bank*, Oxford University Press, UK.

Barr, N. 2007, Interest subsidies for income-contingent student loans, Mimeo., London School of Economics and Political Science, UK.

Carneiro, P. and Heckman, J. J. 2002, 'The evidence on credit constraints in post-secondary schooling', *The Economic Journal*, vol. 112, no. 482, pp. 705–30.

Chapman, B. 2006, *Government Managing Risk: Income contingent loans for social and economic progress*, Routledge, London.

Chapman, B. and Leigh, A. 2006, *Do very high tax rates induce bunching? Implications for the design of income-contingent loan schemes*, Discussion Paper No. 521, Centre for Economic Policy Research, The Australian National University, Canberra.

Chapman, B. and Lounkaew, K. 2008, 'HECS is in need of reform', *Campus Review Weekly*, January.

Dynarski, M. 1994, 'Who defaults on student loans: findings from the national post-secondary student aid study', *Economics of Education Review*, vol. 13, pp. 55–68.

Finnie, R. and Schwartz, S. 1996, *Student Loans in Canada Past, Present and Future*, C. D. Howe Institute, Toronto.

Freidman, M. 1955, 'The role of government in education', in A. Solo (ed.), *Economics and the Public Interest*, Rutgers University Press, New Brunswick, NJ, pp. 123–44.

Harding, A. 1995, 'Financing higher education: an assessment of income-contingent loan options and repayment patterns over the life cycle', *Education Economics*, vol. 3, pp. 173–203.

Lathapipat, D. 2008, The changing educational distribution and its impact on the evolution of wages in Thailand, 1987–2006, Paper prepared for Student Loans in South and East Asia Conference, Bangkok, 15–16 July.

Palacios, M. 2004, *Investing in Human Capital*, Cambridge University Press, UK.

Piruna, P., Sarachitti, R. and Thitima, S. 2008, Thailand's Student Loan Fund: an analysis of interest rate subsidies and repayment hardships, Paper prepared for Student Loans in South and East Asia Conference, Bangkok, 15–16 July.

Psacharopoulos, G. and Patrinos, H. A. 2002, *Returns to Investment in Education: A further update*, The World Bank, Washington, DC.

National Statistical Office 2006a, *Labour Force Survey, 3rd Quarter*, National Statistical Office, Bangkok.

National Statistical Office 2006b, *National Statistical Year Book 2006*, National Statistical Office, Bangkok.

Wooldridge, J. M. 2006, *Introductory Econometrics: A modern approach*, (Third edition), South-Western Thomson Learning, Sydney.

Ziderman, A. 2003, *Student Loans in Thailand: Are they effective, equitable, sustainable?Volume 1. Policy Research and Dialogue Student Loans Schemes in Asia*, United Nations Educational, Scientific and Cultural Organisation, Bangkok.

Appendix 11.1

Table A11.1 Years-of-schooling model

Variable	Female		Male	
	Coefficient	t-stat	Coefficient	t-stat
Schooling	0.129**	138.79	0.112**	113.58
Experience	0.036**	34.39	0.037**	34.60
Experience^2/1000	−0.1186**	−5.17	−0.178**	−8.13
Constant	1.692**	133.93	1.979**	164.27
n	17 491		19 856	
R^2	0.6146		0.5436	

* statistical significance at the 5 per cent level

** statistical significance at the 1 per cent level

Table A11.2 Dummy variables and interaction terms model

Variable	Female		Male	
	Coefficient	t-stat	Coefficient	t-stat
Experience	0.063**	32.34	0.077**	47.46
Experience^2	−0.001**	−34.55	−0.001**	−42.79
Primary	0.150**	3.65	0.146**	3.83
Lower secondary	0.254**	7.28	0.221**	5.49
Upper secondary	0.315**	9.64	0.350**	8.33
Diploma	0.577**	11.79	0.548**	9.26
Undergraduate	0.776**	28.39	0.859**	19.37
Postgraduate	1.025**	15.95	1.104**	11.48
Experience*Primary/100	−0.019**	−4.12	−0.018**	−4.34
Experience^2*Primary/10 000	0.006**	4.92	0.007**	3.58
Experience*LowerSecondary/100	−0.023**	−4.79	−0.018**	−4.14
Experience^2*LowerSecondary/10 000	0.810**	8.31	0.734**	9.14
Experience*UpperSecondary/100	0.008**	4.14	0.005**	3.60
Experience^2*UpperSecondary/10 000	−23.351**	−9.11	−30.058**	−9.39
Experience*Diploma/100	−0.003**	−4.13	0.023**	3.90
Experience^2*Diploma/10 000	0.646**	4.53	−0.205**	−1.51
Experience*Undergraduate/100	−0.009**	−2.66	−0.025**	−6.08
Experience^2*Undergraduate/10 000	0.845**	10.19	0.822**	7.70
Experience*Postgraduate/100	0.026**	2.31	0.028*	1.93
Experience^2*Postgraduate/10 000	−0.487**	−1.49	−0.861**	−2.24
Constant	2.860**	145.93	2.720**	155.52
n	17 491		19 856	
R^2	0.6146		0.5106	

* statistical significance at the 5 per cent level
** statistical significance at the 1 per cent level

Table A11.3 Truncated OLS by income groups

Variable	Male			Female		
	Q25	Q50	Q75	Q25	Q50	Q75
Constant	2.5382**	2.5804**	2.6332**	2.5621**	2.6190**	2.6571**
Educational attainment						
Primary	0.1117**	0.1553**	0.2443**	0.0744**	0.1154**	0.1840**
Lower secondary	0.2314**	0.3002**	0.4367**	0.1857**	0.2735**	0.4003**
Upper secondary	0.3874**	0.5331**	0.7328**	0.3542**	0.4740**	0.6615**
Diploma	0.6875**	0.8419**	1.0061**	0.6610**	0.8331**	1.0663**
Undergraduate	0.8647**	1.0676**	1.2960**	0.8280**	0.9467**	1.1260**
Postgraduate	1.7256**	1.6819**	1.5987**	1.7043**	1.8011**	1.8186**
Experience						
Experience	0.0337**	0.0454**	0.0506**	0.0253**	0.0312**	0.0354**
Experience^2	−0.0004**	−0.0005**	−0.0004**	−0.0003**	−0.0003**	−0.0002**
Undergrad*Exper	0.0262**	0.0196**	0.0142**	0.0266**	0.0376**	0.0389**
Undergrad*Exper^2	0.00001	−0.0001	−0.0004**	0.0002**	−0.0003**	−0.0006**
Observations		19 856			17 491	
R^2	0.2838	0.3736	0.4341	0.3950	0.4950	0.5301

* statistical significance at the 5 per cent level

** statistical significance at the 1 per cent level

www.ingramcontent.com/pod-product-compliance
Lightning Source LLC
Chambersburg PA
CBHW050100220326
41599CB00049B/7209